D0233002

The Presidency of
DWIGHT D.
EISENHOWER

N.D.
BOTTINEAU BRANCH
LIBRARY

AMERICAN PRESIDENCY SERIES

Donald R. McCoy,
Clifford S. Griffin,
Homer E. Socolofsky,
General Editors

The Presidency of
DWIGHT D.
EISENHOWER

by

Elmo Richardson

BOTTINEAU BRANCH
LIBRARY

THE REGENTS PRESS OF KANSAS
Lawrence

027171

© Copyright 1979 by The Regents Press of Kansas
Printed in the United States of America

Library of Congress Cataloging in Publication Data

Richardson, Elmo R.
The Presidency of Dwight D. Eisenhower.

(American Presidency series)
Bibliography: p.
Includes index.
1. United States—Politics and government—1953–1961.
2. Eisenhower, Dwight David, Pres. U.S., 1890–1969.
3. Presidents—United States—Biography.
I. Title.   II. Series.
E835.R53   973.921   78–17923
ISBN 0–7006–0183–X

To

my mentors,
Frank Freidel and George Mowry,
great-hearted men

Editors' Preface

The aim of the American Presidency Series is to present historians and the general reading public with interesting, scholarly assessments of the various presidential administrations. These interpretive surveys are intended to cover the broad ground between biographies, specialized monographs, and journalistic accounts. As such, each will be a comprehensive, synthetic work which will draw upon the best in pertinent secondary literature, yet leave room for the author's own analysis and interpretation.

Each volume in the series will deal with a separate presidential administration and will present the data essential to understanding the administration under consideration. Particularly, each book will treat the then current problems facing the United States and its people and how the president and his associates felt about, thought about, and worked to cope with these problems. Attention will be given to how the office developed and operated during the president's tenure. Equally important will be consideration of the vital relationships between the president, his staff, the executive officers, Congress, foreign representatives, the judiciary, state officials, the public, political parties, the press, and influential private citizens. The series will also be concerned with how this unique American institution—the presidency—was viewed by the presidents, and with what results.

All this will be set, insofar as possible, in the context not only of contemporary politics but also of economics, international relations, law, morals, public administration, religion, and thought. Such a broad approach is necessary to understanding, for a presidential administration is more than the elected and appointed officers composing it, since its work so often reflects the major problems, anxieties, and glories of the nation. In short, the authors in the series will strive to recount and evaluate the record of each administration and to identify its distinctiveness and relationships to the past, its own time, and the future.

Donald R. McCoy
Clifford S. Griffin
Homer E. Socolofsky

Preface

Trying to make sense of the Eisenhower presidency at the present time is not unlike the task of Sisyphus. No sooner is the rock of objectivity rolled up the hill by scholarship than it is swept back down by a fresh tide of partisanship. Before taking up this project, I too felt disdainful toward the man and his role in the events of mid century. Those hard feelings were accretions from the academic climate in which I had been trained during the early 1950s. As I began my work, I observed that many fellow historians, some fair and compassionate teachers, still nursed the conviction that Eisenhower had been the epitome, if not the source, of the paranoia, hypocrisy, and banal materialism of our time. Their clever denigrations discouraged my hope of convincing college-educated readers, as well as those who would pick up this volume out of mere nostalgia.

Could such doubt and hostility be successfully refuted? Whether or not such bias could be demolished, the limited format of this series would not sustain that kind of exploit. Instead, I concluded that adversities in human affairs, whether those of a nation or of an individual, ultimately contributed to acts of faith. During the short span of five years that I worked on this study, for example, Americans discovered flaws of various dimensions in the presidencies of the men who preceded and followed Eisenhower; with reexamination came a better understanding. I recognized, therefore, that my purpose need not be to convince but rather to stir the reader to take new measurement of the subject, to look for analyses undented by the well-ground axes of partisans of other heroes and other causes.

In the same sense, this book is an act of faith in me expressed by many friends. It was begun because my great friend Donald R. McCoy had confidence in my past and future as a scholar. Max Savelle, Professor Emeritus of the University of Washington, read each successive draft with the acuity of the fine, skilled scholar that he is. Professors Mark Rose and Clifford Griffin of the University of Kansas pointed out many ambiguities, imprecisions, and delusions, encouraging me to sharpen the focus of the final version.

From Phillip Paludan, another former colleague in Lawrence, I gained a better understanding of the constitutional matters involved in civil rights policy. In correspondence and conversations, Wilbur C. Eveland, Jr., who was on high-level intelligence assignments during the 1950s, pointed out important circumstances involved in the several Middle East crises. The staff of the Eisenhower Library in Abilene, Kansas, gave me every assistance in my search through the primary sources there. The Research Committee of the University of Kansas twice bore the cost of typing the manuscript. Marjorie O'Gorman and Lois Clark steadfastly deciphered the runes (ruins) of those pages to type the last two versions. Still undismayed, Lois went on to insert my ragged corrections and additions. Most importantly, in those five years of work and thought, I found a personal regeneration from the lessons of the spirit shown me by Reed Christiansen in brief but profound encounter, and I have moved on down the path since then.

Elmo Richardson

Seattle, Washington
September 1977

Contents

1

★★★★★

A SOLDIER'S DUTY

In the summer of 1951, General Dwight D. Eisenhower was reported to be in a cold sweat, losing weight, and wracked with stomach pains. At his Paris headquarters as commander of the military forces of the North Atlantic Treaty Organization (NATO), his aides warned visitors that the boss did not take shoving. Nevertheless, a long line of American businessmen and politicians persisted in carrying their urgent message into his office. The issues of an unpopular war and a controversial administration had divided the nation back home, they told him. Individual freedom, the two-party system, and capitalism itself seemed threatened with extinction. While the power and prestige of the United States were declining, communism was on the march throughout the world. There was only one hope for freedom at home and abroad, the visitors claimed: Eisenhower must run for the presidency of the United States in 1952.

The general was courteous but barely patient with these callers. In public remarks he rejected the possibility of becoming a candidate; in private conversations he was more specific. He had never run for any job in his life, he said; he was too old (he would be sixty-two by the time of the election); he did not want to give up the privacy of his retirement years to take on a job that was nothing like the command he had exercised during World War II. Public acclaim and political prestige held no attraction for a man who was already a hero in his own country and a friend of many world leaders. He felt that he had reached his peak in history seven years before, when he accepted the surrender of Nazi Germany.

1

These objections were, however, merely secondary considerations. The main reason that he rejected all suggestions of running for the presidency was the fact that he was a soldier. In the American tradition, the military was properly separated from, and subject to, civilian leadership. From time to time, some generals toyed with the conviction that they could do the job of government and diplomacy better than civilians, but rarely had any of them convinced a large portion of citizens of their ability. The dismal record of Ulysses S. Grant's presidency and William T. Sherman's categorical refusal to be a candidate were the lessons military men read when Eisenhower had entered West Point before World War I. John J. Pershing, leader of the American forces in that struggle, had disdainfully ignored political proposals that he run for the office in 1920; this greatly impressed Eisenhower, who was then a young officer attached to Pershing's staff. Years later, the political tendencies of another superior, Douglas MacArthur, confirmed Eisenhower's feeling that politics destroyed the qualities of soldiering. Yet it is precisely because he thought of himself as a soldier before all other things that he finally decided to seek the presidency. The experiences of his own career had convinced him that there was only one proper ambition for a soldier: to serve. When he told his friends that he had never run for any job, he was both accurate and self-revealing. Throughout his life, he had been the beneficiary of admiration and trust, and those gifts in turn had propelled him forward into ever greater responsibilities.

Born October 14, 1890, in Denison, Texas, Eisenhower grew up in Abilene, Kansas, a small farm town located geographically on the eastern edge of the Great Plains and spiritually in the landscape of what used to be described as "the American dream." His father, David, a stern and morally upright man, managed a creamery; his mother, born Ida Stover in Virginia, was a fundamentalist, a religious pacifist who taught her six sons that the sole distinction among people was to be measured by their exercise of Good and their perception of Evil. Along with nightly family Bible readings, the brothers found a framework of certainty in their father's firm instructions and their mother's favorite axioms. Living in a small house across the railroad tracks (literally and figuratively), each child assumed an equal share of responsibility for the serenity and orderliness of the home. "Ike," as Edgar—Dwight's next older brother and closest boyhood friend—nicknamed him, showed a deliberate cast of mind at an early age, a seriousness leavened by the delight he took in acting out the adventures of heroes and villains in Abilene's mythical past. Dwight became such an avid reader of historical epics that his high school yearbook predicted he would become a professor of history. (Edgar, that oracle said, would be president of the United States.) In 1911, an appointment to the United States Military Academy at West Point, New York, provided Dwight with the opportunity for a college education.

Eisenhower began his military career at the age of twenty-one, holding significantly different opinions from those of his younger classmates. While many plebes had an heroic vision of soldiering, his own view of the profession reflected a more mature motivation. Deeply impressed by his mother's belief that killing was a mortal sin, he had to reconcile his family heritage of concern for the value of human life with the realities of his chosen profession. At some point during the course of his early career, Eisenhower found it possible to consider military power primarily as a means of preventing bloodshed. Force directed by men who believed in the human spirit, he reasoned, would shield that spirit from the assaults of those who believed only in the sword. That same concept of soldiering had, of course, motivated crusader and Roundhead alike, among others in history. Eisenhower would indeed think of himself as a participant in a great crusade during World War II and later expressed admiration for the dedication of Cromwell's troops. But even in the enthusiasms of young manhood, he viewed zealousness as a superficial emotion. Nor did army ceremonials and West Point elitism appeal to him as they did to most of his associates. The soldier's way, he believed, was a matter of self-effacement; he viewed the posturings of the "brass hat" as unnecessary and improper behavior.

As a plebe, Eisenhower's bouts of stubbornness and flashing temper relegated him to the lower quarter of his class in discipline. But his genuine regard for people earned him a wide circle of friends. Always ready to throw off his usually solemn—sometimes dour—demeanor, he could flash an appealing smile and join in the bantering humor of the barracks. Off duty, he relished card games and surreptitious romances, but football was the real love of his life during those four years. Just when he demonstrated enough skill on the gridiron to attract outside notice, however, he sustained a leg injury that ended his athletic career. Later, he would channel his enthusiasm for the sport into organizing and coaching football teams wherever he was stationed.

Eisenhower eventually ranked in the top third of his class scholastically. Perhaps his avid interest in history contributed to

3

that achievement. In American history particularly, he studied the lives of several men who had the personal qualities he most admired. Foremost among them was George Washington, the modest, patient harmonizer of factions who subordinated his own feelings to the higher cause of his country's needs. Abraham Lincoln, the hero of Eisenhower's father's generation, had used his enormous powers with restraint and had shown a deep concern for those whose lives depended on his decisions. The lives of both leaders confirmed Eisenhower's belief that strength and compassion could be successfully blended in a man's character. His readings in biography reflected a personal interest in the role of the individual in human affairs, and that, in turn, was the basis for understanding the events of his own time. The exciting issues of those progressive reform years in America seemed to depend more on men of principle than on partisanship. As a boy, he had marched in a rally for William McKinley, but he was not thereafter interested in Republicanism so much as he was in Theodore Roosevelt's version of that political tradition. In 1913, Eisenhower was part of the West Point contingent that participated in Woodrow Wilson's inauguration ceremonies. Perhaps as a result of that experience, he paid particular attention to the president's subsequent conduct and policies.

After graduating from West Point in 1915, the new lieutenant was stationed in Texas, where he met and married a Denver girl, Mamie Doud. The early death of their first child, a son, would shadow Eisenhower's thoughts to the last years of his life. A second son, John, was born in 1922 and raised with all of the discipline and none of the indulgences of an army child. By then, Eisenhower had started on a series of duty assignments that taught him to curb any personal ambitions for the future by concentrating on the requirements of the present. His desire for active battle duty in World War I was thwarted when the Armistice was signed a week before he was scheduled to go overseas. At army training camps in the East, however, he developed friendships with men who had had wartime field experience. One of them was George Patton, a cavalry officer who preached the revolutionary advantages of the new weapons called tanks. In the early 1920s General Pershing sent Eisenhower to France to survey American cemeteries near the battlefields of the war and thereafter assigned him to a staff position in Panama.

Eisenhower's superior in the Canal Zone was General Fox Conner, a man who always put duty before any personal satisfaction. Conner also taught his junior officers the value of the written word: that is, the militarily vital difference between factual information and opinion. With Conner's recommendation, Eisenhower was later sent to General Staff and Command School at Fort Leavenworth, Kansas, to study war-games theory. In 1925, he graduated first in his class. Instead of putting theory into practice as a field commander, however, Eisenhower was sent to Washington, D.C., and ultimately was chosen as a personal aide by General MacArthur, the army chief of staff.

During the depression years, Eisenhower's livelihood was not affected by the economic strains that touched most Americans. As a result, he was far less enthusiastic than many about Franklin Roosevelt's New Deal. In comparing his views with those of his military associates, however, he thought of himself as a liberal, or at least as a humanitarian idealist. He was also impressed by the pragmatic arguments of his youngest brother, Milton, an assistant to the secretaries of agriculture during these years. While serving in the nation's capital, Eisenhower acquired firsthand familiarity with the frustrations and temptations experienced by military men in peacetime. He formed distinctly negative impressions of the politicians he encountered while testifying on army budgets before congressional committees. Their antimilitary views were especially aroused in 1932 when MacArthur led a rout of unemployed veterans camped near the capital. Eisenhower thought that by taking personal command, MacArthur would degrade himself or the army's public image, but he was ever after impatient with what he described as ill-informed criticism of that action. Soldiers, he believed, could do only what the civilians required of them.

Eisenhower stayed with his chief when MacArthur took up a new command in the Philippines in 1935. During the next three years, his duties ranged from organizing the commonwealth's army and air force to polishing the general's speeches and correspondence. MacArthur valued Eisenhower's dedication and staff abilities, but privately denigrated his aide as lacking toughness. MacArthur also seemed willing to shift to the subordinate blame for errors that he himself made. His own indulgence in self-promoting politics caused his aide to welcome reassignment. In 1938, Eisenhower was appointed chief of staff of the Third Army Division stationed at Fort Lewis, near Tacoma, Washington.

As the United States began to prepare its defenses after the outbreak of war in Europe, Eisenhower finally obtained the field command he had wanted for so long. At the army's peacetime maneuvers in Louisiana, he was acting commander of the "Blues."

(His force ultimately defeated the "enemy" led by his old friend Patton.) That experience, however, did not lead to further field duties. Instead he was ordered back to Washington, D.C., to work in the war plans divisions of the War Department. In 1940, he joined the staff of George C. Marshall, army chief of staff. General Marshall had watched Eisenhower's professional growth for several years and now took him under his wing as a protegé. Eisenhower, in turn, found in Marshall's modest, courtly personal manner and scrupulous professional principles the finest model for his own behavior. After the Japanese attack on Pearl Harbor in 1941, the two men worked long hours together planning the army's mobilization for combat. From that close association, Eisenhower learned the two interlocking axioms that constituted the keystone of Marshall's managerial philosophy: first, the decision-maker must not be distracted by problems his subordinates should resolve for themselves; and second, the subordinates must have ready the precise information needed as the bases for decisions.

Marshall did not grant his assistant a coveted field command, but sent him instead to London to serve as the liaison between American and British strategists. Eisenhower's analyses of Allied plans for the defeat of Germany were passed on to Secretary of War Henry Stimson and to President Roosevelt. Winston Churchill, then prime minister, was also impressed by these expositions and agreed with Roosevelt that Eisenhower would be a good choice to oversee the preliminary Allied offensive operation, an invasion of North Africa. Although he was a staff officer with no more than a few months of field experience after twenty-six years in the army, Eisenhower was given the post and promoted to major general over 810 other qualified senior officers.

In effect, wartime command was Eisenhower's political education. From the outset, his deliberative procedures and personal self-effacement were interpreted by Allied associates and war correspondents as signs of timidity. He quickly became skilled in selecting subordinates in field and staff positions, however, and was most successful in bringing together men of many nationalities and unproven abilities to work for the common cause of victory. The most troublesome of these men were Admiral Jean Darlan, commander of the forces of Occupied France in North Africa, and General Charles de Gaulle, leader of the Free French in exile. While de Gaulle was something of a popular symbol of the Allied cause, Darlan was the only man with enough authority to prevent French forces from opposing the Anglo-American armies. When Eisen-

6

hower secured the admiral's agreement to cooperate, many critics at home denounced this "Darlan deal" as appeasement of the fascists. For Eisenhower the incident was a convincing indication of the way in which military pragmatism would invariably be subject to political judgments. In any case, these detractions did not offset the fact that by 1943 he was the Allies' most knowledgeable manager of military operations. By then, Roosevelt and Churchill had agreed that it must be an American who would oversee the "second front," the invasion of Nazi-occupied Europe. General Marshall was the most likely choice for that post, but he withheld his hopes for it in the face of Roosevelt's desire to have him continue as the organizer of victory. Marshall thereupon recommended Eisenhower and was gratified when his onetime protegé was named supreme commander.

In that high position, Eisenhower was no solitary Napoleon, deciding grand strategy while surrounded by obsequious lieutenants. Instead, he was the instrument of Roosevelt and Churchill and the executor of strategic operations formulated by the combined chiefs of the Allied armies and navies. Moreover, a phalanx of field commanders made their own on-the-spot tactical judgments within the framework of those strategies. Eisenhower's role would later be described by critics as that of a glorified chairman of the board, but the manner in which he performed his task belies such a description. Most importantly, the two Allied leaders never overruled his military recommendations in any major instance. Although Eisenhower admired Roosevelt's ability to inspire Americans to a united effort, he rarely had direct contact with the president. But he frequently spoke and corresponded with the British prime minister after invasion headquarters were set up near London. Although Churchill often disagreed with him on matters of overall strategy, the prime minister set aside several pet schemes when confronted by Eisenhower's objective assessments. Because both men shared a deep concern for preserving the Anglo-American alliance, their association quickly ripened into a close friendship that continued until Churchill's death more than twenty years later.

Working with military chiefs from several nations, the supreme commander was mindful of the fact that he was the newcomer, an outsider with the obligation of gaining respect from all of his associates. Under the circumstances of unified command, Eisenhower could not merely give orders. He believed that leadership was basically a matter of inspiring men to want to follow; it was the art of persuading by one's example, not by force or eloquence. A man would demonstrate his own ability or lack thereof; neither pushing nor pulling him could improve his ability; to do so would mean doing his job for him. Eisenhower, therefore, kept the reins of command loose enough to permit his colleagues to exercise their best judgments.

He used this method in dealing with the principal Allied commanders in the field. In Omar Bradley, his West Point classmate who now led the American forces in the conquest of Nazi-occupied countries, Eisenhower had a self-reliant yet dependable colleague. But Field Marshall Bernard Montgomery, overall commander of the British troops, was a cross to bear. Contemptuous of the supreme commander and nearly everyone else, "Monty" rode his own self-esteem in pursuit of independent, sometimes dangerously unwise, tactics. Eisenhower chose not to respond to Montgomery's rudeness, checked his own temper, and repeatedly asked for cooperation. The field marshall's contribution, he reasoned, was essential to the cause of Allied unity if not to the final victory. But Eisenhower's self-restraint with Montgomery contributed to the feeling held by some American generals that he was not tough enough for a position of overall command.

Another, more personally painful test of Eisenhower's technique was his dealings with George Patton. Upon learning that his old comrade had slapped a hospitalized enlisted man, he was willing to remove Patton from command of the Italian campaign; but he greatly preferred to bring that master of armored thrust and pursuit into the main European theater of operations. In private communication, Eisenhower rebuked the general by pointing out that any further lapse of self-control would deprive the Allied cause of Patton's abilities. Using the same argument, he secured the silence of war correspondents who knew of the slapping incident. On his recommendation, Patton was appointed soon after to the new command over the opposition of several Allied officers. His subsequent bold actions in sweeping back the Nazi forces proved the wisdom of Eisenhower's forbearance.

In other instances as well, the supreme commander preferred to respond to pressures with firmness. For example, he rejected the contention of American army air force officers that massive bombing alone would provide a short-cut to victory. Instead, he utilized every force available and applied the enormous power at his command in a measured but relentless manner. He was also anxious to prevent disorder in the lower ranks from undermining the morale and discipline essential to military action. When Eddie Slovik, an American private, was tried and sentenced to death for disobedience during the desperate German counteroffensive of 1944—the Battle of the Bulge—the supreme commander refused to stay the man's execution. Slovik seemed to him to be the "barracks-lawyer" type who fomented trouble in many military units. Such behavior had to be unmistakably checked, and the decisions of military courts in time of war had to be upheld unconditionally. The incident was, of course, on the periphery of Eisenhower's paramount concerns.

The invasion of Europe on D-Day, June 6, 1944, was the product of general systems analysis, of multi-level, integrated assessments of every fact and option involved in moving many thousands of men, ships, aircraft, weapons, and supplies. But it was up to just one man to decide when the plan would be set in motion. Eisenhower's terse "OK. Let's go" was the most admired of all his wartime decisions. In contrast, he never heard the end of criticism about withholding Anglo-American units from capturing Berlin before the Russians took the German capital. On many occasions later in his life, Eisenhower would have to explain the circumstances behind that judgment. (They were that the Russians were much closer to the city; an advanced striking force of his own troops would have been vulnerable to flank attacks and to being cut off from their supplies; and, finally, the decision was in keeping with an agreement made by Roosevelt, Churchill, and Joseph Stalin, the Soviet Union's leader, to place Berlin and its environs in a postwar zone to be occupied by Russian troops.) From the outset of his command, Eisenhower was determined to fight a military—not a political—war. His decision on who should capture Berlin was consistent with that soldierly priority. He always thought that the controversy over the decision was a fine example of armchair strategists' reasoning after the fact.

When the forces of Nazi Germany surrendered at his field headquarters, Eisenhower gladly put down the grim burden of making life-and-death decisions. But his managerial duties continued. In June 1945, he was appointed to be military governor of the American occupation zone. Because he initially had opposed dividing Germany and Berlin into zones and believed that the military should not participate in political administration, he was not happy with the assignment. As he expected, his responsibilities took him further into political controversy than he cared to go. Among his recommendations was support for the economic reconstruction of western Germany; and one of his orders was for the return of displaced persons to their homelands, even if those countries were now under Soviet control. Both actions drew fire from members of

Congress and others at home who differed on the question of how to deal with the Russians.

When the leaders of the United States, Britain, and the Soviet Union held their final Big Three conference in July, Eisenhower learned that the newly developed atomic bomb would be used to force the surrender of Japan. He thought the strategy faulty: Japan was already making overtures for peace; in a few more months or even weeks, use of the bomb would be unnecessary. He was especially concerned with the moral impact this devastating weapon would have on the international image of the United States. Truman usually relied on the advice of the military chiefs, but in this instance he did not accept Eisenhower's reasoning; Secretary of War Stimson, who was angered by the general's opposition, supported the president's decision to use the bomb.

Eisenhower was relieved of his post as military governor in October 1945 and returned home to accept the honors of a grateful nation and the cheers of an admiring citizenry. He was then fifty-five years old, still nine years short of the army's retirement age, but his thoughts already inclined toward possible civilian occupations. Perhaps, he confided to close friends at this time, he could head some small college in the Pacific Northwest or the Great Plains. There, he might become something of a respected campus character, teaching young people what he believed was the proper basis for the nation's role in any future wars. The dream was pleasant but premature. Away from challenging wartime responsibilities, he soon felt a distinct let-down. He was gratified, therefore, when President Truman appointed him late in 1946 to be army chief of staff.

Succeeding his mentor, General Marshall, Eisenhower took the job on a one-year provisional basis. He soon found the work onerous. The task of juggling military budgets brought him into contact once again with politicians and bureaucrats. He observed that some congressmen were still just as anxious to reduce the size and expense of the nation's armed forces as their predecessors had been a decade before. Many of his recommendations became the casualties of political warfare: for example, when he endorsed the idea of universal military training based on peacetime conscription, old-line Republicans cited his testimony as proof that the Democratic administration intended to transform the nation into a "garrison state." He also faced dissent from his own army colleagues. Some generals feared that Truman's proposal to combine the War and Navy departments into a single department of defense would diminish their influence. Eisenhower, on the other hand, welcomed the plan because it would end wasteful interservice rivalries. Recalling past administrations, he also expected that the new agency would mix politics into decisions on strategy and military contracts.

Although critical of the distribution of executive authority in the Defense Department, he accepted the president's appointment as provisional chairman of the new Joint Chiefs of Staff. Eisenhower and his immediate superior, James Forrestal, a former naval officer who had been named as the first secretary of defense, soon found themselves in full accord on the subject of deteriorating Soviet-American relations. Eisenhower believed that Russia would not initiate a war (short of a blunder or stupidity) for at least five years. He felt that politicians and diplomatic advisers were basing long-range policies on fearful assumptions about the Communists. Defense should be based on military knowledge, he believed, not on suspicion. In 1947, consequently, he supported Forrestal's recommendations for a nuclear detection/warning system and for the establishment of a central intelligence agency (CIA). When Congress called for drastic cuts in the nation's defense budget, however, Eisenhower resigned his temporary post.

In November 1947 he had attained the highest American military rank, but Eisenhower did not think that his duty as a soldier was finished. Although now on inactive status, he had been too close to events and decisions to be inactive in any real sense. Freed of official restraints, he set to work in the spring of 1948 to expand a short piece he had written at the war's end. Expressing his own feelings about the nature of that great struggle, he titled his account *Crusade in Europe*. Because of its author's prestige and influence, the volume quickly became a best seller, ultimately earning $250,000 in royalties. Eisenhower's purpose in writing the book was to remind Americans of the strength afforded by collective security. But *Crusade in Europe* also served to conduct him into a new field. Just as it was finished, his publisher, Douglas Black, together with Thomas Watson, head of International Business Machines, induced their fellow trustees at Columbia University in New York City to offer Eisenhower the institution's presidency. It was hardly the college of his earlier dream, but the trustees assured him that at Columbia he could better pursue the Holmesian purpose of instructing the younger generation in matters of war and peace.

As Columbia's president, Eisenhower was not generally success-

11

ful in communicating with the university population. Although he defended faculty and academic integrity in that time of loyalty oaths and urged students to seek opportunity rather than security, many remained biased against his military background. On the other hand, he was remarkably successful in presenting the university's best features to the public and in soliciting funds for its growth. Traveling across the country, he met with hundreds of alumni, most of them wealthy and prominent men. In the public speeches he made and the private conversations he held, Eisenhower naturally touched on domestic issues and international tensions. While he echoed his listeners' distrust of liberalism (in the New Deal sense of that word), he insisted that he was neither a conservative nor a liberal. Both ideologies, he argued, tended to rely on theories and shibboleths instead of deciding each question on its own merits, within the framework of what was best for America. In 1948, an election year, these centralist views attracted considerable attention.

A war correspondent whose name has been lost to history was the first to broach the subject of a presidential candidacy to Eisenhower. That event occurred in North Africa in June 1943, and the general responded by suggesting that the man had been out in the desert sun too long. "Once this war is over," he wrote to a friend at about this time, "I hope never again to hear the word 'politics'."[1] But a year later, several British and American officers who worked closely with the supreme commander were certain that he very much wanted to be president. After the war, the question of his candidacy followed Eisenhower as the war hero toured cities all across the United States. In 1946, former superiors as diverse as Marshall and MacArthur urged him to run for the office, and Secretary Forrestal assured him that he could not help being president. In 1947, Truman considered him for the post of secretary of state (before appointing Marshall) and afterwards suggested to him the idea of a Truman-Eisenhower ticket in 1948, designed to close the rifts in the Democratic party. By adhering to Sherman's stance, which present circumstances had rendered "academic," Eisenhower privately admitted, "I am merely punishing myself."[2] His rejections of these solicitations were noticeably oblique. For example, he said that he could not see any circumstances that would elicit his permission to be considered for candidacy. But in January 1948, he made public a letter to Leonard Finder, a New Hampshire newspaper publisher who was drumming up support for him. In it, Eisenhower underscored his belief in the separation of military men from civilian office. Moreover, he said, he did not think that the American people wanted a soldier as president.

That summer, Senator Arthur Vandenberg, Jr., of Michigan submitted Eisenhower's name to the Republican national convention. The gesture was primarily an effort to head off the nomination of Senator Robert A. Taft of Ohio, an isolationist, and the boomlet quickly faded when the delegates chose Governor Thomas E. Dewey of New York. After Dewey went down to unexpected defeat in November, Eisenhower's admirers renewed their speculations. Their interest was whetted by the distinctly political overtones of his speeches as a university president. He referred to the "paternalistic measures" of a government "swarming with bureaucrats" and to a nation divided by pressure groups "organized in opposition to the whole." There were some citizens, he said, who believed themselves to be liberals but who, in fact, "work unceasingly" for ideas that would advance American civilization "one more step toward total socialism, beyond which lies total dictatorship."[3]

Eisenhower was undoubtedly giving serious thought during 1949 to the conditions and possibilities of political life. In August, several friends presented him with an analysis of the health of both major political parties. They described the Democrats as hopelessly socialistic and the Republicans as critically weakened by intransigent, ineffective leadership. Their report claimed, however, that the Republican tradition was closer to Eisenhower's own beliefs and concluded that its salvation meant the preservation of the two-party system in America. Such an important task transcended mere partisanship, Eisenhower reasoned. A victorious candidate must, therefore, secure both party unity and bipartisan support among the voters. This speculative analysis suddenly ended, however, when he left Columbia to resume his military career; any further political considerations, he told friends, were now out of the question.

In 1949, the United States became a founding member of the North Atlantic Treaty Organization over the opposition of isolationists led by Senator Taft. As Eisenhower saw it, NATO was nothing less than Western civilization's last chance for survival. But when President Truman asked him to take command of the armed forces being assembled by the NATO members, he accepted with some regret. The work at Columbia had interested him greatly, and he felt such tremendous personal disappointment in having to give it up that he asked for an indefinite leave of absence instead of resigning. Just as he was moving to NATO's Paris headquarters, the United States once again faced war, this time in the Far East.

ıne 1950, Truman ordered General MacArthur to use Amer-
ɔrces in Japan to halt a Communist invasion of South Korea.
ɩnhower believed that the aggression would never have occurred
the United States had not dismantled its wartime military strength;
but as one of the president's principal military advisers, he supported
the so-called police action. Here was an opportunity, he thought,
for showing free nations everywhere that peace and freedom were
in constant jeopardy. The subsequent participation of other members of the United Nations would, like the formation of NATO,
demonstrate the necessity for collective security. These were the
subjects of his own pronouncements when he assumed his new command. Thinking of himself as a modern Peter the Hermit, he
preached the message of international cooperation, but in the streets
of Western European capitals, he encountered nationalistic jealousies and "Go home, Ike" signs. Far more disturbing was the criticism back home directed against both the UN and NATO.

Confronted by conditions of the recent war years—the draft,
shortages, curtailment of business expansion—Americans grew increasingly dissatisfied with the Truman administration. They were
further shocked by the Communists' near expulsion of American
troops from Korea and by the president's removal of MacArthur
from his command there. In a climate of growing discontent, the
fear-mongers plied a lively trade. Public officials discussed crash
programs for air raid shelters, and citizens debated the ethics of
turning away unsheltered neighbors. General James Doolittle, hero
of the famous World War II air raid on Tokyo, advocated a preemptive nuclear attack on the Communists. Republican Senator
Joseph McCarthy of Wisconsin blamed the Democrats for sheltering
traitors and allowing nations in Europe and Asia to fall to Communist conquest.

Eisenhower was contemptuous of these men who peddled fear
and hatred in the guise of patriotism. When he returned home in
June 1951 to report on NATO's first year, he learned of the growing
influence in Congress of a small but powerful faction of those he
called extreme nationalists. While he was at the Pentagon, their
leader, Senator Taft, asked to talk with him. The two men agreed
on the need to preserve individual liberties against the domination
of big government, but Eisenhower concluded that the senator was
very stupid in advocating withdrawal to a "fortress America" stance
in world affairs. Eisenhower was ready to issue a statement removing his name from further political consideration if Taft had expressed even a general commitment to collective security. The

general was not taking a chance with his own future; it was very unlikely that his visitor would abandon long-held convictions. The statement was a characteristic gesture of self-denial, indicating how strongly he felt about using his own influence to turn the nation away from neo-isolationism.

In that agitated frame of mind, he returned to Paris to be confronted by the long line of well-wishers visiting his office. He knew of the crises at home and abroad as well as any of them, but he was interested in their assessments. The views of two professionals particularly impressed him. John Foster Dulles, a career diplomat in the State Department and Dewey's former foreign affairs adviser, presented an analysis of international problems that prompted Eisenhower to think of him as a likely secretary of state. A second expert was Senator Henry Cabot Lodge, Jr., of Massachusetts, who had been Dewey's campaign strategist. Lodge had served as political liaison with the Allied command during the war and had met Eisenhower then. He knew the general's wartime reasoning about the requirements for a successful candidacy. Now he showed Eisenhower a private poll that indicated Americans did not object to having a soldier as president; he described the bipartisan membership of the "Citizens for Ike" clubs mushrooming across the nation; and he pledged the assistance of Dewey and his followers. When Eisenhower asked why he—Lodge—or Dewey did not run for the nomination, Lodge replied that they could not win. Only Eisenhower could win, he argued, because only he commanded sufficient respect at home and abroad to deal with the dual crises in freedom.

At the end of their meeting, Eisenhower agreed not to disavow any efforts on his behalf, as he had in 1948. The senator then returned home to enter the general's name on the ballot for the New Hampshire primary in January 1952. The results there and from a write-in vote in Minnesota were very gratifying. Eisenhower and his wife were also deeply moved when they saw a film made at an enthusiastic rally for him, held in Madison Square Garden in New York City. Further encouragement came from Truman's announcement that he would not be a candidate for reelection. The soldier's doubts about the embarrassing prospect of having to publicly criticize the commander-in-chief were thereby allayed. He made a few last gestures of reluctance. One was a plaintive letter to a friend: "How happy I'd be," he exclaimed, "if all the people who believed a change is necessary would agree on some young, vigorous leader— and forget old soldiers."[4] But General Lucius Clay, his wartime political adviser, told him the time had come to fish or cut bait.

After the decision was made, Eisenhower took up his new challenge eagerly. In April, he announced that he would resign his NATO command in June and return to the United States to campaign for the Republican nomination.

Long after he left the presidency, he told an interviewer, "My hand was forced by Lodge."[5] It was not. He had already decided on a set of requirements that had to be met before he would venture into partisan politics; and the senator's political intelligence assured Eisenhower that the required circumstances were at hand. Those circumstances, however, did not lay the foundations for his receptivity; they put the finishing touches on it. During the preceding years, domestic and international issues had caused Eisenhower to enlarge his concept of a soldier's duty to include a dimension beyond military responsibilities. As early as September 1948, he wrote to advise Forrestal that the time had arrived "when everyone must begin to think in terms of his possible future duty and be as fully prepared for its performance as possible."[6] For Eisenhower, the NATO command was both that duty and a time of preparation. While in Paris, he wrote to his brother Milton about the possibility of a larger duty; and in December 1951 he admitted to Lodge that he hoped he would always be ready to accept any duty, including one "which would, by common consent in our country, take priority over the one I am now performing." With characteristic self-denial, however, he hastened to add that "realization of such a hope certainly does not require occupation of political office."[7]

But political office was the only responsibility pending, and while he had never run for any job in his life, he also had never refused any assignment in his life. His earlier confidence "that I alone should make a negative decision" was worn away by the repeated arguments that it was his duty to run. "I have always been particularly sensitive" he recalled in his diary seven years later, "to any insinuation that I might recoil from performance of any duty, no matter how onerous." He had been close enough to the presidency to know that "any serious-minded incumbent of that office is bound to feel . . . [that] its frustrations and disappointments far outweigh any possible satisfaction. . . . Consequently I had no struggle with any personal ambition of my own."[8]

Having entered the political arena by waiting until circumstances caught up with his scruples, Eisenhower hoped that the nomination would seek him. Perhaps the ideal of George Washington was in his mind—as well as Wendell Willkie's sweep of the Republican convention in 1940. He now recalled the earlier predictions by his supporters that both parties might nominate him. Perhaps that is why he waited until the last minute to declare himself a Republican. If he held that naive hope, it was rudely shattered—not only by defensive Democrats, but by aggressive Taft Republicans as well. Stooping to conquer the nomination and certain victory, the Taft men cried that Eisenhower was a pig-in-a-poke, put forward by a modern Conway's Cabal (the alleged conspiracy to remove George Washington as commander-in-chief of the Continental army) in an un-American coup d'état. "Draft Ike," they mocked, "and he will draft you." They scoffed that Eisenhower was "a good-looking mortician" who would bury the party's tradition of "America first."[9] Eisenhower, they whispered, had had an affair with his wartime chauffeur, Kay Summersby, and had asked General Marshall to approved a divorce from Mamie so that he could marry the woman. A delegation from one midwestern state even flew to Paris to ask the general if his wife was an alcoholic. "No, it's not so," he reportedly told them without flinching, "the truth of the matter is that I don't think Mamie has had a drink for something like eighteen months."[10]

Eisenhower, used to the customs and behavior of army life, was bewildered by the political bitterness and desperation he found in the summer of 1952 at the Republican National Convention in Philadelphia. He wisely stayed away and watched the proceedings on television in his hotel suite while his professionals worked to wear away Taft's apparent majority. Leading the Eisenhower forces were Dewey's former strategists, Senator Lodge and Herbert Brownell, Jr. At the outset, they seized upon the fraudulent selection of Taft delegates in Texas and protested that the party could not stand before the voters promising to end Democratic corruption if its own hands were unclean. To their surprise, Taft agreed to a "fair play" resolution calling for the examination of disputed credentials. Combining their appeal to morality with the prediction that "Taft can't win," the Eisenhower team steadily gained strength among delegates pledged to favorite sons. On the third ballot, the general emerged with a slight margin, enough to win the nomination.

By that time, Eisenhower was completely worn out and heartily sick of the whole business. Mamie was ill, and he himself was suffering from long-standing stomach troubles. Still not certain whether his decision to become a candidate had been a wise one, Eisenhower was at first more dazed than elated by his nomination. When he asked Taft for future support, he appeared to be so agitated that the senator's friends wondered if he feared the task ahead. Looking back on that day, Eisenhower remembered how sad he felt as he wrote out a letter resigning his five-star rank, thereby becoming a civilian for the first time in over forty years. The evening of the same day, however, he appeared before the convention beaming and resolute and promised the cheering crowd that he would lead another crusade, this one for freedom in America.

Eisenhower appointed Brownell as his campaign manager, but he alone determined what he would do and say, in keeping with his own values and priorities. Resenting the Republican National Committee's obvious intention to campaign on the basis of his wartime popularity and contemptuous of the party's past electoral record, Eisenhower turned for substantive advice to political analysts, economists, and businessmen who had extensive experience with federal programs. But it was his decision to invite the still-brooding Taft to his home to find common ground for future legislation. And it was his decision to campaign in the southern states, although party professionals had crossed off that region as irretrievably Democratic.

Eisenhower made a slow start, perhaps because he had to adjust his personal code of conduct to the demands of campaigning. But in time, he learned the rhetoric that Republicans had honed to perfection during the past four years. While he focused on the main issues of Korea, communism, and corruption, he preferred to discuss consequences rather than personalities. He refused to attack the president, lest his words undermine respect for the presidency and diminish his own potential use of that office. In his presentations, Eisenhower posed neither as savior nor as architect. Instead he concentrated on three themes: the dangers of power centralized in the federal government; the debilitating influence of government domination of the economy; and the inadequacy of America's response to Communist threats to freedom around the world. In these matters he urged the restoration of initiative to the states and local communities; an equitable partnership between the federal government and private enterprise in the development of the economy; responsible federal funding of the nation's essential needs; and in foreign affairs, the substitution of deliberation for isolationism and selectivity for indiscriminate commitments of the nation's influence. To the disappointment of many members of his party, Eisenhower did not advocate dismantling the twenty-year accretion of federal power nor would he indulge in what he considered the demagogic promise to cut taxes. He also refused to attack his Democratic opponent, Governor Adlai Stevenson of Illinois, by name. (Although he would later revise his opinion, he initially considered Stevenson a statesman rather than a politician.)

Although his scrupulous campaign conduct was inspirational, Eisenhower's supporters wondered anxiously how he expected to win with it. Early in the fall, public opinion polls were giving him only a slight edge over Stevenson when two incidents seemed to erode that potential margin of victory. The first of these involved Joseph McCarthy. Angered by the way in which the senator and his adherents had branded General Marshall as a traitor who had abandoned China to communism, Eisenhower delivered a moderate but certain defense of his mentor in a speech in Denver. As he moved on to McCarthy's home grounds in Milwaukee, Wisconsin, Walter Kohler, the state's Republican governor, urged him to remove a similar passage from the remarks he would make there. The candidate's feelings about Marshall were already on record, Kohler argued, and to raise the matter again would point up intraparty differences and embarrass everyone else on the platform.

Eisenhower accepted that counsel, in part because he thought that General Marshall would be embarrassed if the subject was transformed into a political issue. He was obviously angry when he ordered the reference taken out of the speech. Newsmen on the campaign train did not know of the deletion until they heard the speech; nor did the public know, until many years later, that Eisenhower gave McCarthy a private bawling out that evening at his hotel. The next day Democrats seized on the deletion as shameful evidence of ingratitude and disloyalty. Having already put the matter out of his mind, Eisenhower was surprised and chagrined by the criticism. Six years later, after McCarthy was dead, he broke his public silence about the incident to say that he would never permit anyone to traduce Marshall "in my presence."[11]

The second campaign incident was far more grave. After his nomination, Eisenhower had accepted the recommendation of Dewey, Brownell, and Republican National Committee chairman Arthur Summerfield that Senator Richard Nixon of California was the man most qualified for the vice presidential slot on the ticket. He later publicly repeated their private assurances that the senator's past prosecution of alleged Communists had been scrupulously fair. Nixon's presence on the ticket would, of course, ensure that all party factions were represented in the inner circle. But Eisenhower's personal interest was in the senator's youth. (Nixon was thirty-nine and looked even younger.) The general hoped Nixon would appeal to the great number of new voters and serve as a symbol of Eisenhower's determination to rejuvenate the party's ranks.

In the midst of the campaign, Nixon became the target of charges alleging that he was the beneficiary of a secret slush fund raised by wealthy California industrialists. Eisenhower was at first disgusted to learn that such things were used by politicians; had it been a matter of a subordinate's misbehavior in the army, he said later, he would have dismissed the man at once. But he was also contemptuous of those advisers who hysterically urged him to drop Nixon from the ticket in order to preserve his own image and electoral chances. In any crisis, Eisenhower thought deliberation was essential. He first secured an accounting firm's quick evaluation of Nixon's finances; it revealed nothing that substantiated the charges. His political advisers assured him that such slush funds were common—even Stevenson had one, they said. He also recognized that mudslinging was a favorite political pastime and that Nixon had made vengeful enemies in the course of his anti-Communist campaign. If the senator was dropped from the ticket, Eisenhower reasoned, party unity would be shattered. If Nixon was guilty of wrong-doing, the party's appeal to morality would be besmirched. In either case, victory would be impossible. One more factor remained to be evaluated before a decision could be made: whether or not the man showed himself worthy of trust. In a telephone conversation, Eisenhower advised Nixon to defend himself before the whole nation. After watching the so-called Checkers speech on television Eisenhower told an audience in Cleveland that he "would rather go down to defeat with a brave man," than to win with "a bunch of cowards." He sent a telegram at once to the senator declaring his continued confidence and later met Nixon with the gladsome greeting: "You're my boy."[12] Thus, in reaching a decision there was no disruptive confrontation, nothing was done impulsively or desperately, and all options were duly evaluated. That resolution of the crisis apparently satisfied a majority of the electorate.

Referring to the Nixon and Marshall episodes, the Democrats added timidity and indecision to their portrait of Eisenhower. Their caricature also showed him to be dim-witted and, compared to Stevenson, lacking in executive experience. These distortions were not only incredible, they were ineffective. The repeated warning that Eisenhower was a militarist also rebounded with immeasurable effect. No campaign issue better summed up the nation's disenchantment, doubt, and dislocation than the war in Korea. It had cost men, money, and resources, yet after two years of fighting there had been only retreat and a stalemate. Many were prone to ascribe those dismal circumstances to what they believed was the ineptitude and disloyalty of the decision-makers in the Truman administration. Instead of making Americans distrust military men, the war made them view the prospect of a soldier in the White House as desirable.

Because of his NATO assignment, Eisenhower had not evaluated the situation in Korea firsthand. Early in the campaign, therefore, he decided that he would go to the battle front once the people had elected him. He waited until other candidates raised the issue of the Korean War late in the campaign and then announced he would make the trip. The overwhelmingly favorable response buoyed Republican hopes, of course, but Democrats denounced the pledge as demagoguery, evidence of a militarist's one-track solution to all problems. Having called him timid, they liked his boldness even less. In private, Eisenhower himself expressed doubts about the wisdom of the statement. Some citizens, he thought, might conclude he could bring victory in Korea. Worse, he feared, they might assume that all other national security and foreign policy matters would be handled that same way. Political analyst Samuel Lubell later judged that the pledge to visit Korea was the most important factor in Eisenhower's election.

On November 4, 1952, the newcomer to politics received 21.5 million votes out of more than 39 million votes cast. He won the electoral votes of every state outside the South; four Border States went Republican for the first time since Reconstruction. The morning after, a banner was hung from the window of an old brownstone house in the Beacon Hill section of Boston; it read simply: "Thank God."[13] Across the nation in the Pacific Northwest, citizens felt that "the course of history" had been changed by an election that was "so very necessary."[14]

Much was said subsequently about the personal nature of Eisenhower's victory. While the majority of Americans signified that they "liked Ike," they gave only a slight majority to Republican candidates for Congress. But the word "personal" also referred to the fame of the war hero. To be sure, many voters were members of the World War II generation who eagerly registered their admiration for the onetime supreme commander. Moreover, his photogenic smile and soldierly bearing was enhanced by television in that new medium's first coverage of a presidential campaign. Yet, Eisenhower did not exploit his popularity and always resented the implication that Americans were so gullible that they would vote on that basis. Political analysts would later suggest that the Amer-

BOTTINEAU LIBRARY

027171

ican people saw in his character and experience a reflection of their own ideals and aspirations. He was indeed a comforting set of contradictions: a soldier of peace, a plain-spoken intellect, a manager of power who advocated harmony and equity. Perhaps they voted for Dwight Eisenhower because they shared his conviction that strength and respect for human values can be successfully combined not only in the character of a man, but in the character of a nation as well.

2

★★★★★

GOVERNMENT IS PEOPLE

The Eisenhower era began with high expectations and certainties. At the outset, economic experts assured Americans that the nation's enterprise would not again falter, that socialism had been safely by-passed, and that even the Cold War had a bright side: it would stimulate trade and production at home and abroad. The total wealth of the United States was then reckoned in excess of $1 trillion. During Eisenhower's two terms the gross national product grew by 25 percent to well over $400 billion. The hucksters of advertising dazzlingly displayed the immediate prospect of a magical technology. There would be prefabricated dream houses in the suburbs, futuristic cars, plastics and fabrics made by chemistry, television sets to bring grand opera as well as sports into every living room, more and better food with less work, and income and leisure time to devote to all of these things. And the predictions appeared to be quickly fulfilled. In 1955, for example, General Motors made a profit of $1 billion. The number of television sets climbed from a million at the beginning of the decade to fifty million at its close.

While the great middle class—a term subsuming everyone's ambition if not their status—happily embraced the new prosperity, they were mindful of a second concern. As they had learned during the Great Depression and war years, they taught their children the equation of material success and the moral heroics of individualism. As a result, church memberships and attendance boomed during the 1950s; a new evangelicalism appeared clad in the modernity of "positive thinking"; and young adults found a new piety in social respectability. Yet these beliefs were simultaneously being undermined by the mobility and rootlessness required of all who took advantage of the new economic opportunities. Moreover, by 1955, American literature, art, films, music, and drama turned increasingly to existential themes and portrayed the futile efforts of anti-heroes.

The weakening of traditional American faith in individual worth may be explained by recalling a single statistic: by the end of the decade, the population of the United States had reached almost 180 million, up 22 million from 1950. Indeed, in just one year, 1955, it increased by nearly 3 million. Over two thirds of these people lived in cities or new suburbs. The 25 percent rate of urban growth, for example, doubled the population of Los Angeles during those ten years. In order to meet the multiple requirements of that massed society, the nation's political, economic, and social systems had to deal in human quantities not human qualities. Organization was essential in every phase of activity from planning to public response. Coping with any problem became a matter of computation and collaboration. Even such old antagonisms as capital versus labor gave way to the symbiosis that would be called countervailing power. Interdependence was in turn facilitated by instant replication and easy conformity, epitomized in the "buttoned-down" look in men's fashions and the homogeneous wares offered in the supermarkets and shopping centers upon which mobile urbanites and suburbanites depended.

If material progress transformed conformity into the new orthodoxy, what could remain of the belief in individual initiative and choice? That question was central to the citizens' view of the national political process and the affairs of the world beyond. They expected their representatives in the federal government to continue to generously support farm production and resource development—matters affecting masses of people—yet to prevent enlargement of federal regulation in those areas. Americans were especially anxious to protect the private sector from government in such matters as social welfare and education, areas deemed the proper realm of private citizens. It was this underlying anxiety that accounted for the rigidity of popular convictions about the Cold War, McCarthyism, and civil rights. But the people acted inconsistently. While many were fervid about anticommunism, over 40 percent of the electorate failed to vote for any candidates in the elections held during that decade. If their main concern, therefore, was to retain both the values of the past and the promise of the future that was at hand, then their principal need was for a clear sense of national purpose. In January 1953 they turned to the new president to fulfill those expectations.

Dwight Eisenhower used the presidency not as a sword of power, but as a set of scales. Instead of thrusting the executive branch of the federal government into conditions and events, he marshaled its authority to restore a balance between citizens and the state. That difficult feat called for the exercise of executive power, of course, but the command experiences of war and peace had convinced Eisenhower that restraint was the key to the effective use of power. Restraint, however, was more than a matter of scruples; it was a matter of deliberation and judicious choice. Instead of continuing his Democratic predecessors' portrayal of the president as a "great white father," Eisenhower chose to act as the nation's teacher. Rather than assuring Americans that an omniscient and omnipotent government would solve their problems, he urged them to express their sensibilities and defend their initiatives, to be participants in every aspect of the nation's life.

In presenting that lesson, Eisenhower expressed his fundamental faith in the eminence of God as the wellspring of individual strength. From the outset of his administration, he directed public attention to the spiritual base of government. He opened his inaugural address with a prayer recognizing the spiritual equality of all men and began each cabinet meeting with a moment of silent prayer. He frequently spoke to religious gatherings and expressed admiration for religious leaders who understood that "any advance in the world has got to be accompanied by a clear realization that man is, after all, a spiritual being."[1]

Eisenhower organized the executive branch on the basis of his belief in the worth of the individual as the essence of any organization. Reminding Americans that "we must always think of government as persons,"[2] he projected presidential leadership as a matter of teamwork. "Now look," he explained, "this idea that all wisdom is in the President, in me, that's baloney. . . . I don't believe this government was set up to be operated by any one acting alone; no one has a monopoly on the truth and on the facts that affect this country. . . . We must work together."[3] Rejecting the appeals of special interest groups because he believed that they accentuated differences and created friction, his aim was "to bring people together so we can actually achieve progress . . . for the United States."[4] As a first step, he organized a White House administrative staff.

In the course of his military career, Eisenhower had been im-

25

pressed with the management process called general systems analysis—a systematic, interlocking, regenerative scrutiny of all available information and functions applicable to the operations of every large organization. Now, as president, he selected assistants who were familiar with such procedures, men who had held positions in business and planning during the war and after, and those who were particularly experienced in finance and management. Most of them came from the East and Midwest and had been educated at Ivy League schools or private universities. Few of them were chosen because of their political associations; in fact, politics was the least of their interests. Expressing a sense of honor to be a part of the president's crusade to restore harmony and equity to the nation, they rarely indulged in the jealousies and backbiting common among men close to the sources of power.

The dozen members of the top-echelon of the White House staff were men with whom Eisenhower had recently worked. Among them were his wartime associates, Walter Bedell Smith, Wilton "Jerry" Persons, and Andrew Goodpaster; others were Bryce Harlow, Gabriel Hague, and C. D. Jackson, men from government, academia, and business whom he had met during the postwar period. The responsibilities of these presidential assistants were grouped under four headings: domestic affairs (cabinet secretariat, departmental liaison, congressional liaison, state and local relations); foreign affairs (defense, national, and mutual security, intelligence); special projects established by order of the president or Congress; and routine scheduling and coordination.

Like everyone else, members of the White House staff had access to the president through a single person: Sherman Adams. The former New Hampshire governor who had encouraged Eisenhower to become a candidate and had helped him win the nomination was given the ambiguous title "assistant to the president," but in a more precise term, he was the "ramrod" to the "trail boss." Adams made staff assignments and personnel changes and decided what subjects would appear on the president's daily agenda. He gave and withheld permission to enter the Oval Office on the basis of whether the information was vital and the president receptive. He also sat in on cabinet meetings and monitored most of the president's conversations with advisers and delegations. He did not participate in those discussions unless called on and did not have personal expertise in any major policy area.

Observers who mistook propinquity for influence thought that Adams was a "grey eminence," an "assistant president" who made most of Eisenhower's decisions. Some Republican leaders resented his laconic, negative responses to their requests to talk with the president, and together with Democratic critics, they bitterly repeated the joke that answered the question, "What if Eisenhower died and Nixon became president?" by asking, "What if Adams died and Eisenhower became president?"

Yet Adams was no more and no less than what Eisenhower required him to be: a fair but firm chief of staff, totally preoccupied with guarding the president's interests. He handled procedural decisions so that Eisenhower could devote his full attention to important substantive decisions. He said no often so that Eisenhower would not have to. To be sure, Adams misjudged some topics as irrelevant. Although the president later expressed an interest in several subjects that had been omitted from his agenda, he assumed that his lieutenant had had good reasons for rejecting them. In short, Adams had the president's trust. Perhaps that was why Adams cultivated no other allies.

While Sherman Adams had little substantive influence on the president's thinking, Milton Eisenhower served without portfolio as his brother's principal confidant. He had been the right-hand man to secretaries of agriculture for many years and more recently had been president of two universities. His understanding of the problems of federal administration and organization had been highly regarded by a succession of presidents of both political parties. Apparently he added a liberal leaven to Eisenhower's political and economic conservatism and reinforced his brother's faith in the human spirit. The president turned to him on many occasions, confident that he would receive a completely unselfish reply to any question. Despite that special relationship, Milton Eisenhower was as sensitive as the president about the appearance of nepotism and undue influence and was careful to use proper procedural channels.

Eisenhower's view of the executive branch as "a great organizational body" and his emphasis on teamwork as the basis for leadership convinced some Americans that he was unable to realize the heroic potential of the presidency. One kind of criticism directed against his conduct alleged that he was an unlettered boob, an indecisive leader overwhelmed—or bored—by duties that called for intellect and firmness. The real nature of the man stands in distinct contrast to that caricature: Eisenhower was not an intellectual, nor did he read widely, but he was well-briefed. As he once explained, a soldier had no spare time in which to read extensively or speculate idly. He had always been in a position

where information was assimilated for him, and he had perforce
dealt with practice not theory. As a result, he usually called for
prepared evaluations of a few pages in length and preferred to be
briefed orally. Relying on associates to bring books and articles to
his attention, Eisenhower usually read selected portions of the
works. He preferred newspaper and magazine articles he felt were
based on facts, not opinions—pieces that were expositions, not po-
lemics (yet he especially admired the editorials of David Lawrence
in *U.S. News and World Report*). The allegations contrived by
popular syndicated columnists disgusted him. He even gave up
reading Walter Lippmann after that widely respected pundit wrote
about postwar Germany without personal knowledge of the subject.
Eisenhower preferred to read books by men who had carried out
responsible tasks or who wrote about such men. (One of his favorite
authors was longshoreman-turned-philosopher Eric Hoffer, whose
The True Believer expressed the president's own attitude on indi-
viduality endangered by a mass society.) Because he rarely discussed his reading interests in public, the president's most uncharitable detractors dwelled on the fact that he read western adventures
for relaxation, claimed that they were all he ever read, and cattily
remarked that he had to move his lips to do even that.

The president's private papers reveal a predilection for precision and logic. His official statements were the product of work by
several writers, but he issued lengthy and specific instructions to
them, mercilessly edited their drafts, and just as savagely edited his
own revisions up until the moment a statement was issued. Removing every vestige of what he disdainfully called "federal prose,"
he wrote in a simple style so that everyone would be able to understand his meaning. (He also sporadically dictated notations for a
diary, giving the precise circumstances of his actions in certain instances.) Eisenhower was unable to speak with any facility in the
foreign languages he had studied, but he was adept at arranging the
words in a written translation.

To a great extent, innuendoes directed against the president's
intellect were based on his performances at the news conferences he
held two or three times each month. Although he distrusted columnists and editors who distorted facts, Eisenhower had a high
regard for working correspondents. Shortly after the election, he
asked James Hagerty, Governor Dewey's former press secretary, to
take that same post in the White House. "You'll know everything
I'm doing," he told Hagerty, "and I'll keep you fully informed. If
you get any questions, don't shoot off your mouth before you have

the answers. If you have anything you don't know the answer to, come to me and I'll tell you."[5] In turn, Hagerty encouraged the president to expand the format of the news conferences by using a room large enough to accommodate audio-visual equipment and by permitting live television coverage and direct quotation of his statements.

Eisenhower welcomed the chance that these meetings with the press gave him to brush up on a variety of detailed matters and to clarify actions he had taken. "My good man Friday here," as he referred to Hagerty, refreshed his recall beforehand, anticipating 90 percent of the subjects that were raised by the reporters. The president nevertheless took great care not to reply impulsively. Precision, not style, was his concern. A perfectionist with the written word, he also tried to edit as he spoke. The resulting tangle of qualifiers and mid-sentence changes in person and antecedents sometimes resembled a literal translation from a foreign language. These responses were easily ridiculed, but none of his critics noted that the questions themselves were often poorly expressed, nor did they understand that the president frequently had to be wary of references to national security or other administratively confidential matters. In those instances he would often employ circumlocutions or use phrases such as "I'll have to look that up," or he would urge the correspondents to take their question to the official directly in charge of the subject. His critics seized upon such responses as evidence that he did not know what was going on in his administration or in the country.

A second type of criticism leveled against President Eisenhower insisted that he was a "captive hero" in the clutches of his "palace guard" of unelected assistants and millionaire cabinet advisers. The later testimony of members of the White House staff belies part of that allegation. At work in the Oval Office, the president proceeded steadily—occasionally with what he described as "ordered haste"—but never impulsively. As he listened to briefings by an assistant, he gave the impression by frowning or doodling that his thoughts were wandering; then he precisely recapitulated the main points and fired questions that would put his staff member on the spot. "What do you think I should do about it?" he would say, or "What do you think they will do if we . . . ?" Such behavior seemed contentious, but he was actually encouraging his subordinate to consider the alternatives and consequences involved in the problem. He might then indicate disagreement, saying, "I don't see how you can . . ." or he might assent, replying, "Why haven't I heard of this before?" or

"What are we waiting for?" At the close of some discussions he would gently make suggestions that were, of course, instructions, saying, "Well, this is what I would do . . ." or "You may want to . . .".[6]

Former President Truman once expressed the widespread public assumption that a man long used to military command would try to run the presidency by snapping out orders, and he predicted that if Eisenhower did so, nothing would happen. But Eisenhower's associates in war and peace knew that his real manner was far from the stereotype of the military martinet. He insisted that he did not want a bunch of yes men around him. His assistants were supposed to defend their point of view, but they were also expected to abide by decisions once they had been made. From the habit of his career, their chief expected each subordinate to master tasks specifically assigned and to report on those subjects only. Staff members consequently avoided any actions that would displace the lines of responsibility. Under Eisenhower, there was a marked absence of the competition for favor and influence often present in preceding, Democratic administrations. Judging from their record in the Eisenhower White House, these men may have been impressed with what might be called the mystique of military organization: that is, the attitude that discipline elevates the natural human desire for order into righteous conviction and devoted effort.

In return for their devotion, the president offered his personal confidence and an extra measure of solicitude. "Well, seems like a tough battle," he would say. "I'd like to get into it. How can I help? What do you want me to do?" Recognizing that from time to time everyone was subject to pressures and tempted to give up too easily, he expected of them no more than he expected of himself. "God," he would sometimes sigh before turning in at night, "I did the best I could today."[7]

To be sure, there were times when the president felt very sorry for himself. Whenever a goodly portion of his day included criticism from several sources, he had to work at checking his temper. There were warning signs: "I'm in a dark mood," he would say, or he would growl, "I told you, mister, . . ." or he would glare over his reading glasses and bring his open hand down—once—on the desk top. He would remark, "That's fine, but that's not what I wanted to say" to a speech writer, but to his son John he would blurt out: "What the hell is this? Do you expect a President to sign a bunch of garbage like that?"[8]

On some occasions, the insinuations of the press would test his self-control. When one reporter's question implied that the president did not know what had just occurred in Congress, Eisenhower's usual courtesy gave way. "As a matter of fact, I didn't know about that," he replied sarcastically. "Maybe I was fishing that day, I'd not know."[9] But the euphemisms such as "bozo" and "gosh" which he employed in public were abandoned on private occasions, replaced by selections from a soldier's well-worn vocabulary. He had never lost a battle, and he hated to lose at anything. When an opponent once bested him in a legislative matter, he took up the bill, gouged his signature on it, and exclaimed: "God damn it to hell! Jesus Christ, I hope the son of a bitch dies!"[10]

Eisenhower was more sensitive to these lapses of self-control than were those around him. He distrusted anger, hatred, and fear as useless distortions of the clarity required to deal with a subject. Asked by newsmen why he did not strike back at his detractors, he replied: "Look, I did a great deal of boxing as a young fellow, and that would probably be my natural reaction. I believe that there is a very great responsibility resting on the man in this office to preserve the dignity of the office. I believe it is good practice, at least for me, to avoid [the] calling of names."[11] Refusing to impugn anyone's motives, Eisenhower would not denigrate others, no matter how much he disagreed with them.

It was not enough for the president merely to check his emotions; he would go farther. Whenever he felt strongly about something or someone, he would instinctively cover his feelings with noncommittal, often polite words, or he would certify his response by exaggerating his facial expression. Such behavior was part of what close observers referred to as his "act." Eisenhower's apparently fearful appeal to Taft just after the nomination in 1952 was one example of this device. Another was his stance of helpless resignation. "I've been trying to appoint some friend, any friend, of my brother Edgar to some important position," he once remarked to an aide. "It looks as if I've failed again."[12] Those who knew his contempt for nepotism and political spoils saw through the sarcastic remark at once, but in such instances less perceptive observers concluded that Eisenhower was either disingenuous or hypocritical. The president was neither; his manner was merely disarming.

The allegation that Eisenhower was a "captive hero," a pawn in the hands of his advisers, does not hold up when his relationship with his cabinet officers is considered. Shortly after the election in November 1952, he asked Herbert Brownell and Lucius Clay to serve as a talent search committee. Instead of consulting congressional party leaders, they relied mainly on suggestions by prominent businessmen and public administrators across the country. None of the men they recommended had asked for a cabinet position, and none of them declined the president's invitation to take a portfolio. As equals in experience, Eisenhower hoped that they would more readily pool their best judgments. In reality, of course, they were not equals.

The secretary of state, John Foster Dulles, awed some of his colleagues by his knowledgeable expositions and his special relationship with the president. Two other men also carried great weight in cabinet discussions. George Humphrey and Charles Wilson were thought to be geniuses at organization. The former had been chairman of the Marcus Hanna Company of Cleveland, Ohio, a corporation that for half a century had been a leading influence in the economic world and also in Republican politics. As secretary of the treasury, Humphrey made every effort to restore a free-market economy to the nation. He was especially anxious to encourage business initiatives through federal tax and credit incentives, but he privately doubted whether businessmen would exchange security for opportunity. Eisenhower had great admiration for this solemn, quietly earnest man, although some White House staff members thought Humphrey stubborn and conceited.

As chairman of the General Motors Corporation of Detroit, Michigan, Charles Wilson had held one of the most highly paid jobs in the nation. Because of his wide experience in procurement and allocation, he seemed the perfect choice to preside over the Defense Department. But Wilson soon proved to be the president's greatest cabinet disappointment. A bundle of banalities and suspicions, Wilson habitually wavered between moments of self-doubt and bouts of truculence. Impervious to briefings by his subordinates, he blurted out his personal opinions in public as well as in private. But it was his surprising timidity that most exasperated Eisenhower. Despite his pleas for Wilson to make his own decisions, the president ultimately had to rely on the department's military chiefs to inform the secretary of the problems he was supposed to resolve.

Although Wilson's gaffs made entertaining headlines, Secretary of Agriculture Ezra Taft Benson was the most controversial cabinet member. A high official in the Mormon Church, he pursued his task of renovating federal farm policy with an appropriate righteousness. Eisenhower counseled the Utahan to do "a lot of zigging and zagging" because "that's the way you run a military campaign . . . that's also the way you run a political enterprise."[13] When Benson achieved remarkable success with a more straightforward approach, however, the president gave him unwavering support.

Secretary of Commerce Sinclair Weeks, former finance chairman of the Republican National Committee, held economic views that were even more conservative than Humphrey's. Although Eisenhower did not think of him as a spokesman for special interests, Weeks sustained his department's traditional role as defender of the nation's businessmen. Weeks had inherited his wealth; his colleague Douglas McKay epitomized the Republican ideal of rags-to-riches. The folksy former automobile dealer and long-time governor of Oregon was chosen to be secretary of the interior because of his apparent familiarity with the resource problems of the western states. In office, however, McKay was another Charles Wilson. He suffered from the same foot-in-mouth affliction, depended on his subordinates to run the department, and proved to be an ineffective salesman of the administration programs.

The only mistake Eisenhower admitted in the selection of his cabinet was his choice of Martin Durkin as secretary of labor. As a Democrat and a Catholic, Durkin stood in bewildering contrast to the other members; as a leader of the international plumbers' union he incurred the palpable hostility of his business-oriented colleagues. From Eisenhower's viewpoint, Durkin seemed oblivious to administrative procedures and unable to divorce himself from his union connections. When the secretary failed to support the administration's recommendations for labor legislation, the president asked others to act in his place at the congressional conferences. For his part, Durkin decided that Eisenhower's behavior was devious; he resigned, citing poor health, eight months after taking office.

Determined to avoid another mistake, the president selected James Mitchell to head the Labor Department. Although not a union member, Mitchell had shown that he was a friend of the workingman while serving as mediator between the army and federal manpower agencies. A serious-minded loner who was quite familiar with administrative responsibilities, the new secretary was able to defend his jurisdictions without provoking cabinet colleagues or congressmen. Eisenhower was especially impressed with the facility Mitchell demonstrated in settling a steel strike in 1956 and in persuading both union and nonunion voters to support the administration during the election campaign that year.

Republican leaders suspected that Attorney General Brownell exercised a great—some thought a balefully liberal—influence on the president. With Humphrey, Eisenhower could debate the tactics and priorities of economic policy, but the president believed there was no room for contention in the execution of federal law. He therefore accepted Brownell's briefs as the basis for his own decisions. Because the attorney general was a vigorous defender of the equal application of antitrust statutes and of the primacy of federal regulations, he was often out of step with the administration's encouragement of business initiatives and its solicitude for states' rights.

Brownell was particularly helpful in bolstering Eisenhower's determination to improve the composition of the federal judiciary. In general, appointments were made on the basis of recommendations by the American Bar Association. But the two men at once agreed that except for the chief justice of the United States, selections for the Supreme Court would be made from judges who had served on other federal benches or on state supreme courts. The vagaries of fate enabled Eisenhower to make five appointments to the United States Supreme Court. Ostensibly, William Brennan, John Harlan III, and Potter Stewart shared a reputation for judicial formalism but each subsequently acted as swing man on the Court. The disappointing and brief performance of Charles Whittaker may have been foreshadowed by the fact that Eisenhower apparently chose him for personal reasons.

Eisenhower's first appointment to the Court was that of Earl Warren as chief justice. The president quickly grew bewildered and exasperated, however, by the activism and liberalism of the Warren Court. Reports of his dismay leaked out and inevitably reached the chief justice himself. Learning of this, Eisenhower wrote a candid apology: "I have no doubt that in private conversation someone did hear me express amazement about one decision; but I have never even hinted at feeling such as anger. To do so would imply not only that I know the law but question motives. Neither of these things is true."[14] Not surprisingly, the Court's annual dinners at the White House were often strained and embarrassing affairs.

Just as Eisenhower's reliance on Brownell aroused criticism from conservative Americans, his apparent admiration for Richard Nixon disgusted liberals. In an effort to upgrade the traditionally insignificant role of the vice president, Eisenhower asked Nixon to sit with the cabinet and to take on various assignments; these provided a virtual training and proving ground for his young associate. Nixon, in turn, impressed his chief and his cabinet colleagues as an earnest associate who did what was expected of him. Although

Eisenhower used the vice president as a liaison with former cronies in the Senate, privately he regarded Nixon as too political. Because the president defended Nixon's sometimes viciously partisan oratory as nothing more than common political practice, many observers assumed that Nixon wielded a major influence on his chief's thinking. In fact, Eisenhower regarded Nixon as a junior officer whom he hoped would mature, but he did not significantly enlarge Nixon's responsibilities beyond that of special emissary. And when close advisers declined to share his hopes for Nixon's maturation, Eisenhower acted as if he harbored doubts of his own about the man.

In contrast to Humphrey, Benson, and Brownell, most of the members of the Eisenhower cabinet served as coordinators of administration policies rather than as decision-makers. As a result, cabinet meetings were not advisory sessions nor were substantial differences of opinion expressed there. Early in the administration, the president allowed journalist Robert Donovan to record excerpts from those meetings. The notes, later published, revealed the desultory nature of the discussions and quoted some of the less-than-enlightened opinions of certain members. Eisenhower had not read Donovan's book when he acceded to the strident objections of Republican leaders and closed cabinet meetings to outsiders. Soon afterwards, drawing on his familiarity with British practice, the president established a cabinet secretariat. In that post, Maxwell Rabb (and later Robert Gray) gathered suggestions and information from department chiefs and White House liaison men and arranged agendas for subsequent meetings. Thereafter, the cabinet sessions dealt with an impressive number of subjects, and each member was prepared to discuss them with greater understanding. The president guided but did not dominate the discussions, and when they were over, he preferred to have one of the others sum up the sense of the meeting.

At Eisenhower's behest, the department chiefs determined and publicly defended their internal policies and selected their own lieutenants. As a onetime staff officer, the president took special interest in the men of the second rank. At the outset of his administration, he called them into regular meetings at the White House in order to facilitate interdepartmental coordination. In several instances, he assigned his own assistants to the secretaries: General Smith joined the State Department; Robert Anderson was sent to Defense; and Nelson Rockefeller worked with Oveta Culp Hobby, head of the newly created Department of Health, Education and

Welfare. Both of Mrs. Hobby's successors at HEW, Marion Folsom and Arthur Fleming, had been undersecretaries themselves.

There was an almost palpable esprit de corps among the aides and cabinet officers of the Eisenhower administration. In part, their dedication was based on a shared sense of the president's cause. In letters to each of them, he expressed his gratitude for their decision "to drop everything and join our Crusade."[15] But in some cases that sense of righteousness also led to attempted purges of "security risks" in the executive branch (usually Democratic holdovers), belying Eisenhower's directive that career men would be retained and that restaffing not be turned into a vendetta, personal or political. When the purges nevertheless continued, the president explained that he had instructed his assistants to get subordinates they could trust to carry out administration policies. If junior officials could not support their superiors, he said, then they should resign. Eisenhower did not allude to the fact that some who opposed the administration's policies were appointees recommended by the Taft wing of the Republican party. When these new men subsequently expressed intemperate opinions in public and private, he wryly reminded his fellow Republicans of his personal abhorrence of patronage appointments. Party leaders continued to complain, however, that civil service regulations left very few positions open to them.

The president did not like the idea of on-the-job-training, but the Republicans had been out of power for so long that that process seemed unavoidable. Because the party had talked for years of displacing so-called fuzzy-thinking Democratic bureau chiefs with hard-headed businessmen, the Eisenhower team tried to fulfill that dream. They discovered, however, that businessmen were reluctant to accept appointments and that those who did were soon discouraged by the distinctly different purpose of the enterprise. "Whether the thing pays or not," a White House staff member patiently explained to some of them, "is not the primary thing. It's a matter of service, and responsiveness to the public will."[16] Unfortunately, and perhaps because their priorities differed, the best of the businessmen stayed at their government posts for no more than two years.

Because of the administration's solicitude for business enterprise and for businessmen in government, it was constantly confronted by charges of conflicts of interest. Secretary Wilson raised widespread apprehension by divesting himself very reluctantly of his General Motors stock when he assumed command of the department that had extensive contractual arrangements with that corporation. Eisenhower, however, was mainly concerned with what a man could do, not with his connections in the world of business or politics. He approved appointments of businessmen to top-level positions in government, but he did not examine their backgrounds or thereafter monitor their conduct. Until the Sherman Adams affair in 1958, he paid little attention to anyone's involvement in possible conflicts of interest—except his own. In one instance, he tersely referred a business proposal to the head of the appropriate bureau; in another, he had to settle a matter pending before a supervisory agency that incidently involved a political friend. While he conveyed his personal scruples about dealing with federal regulatory commissions to the members of the White House staff, he could not oversee the actions of officials throughout the executive branch. During his administration, more than half a dozen well-publicized instances of influence peddling occurred. He did not countenance such behavior once it was proven, but he waited for the men involved to resign of their own volition. Just as he had viewed the wartime Patton affair, he regarded several of these cases as unfortunate examples of a great cause being deprived of the talents of otherwise honorable and dedicated men.

Perhaps the president underestimated the temptations that accompanied high office because he himself had no interest in further fame or fortune. A wisecrack of the time had it that he was "too true to be any good," but Eisenhower was a genuinely modest man. "It's amazing how much you can accomplish," he liked to say, "if you aren't concerned with who gets credit for it."[17] He took pains to avoid any implication of conceit; for example, he chose times for televised addresses that would not interfere with the normal routines of citizens in their homes, and he fussed about having to wear make-up when he went on camera. After enduring a continental-style *abrazo* at an official ceremony, he confessed to a friend that he found it difficult to show personal emotions in such a manner. His reserve was not a matter of fastidiousness but of practicality. As he once expressed it publicly: "I believe that anyone who does something that is unnatural and artificial for himself is not effective."[18]

As an old soldier, he was similarly detached about his own safety. Personal security measures were tightened after the attempt to assassinate Truman and airplanes replaced trains as the usual mode of presidential travel; but Eisenhower pointed out to his aides that there was really no protection from a marksman shooting from an elevated position. At home, the president and his wife guarded their privacy in order to enjoy the friends and pastimes they had long cultivated. Some wagging tongues insisted that they stayed together only for appearances, but such gossip was belied by the testimony of those close to them and by the fact that they shared a double bed in the White House—as none of their immediate predecessors or successors did. Although charmingly demure in public appearances, Mamie was an ebullient, well-organized woman of strong convictions. She never wanted to be anything more than Ike's wife and thought that her primary responsibility was to make the living quarters of the executive mansion a refuge from his work. She was well prepared by the domestic arrangements of army life to create a tranquil haven. But neither of them ever liked Washington. In 1955, they were delighted to make a first home of their own by renovating an old house and barn close to the Gettysburg battlefield in nearby Pennsylvania. Most of the friends they welcomed there were not connected with government. To entertain official guests, the president used Roosevelt's former retreat in the Maryland mountains; but he changed the name from Shangri-La (which he called "just a little too fancy for a Kansas farm boy")[19] to Camp David, after his only grandson.

Viewing formal receptions as "a form of medieval torture," Eisenhower preferred to relax with family and friends while listening to Fred Waring's singers or watching such favorite movies as *High Noon* and *Luther*. Every few months, he invited about a dozen men to a "stag" dinner, guests who represented a broad spectrum of talents and knowledge. As a result, their postprandial discussions frequently grew into spirited arguments—much to Eisenhower's delight.

Eisenhower's restrained public behavior also gave way to boyish enthusiasm when he joined old friends to fish for trout in the mountain streams of Colorado. Because he insisted on using dry flies, he was notably less successful than his nonpurist companions; when anyone pointed out the smaller size of his catch, he would pretend to be insulted. He hated to be the loser in anything, but he nevertheless loved two games that he was unable to master. At the bridge table he was a frequently uncharitable player, expressing envy for opponents who seemed to know where every card in the deck was. And the challenge of golf so fascinated him that he sometimes carried a putter around the White House and practiced strokes while waiting for his draft revisions to be copied. He looked forward to time on the fairways and established a second retreat on the nationally famous golf course at Augusta, Georgia. He permitted no outsiders to record or publish his scores, perhaps because they revealed his moods so precisely. When one Democratic senator facetiously proposed a fund to protect squirrels from Eisenhower's flying golf balls, the president dryly responded: "I don't see any reason for producing another pressure group."[20] To the surprise of some observers, Eisenhower was also a proud outdoor party chef— specializing in trout feeds, chili, stews, and barbecues—and a solitary artist whose landscapes and still-lifes showed much more sponteneity than his stiffly idealized portraits. Pursuit of these recreations undoubtedly contributed to his remarkable recovery from a sequence of illnesses during his presidency. But recreation was more important than a means to health and sociability: it was for him a spiritual matter.

As if answering critics who were unable to reconcile his puritanical emphasis on self-discipline with his love of play, he once advised a college graduating class to consider such pastimes as essential to the human spirit: "Unless each day can be looked back upon by an individual as one in which he has had some fun, some joy, some real satisfaction, that day is a loss. It is un-Christian and wicked, in my opinion, to allow such things to occur."[21]

Setting aside the sometimes puzzling contradictions in Eisenhower's personality, it is possible to summarize his character. Although his scruples and modesty were genuine, he was also one of the greatest egoists ever to occupy the presidency. As such, he related every problem to the core of his convictions, a concern for the quality of accomplishments and not for the quantity of successes. He would dissemble on unimportant matters or obscure his meaning in order to elicit harmony or give his opponent a way to retreat with honor. He refused to anticipate problems that were beyond his own power to avert, and he declined to seek short-cuts and bargains. While the essential process of deliberation continued, he would gather his forces. When he had made up his mind, he would play out his advantages one by one, always with a keen sense of proportion, ultimately applying only the pressure necessary to secure the outcome he sought. Believing that in war the genius was the man who did the average thing while everyone else panicked in the excitement of the moment, the president adhered to what is best described as not-so-common "common sense."

These attributes were the basis for his procedures in the White House and for his management of the executive branch. They also served as the framework within which Eisenhower promoted a legislative plan for a more balanced government and exercised the nation's influence in world affairs.

3

★★★★★

CONGRESSIONAL SKIRMISHES

If the president was a modernist in enhancing the quality of executive management, he was a traditionalist in his approach to the legislative branch. Like many other Americans, he believed that the balance between Congress and the White House had been upset by his immediate Democratic predecessors. Restoration of constitutional equilibrium called for self-restraint on both sides. In order to demonstrate his adherence to that purpose, he used neither the carrot nor the stick in the manner of a strong chief executive. Instead, he tried to inspire trust by his own scrupulous behavior. He would not berate individual members of Congress in public nor would he judge their work until it had been presented to him for official sanction. He did not try to by-pass them nor modify the sense of their enactments by executive directives. In general, he trusted them to eventually rectify their own sins of omission. Some citizens admired his constant professions of respect for legislative jurisdictions as refreshing evidence that a new day in government had arrived. Others decided that Eisenhower was appallingly naive about congressional motives and his own opportunities.

That contradiction in assessments reflects the fact that the president viewed the Congress in contradictory ways. In general, he had a somewhat textbook-like view of the federal legislature as a great unifier, as the mechanism of democracy bringing oneness out of diversity. Both the executive and judicial branches were properly responsible for upholding that unity of purpose. The American system, however, must continue to be based on the representation of all interests, Eisenhower believed, not just some interests: a truly free society was one in which every citizen's initiatives were encouraged. Each branch, each officer of government must reject the appeals and influences of pressure groups whose demands—however admirable or desirable—short-circuited proper deliberation and the equitable delineation of that fundamental order. "There may be special problems," he said at the end of his first year in office, but "there can be no special rights. . . . there may be special needs, there can be no special privileges."[1]

At the same time, Eisenhower was determined that the evaluations made by Congress should reflect certain of his own emphases. Although the soundness of those emphases was questioned (and is to some extent still questionable), he rightly assumed that Americans believed his goals were both desirable and practical. The first was his conviction that the federal government should confine its activities to subjects that citizens and local governments could not or would not treat with sufficiency. Rejecting the assumption that such areas were immutably defined, he appointed commissions to examine intergovernmental responsibilities, and he called upon state officials to lay claim to topics best understood at the state or local level. Among these were education, housing, health, and social welfare. The fact that governors and mayors continued to come to the federal government for aid only confirmed his belief that the restoration of equilibrium was a long-term, educational task.

Even in those areas deemed necessarily and properly federal, Eisenhower gave priority to legislation that would promote private and local participation in planning and conducting programs. Consultation with all interests involved was to be followed by employment of every available talent and resource, and the ends were to serve a multiplicity of needs. The law as written and executed could not depend upon coercion whether in the form of punishments or bribes; the ready participation of free citizens would instead be secured by legislation that justly sought the public good.

Eisenhower's yardstick in measuring the public good was economy—what he liked to refer to as "fiscal responsibility." A sound economy was the shortest distance to solution of any domestic problem, he asserted, and it was the nation's best defense. The federal government's role in every subject before the Congress should be based, Eisenhower said, on "the plain workings of economic law,"[2] that is, on the common sense philosophy of production capitalism. He did not wholly embrace the laissez faire economics of the nineteenth century, but he did believe that the nation's commerce and industry needed encouragement to venture ever further. Business mergers, in that context, were deemed necessary and proper. He could not abide the arguments of the so-called new economics which held that capitalism should be geared to consumption and which accepted inflation as a desirable means of stimulating and even sustaining prosperity. The claim that "a little bit of inflation every year was a good thing," he once cracked, was "like saying that being a little bit pregnant was good for you."[3] The administration, however, seemed uncertain about which sectors of the economy should transfer such bare-bones economic theory into a workable program. Moreover, Eisenhower assumed that state and local governments could exercise effective influence over the actions of private capital. That confusion of procedure and substance limited the effectiveness of federal economic programs to mere short-run solutions. While claiming to have stimulated an era of prosperity, the administration was unable to sustain it.

The president's first order of business was to ask Congress to rein in the galloping pace of federal spending. In order to guide it in that difficult task, he relied upon three associates: Treasury Secretary Humphrey; Joseph Dodge, the first and most watchful of his directors at the Bureau of the Budget; and Arthur Burns, chairman of the president's Council of Economic Advisers. Eisenhower shared their apprehensions about impending economic paternalism and their abhorrence of governmental intrusion into the private sector. Like them, he thought that expenditures must be proportional to other sources of capital and to other national needs. He agreed with these economists that a tight credit policy initiated by the executive branch would serve to hold down inflation, while prosperity could be promoted by removing restrictions on domestic and overseas trade and investment. Eisenhower was especially concerned with the impact of a domestic economic policy on international developments. Finally, he viewed adequate military expenditures as indispensable.

In his first message to Congress, Eisenhower urged the lawmakers to set aside Truman's proposed $80 billion budget for the coming year and to accept instead his administration's proposals to cut nearly $5 billion from that total. Existing federal obligations could be sustained, he asserted, without being expanded. Like the executive departments, the legislators should take one step at a time; the first step was to call a halt to greater spending. He declared that he would not, therefore, support the cut in federal taxes proposed by members of his own party until they took that first step

43

by approving his budget. Thus, Congress could demonstrate that continuing vigilance—not a short-run gesture—was the price of a sound economy. Because the majority of members of the Eighty-third Congress shared his view, federal expenditures were overtaken by revenues within two years, and the administration happily announced a small but impressive surplus in the treasury. That victory, which would be repeated, was won in part by trimming or eliminating many programs initiated by Democratic administrations. Economy thus neatly served a dual purpose.

The second facet of Eisenhower's relationship with Congress was procedural. As he quickly recognized, partisan support was not the main factor in success or failure. Indeed, his most remarkable legislative achievement was a well-above-average record of recommendations adopted and vetoes sustained during his term by three Democratically controlled Congresses. Because of the "rubber stamp" and "do-nothing" characterizations given Congress in the past, the president adherred to his conviction that legislative leadership was primarily a matter of working with the members as peers in the governmental process; persuasion, not compulsion, was the most effective tool among equals. In some ways, persuasion was enough because most of the Republican members of the Congress shared his belief in a restrained federal role in the economy. Nevertheless, Eisenhower was frequently dismayed to encounter parochialism and even ignorance instead of higher purpose and cooperation among the legislators. "I am always upset," he confided to a friend, "when I know that a politician is putting selfish interests ahead of the interests of his country. So many of them do just that."[4] He frankly commiserated with the congressional leaders of both parties. "I can pick my boys here in the White House," he said, "but you fellows have to take what comes along." Congress, he thought, was "the worst place to go looking for a future President."[5]

He admired those legislators who were experts in their field— that is, masters of evaluation and strategy. By establishing an office of congressional affairs in the White House, and by assigning some of his best assistants to it, Eisenhower maintained a constant liaison with these legislators. He spoke with Republican floor leaders daily and timed personal telephone calls to other members for maximum effect. In these communications he did not refer to his own desires as such, but instead pointed out that the legislators' talents were essential to the implementation of the administration's programs. Perhaps because he emphasized reasonableness on the subject at hand, the president was frequently able to convert members who opposed him on other measures. Thus, he was able to secure harmony for the short sprint, if not unity in the long run.

Republicans held a precarious control of the Eighty-third Congress. Their margin in the House of Representatives was less than a dozen votes; in the Senate it was a majority of just one. This uncertain position was further endangered by factional differences that the recent victory had not diminished. The younger or newly elected (so-called Eisenhower) Republicans were ready to follow the administration's lead in designing legislation. But the members of long tenure, the "Old Guard" scarred by years of battle against Democratic policies, doubted that the president was willing or able to take the lead in dismantling the federal machinery built up by Roosevelt and Truman. Regarding themselves as the true keepers of the Republican covenant, these veterans immediately introduced a sheaf of bills committing the executive branch to withdraw federal responsibilities in many economic and social areas. In some matters, they could even count on the support (or at least the acquiescence) of newly appointed department officials and could thus by-pass the White House.

Although Eisenhower asked every Republican for support, he had no desire to challenge prevailing loyalties. Many party men in Congress still looked to Robert Taft as their real leader. While the senator was outraged by the administration's failure to consult him on high level appointments, the president was, in turn, angered by Taft's legislative priorities and preoccupation with patronage. Nevertheless the two men soon established a better working relationship than either of them had anticipated. Six months after the Eighty-third Congress began its work, however, Taft died of cancer. Had he lived, it is possible that his influence could have closed party ranks to sustain the administration's programs. His successor as majority leader, William Knowland of California, was "cumbersome" in Eisenhower's opinion: "He does not have the sharp mind and the great experience that Taft did."[6] The senator was able to rally his colleagues to support budget cuts, but he also spoke as a member of the "China lobby" to protest the president's "soft" handling of foreign policy. In the House, Speaker Joseph Martin, Jr., of Massachusetts was no better informed and no more effective than Knowland.

Eisenhower was nevertheless ready to work with what circumstances had given him. At the outset, he assumed that congressional application of equity and economy depended on the participation of the Old Guard faction. He soon learned, however, that mutuality of principles did not insure tractability. "It was impossible to do anything just by asking [for] the loyalty of your party," he later complained. Whatever was accomplished was done "by cajolery and argument and secret conferences with the opposition."[7] Eisenhower sought the cooperation of minority leaders as the basis for bipartisan support of administration policies—policies described as being in the national interest.

The Democrats in Congress were led by Senator Lyndon Baines Johnson and Representative Sam Rayburn, both from Texas. Because he had been born in Rayburn's district, the president thought that "you can appeal to Texans on that basis."[8] But neither of these influential legislators felt that Eisenhower fully appreciated the extent to which Democrats supported his recommendations—fifty-eight times, they counted, during the Eighty-third Congress alone. In many instances, the Democratic majority on congressional committees voted funds for departmental programs and then observed with dismay that agency heads declined to spend the appropriations. In private, Eisenhower complained of the Democrats' slavish partisanship, especially during election years. He was, of course, fortunate to have their parliamentary skills in support of some programs, and he was especially grateful to those Democrats who defended his defense and foreign policies.

"Balance" was the administration's watchword in presenting its initial proposals to Congress during the first months of 1953. While the Republican Old Guard seemed bent on reversing the course set by Roosevelt and Truman, Eisenhower focused his recommendations on immediate needs and asked for nothing more than the application of equity and economy. Disdaining those whom he thought meant to "torture" the general welfare clause of the Constitution, he recommended that federal contributions to Social Security be continued but that coverage and individual payments not be enlarged. Similarly, the number of public housing projects was limited, and contracts were based on a pay-as-you-go arrangement. Later in the session, he asked Congress to authorize two projects involving large-scale public works. One of these was the construction of an international seaway linking the Atlantic Ocean and the Great Lakes through the St. Lawrence River. His immediate predecessors had also liked the proposal. Eisenhower endorsed it because it involved federal, state, and private cooperation. Although he was advised that it would eventually require a substantial federal subsidy, the president was willing to spend federal money for works that would stimulate many kinds of local and private enterprises.

That was also the attraction of a second project he proposed to

Congress. While traveling between military assignments during his army career, Eisenhower had been depressed by the condition of American roads and impressed by the *autobahns* of Germany. The latter, he noted, adequately served both commercial needs in peacetime and defense needs in time of war. When he became president, he asked his former military aide, General Lucius Clay, to evaluate the material and financial bases for a nationwide interstate system of highways that could carry the predictably enormous automotive traffic of the near future as well as facilitate the rapid transfer of troops and supplies. When Clay's committee findings were submitted to Congress, however, legislators of both parties found a dozen different reasons for withholding authorization. The multibillion dollar interstate highway system seemed to belie Republican intentions to cut federal spending and restrain the reach of federal government. Furthermore, the project would absorb millions of acres of farm land and real estate, Democratic opponents warned, and would in effect subsidize oil companies and trucking businesses.

Eisenhower customarily left details of legislation to the legislators, but in this case he favored certain specifics. He thought, for example, that the interstate highways should be financed by a system of tolls that could liquidate bonded indebtedness over a short period of time. He also assumed that the routes would by-pass principal cities and that legislation would leave the location of on- and off-ramps to the individual communities. Neither of these provisions was included in the Federal Aid to Highways Act that was passed after three years of congressional debate.

The president's personal interests also accounted for his recommendations on the use of the nation's lands and resources. In a special message to Congress, delivered soon after his inauguration, he proposed an extensive overhaul of federal management of agricultural production. The system of regulation by subsidy, adopted during the depression and expanded during the postwar years, was, in his opinion, anachronistic, wasteful, and politically inspired. As a start in redirecting farm policy, he suggested a statutory redefinition of parity (federal payments given to uphold market prices for agricultural commodities). If parity was trimmed back to practical proportions, Eisenhower argued, retail prices could recede enough to encourage increased consumption and enhance farmers' interests in the long run. Thus, the administration put Congress on notice that it would do its part to redirect past policies. Secretary of Agriculture Benson immediately ordered the reduction of food surpluses stored in federal depots during the postwar period and urged

47

farmers to vote against accepting federal payments for not planting portions of their fields. Eisenhower also favored reforestation of fallow acres even though it would necessitate federal repurchase or regulation of private properties.

Republican legislators from agricultural states warily circled the administration's farm proposals. They were reluctant to incur the possible economic dislocations involved in the reduction of subsidies, but they were even more fearful of political consequences. Neither Eisenhower nor Benson shared the belief that the Democrats' farm policy had accounted for Truman's upset victory in 1948. But whether or not it had been crucial, they reasoned that solicitude for the independence and initiative of farmers could earn political dividends as well as balance the inequities of agricultural economics. Although Congress approved of preliminary reductions in price supports in 1954, the administration would have an uphill fight in every subsequent Congress to secure the remainder of its plan.

In a second special message to Congress, Eisenhower applied his yardstick of proportionate financing and administrative decentralization to what he considered one of the most important problems of the near future: the development of the nation's water resources. During the 1952 campaign, he had used the term "partnership" to describe his intention of rearranging initiatives and participation in resource use. Like "fiscal responsibility," "partnership" was redefined to fit specific issues. Instead of the equal opportunity implied by repeated appeals to fairness and balance, the administration's "partnership" programs appeared to be inconsistent, contradictory, or inequitable. For example, the Republican majority in Congress at once applied that term to the "restoration" of potential offshore oil lands to adjacent states, and the president heartily approved of their action. But when some members from western states also submitted "partnership" proposals to end federal regulation of stock grazing in the national forest, Democrats decried the administration as anticonservationist.

Because Eisenhower had grown up in a relatively arid part of the United States, he thought of conservation primarily as the reclamation of farm land. In smaller projects, private enterprise and state government could meet local requirements for impounding and distributing water and water power, but the management of the nation's larger river systems, serving millions of people, called for federal expenditures and systems analysis. Eisenhower was particularly impressed with a plan formulated during the Truman years for a series of storage reservoirs along the Upper Colorado Basin. The construction of dams throughout that river basin would cost $1 billion and would be supervised by the Interior Department's Bureau of Reclamation. When the president endorsed the Upper Colorado Basin (UCB) project in January 1954, some Republicans objected to the vast federal expenditures involved and, as with the interstate highway system, thought that the proposal would help perpetuate rather than diminish federal domination. Like some Democrats, however, Republicans were mindful of the political impact the project would have in the four basin states—Wyoming, Colorado, Utah, and Arizona.

Eisenhower and his advisers underestimated one other factor in the matter. Already aroused by the Republican members' grazing and forestry proposals, conservationist organizations across the nation pointed out that the UCB project would use Dinosaur National Monument, part of the national park system, as a reservoir and that several proposed dams would endanger other parts of the park system. Like his immediate predecessor, Eisenhower thought that water for agriculture should have priority over the preservation of natural features. Although he declined to refer to the Dinosaur National Monument controversy in public statements, he privately noted that the inhospitable wasteland of the area would be well served by a reservoir used as a recreational lake. Nevertheless, for two years the combination of preservationist publicity together with legislators from eastern states blocked congressional authorization of the UCB project.

When the Eisenhower administration applied "partnership" to the subject of existing water development projects, it encountered other controversies. The first of these was the decision by Interior Secretary McKay to withdraw his Democratic predecessor's objection to the construction by a private utility company of a single-purpose dam in Hell's Canyon on the Snake River in Idaho. Democrats quickly denounced the decision as a "giveaway" of public interests to a private monopoly. Nor were Republicans from the region pleased with the administration's suspension of all new starts in construction of power-producing dams. In effect, they said, "partnership" seemed to be a "takeaway" of contracts, jobs, and electrical energy sources.

The president himself contributed to public doubts about the administration's intentions. While few citizens were familiar with the Upper Colorado Basin or Hell's Canyon, many knew that the Tennessee Valley Authority (TVA) was the showpiece of federal resource management. For some critics, of course, it was the epitome of paternalism. Eisenhower personally believed that TVA smothered private enterprise throughout the seven-state area affected by its flood-control and electric-power production programs. It was, he noted, sustained by taxes from all Americans just to benefit one area. (He did not apply that same concern to UCB—but the project's opponents did.)

At a press conference, Eisenhower used a term popular among opponents of Democratic policies, citing TVA as an example of the "creeping socialism" Republicans meant to bring to a halt. The comment aroused such publicity that neither he nor his staff could wipe away the impression that the administration intended to dismantle TVA. Privately, he acted as if he did indeed want to sell the system, but in public he repeatedly described it as "a going historical concern . . . [that] served a useful purpose"[9] and promised to support it as it stood with all the strength he had. He was ready to preserve TVA because the Supreme Court had designated it as a proper part of the chief executive's responsibilities. But in private correspondence he drew a distinction: "No one has worked harder than I have to stop the expansion of TVA."[10]

In 1954, when the Democratic director of TVA resigned, Eisenhower appointed in his place a former army engineer opposed to suggestions for extending the river authority's operations. About that same time, the Budget Bureau approved of a contract permitting two private firms, collectively known as Dixon-Yates, to distribute TVA power to the city of Memphis, Tennessee. Some Democratic candidates for reelection that year asserted that the contract had been spuriously conceived and described it as a clandestine attempt to begin dismantling TVA. Senators and governors of the basin states urged the president to cancel the agreement with Dixon-Yates, but he preferred to await the outcome of an investigation by the Budget Bureau and White House staff members. When Memphis decided to build its own power distribution system, however, the contract lapsed. Only then did Eisenhower say that he favored the municipal alternative; only then did he explain that he had approved the private contract because his advisers had presented no objections to it. The affair, he lamented, had obscured public recognition of private capital's distress in the TVA region. But like UCB, the Dixon-Yates controversy also revealed the serious drawback of his dependence on staff analyses.

Eisenhower's willingness to play the waiting game in the face of widespread support for federal action on specific subjects also accounted for the congressional stalemate on statehood for Alaska and Hawaii. During the 1952 campaign, he had endorsed the admission of both territories, but when he presented his recommendations to the Eighty-third Congress, he called for immediate approval of Hawaiian statehood and a delay for Alaska's pending resolution of administrative problems. Defense installations in that northern domain, he believed, were better administered while the territory was subject to federal control. "It is one of the great tragedies," he commented privately, with characteristic exaggeration of personal feelings, "to make Alaska a state at this time. It's really a national defense area. . . . It's an outpost."[11] Interior Department officials, some of whom were anxious to open Alaska's land and resource reserves to private development, eagerly defended the president's objections in order to retain full jurisdiction over the territory.

Eisenhower favored the immediate admission of Hawaii because its larger population and advanced economy offered a sound tax base that would preclude federal subsidies. But the idea encountered subtle hostility directed against the territory's racially mixed population. When members of Congress from some southern states threatened to invoke cloture against the statehood debate, they were joined by other Democrats who assumed that Hawaii, once a state, would vote Republican. Admission was further blocked when Eisenhower informed Congress that he would veto any compromise bill granting statehood to both territories simultaneously. Because he refused to alter his assessment of Alaska as primarily a national defense area, and because subsequent Democratic Congresses wanted to admit Alaska before Hawaii, statehood for both was delayed for four more years.

During the initial period of his administration, Eisenhower also brought his personal influence to bear on two congressional issues that threatened to shatter the tenuous unity by which the Republican party had come to power in 1952. The first of these centered on a measure introduced by Senator John W. Bricker, a Republican from Ohio. It called for Congress to initiate an amendment to the Constitution that would profoundly alter a president's authority in the conduct of foreign policy. By its terms, international agreements negotiated by the executive branch would become the law of the land only if they were approved by Congress and did not conflict with state laws. The idea was, of course, a belated response to Franklin Roosevelt's personal diplomacy. Widespread public support for the proposed amendment indicated that many Americans still questioned a chief executive's exercise of initiative in foreign affairs.

As the Senate began its debates on the Bricker amendment, the president maintained a public silence on the subject. The approval of the chief executive was not part of the amending process; that machinery was entirely within legislative jurisdictions. But Eisenhower had good reasons for opposing adoption. First, he felt it would significantly upset the constitutional balance of power among the branches of government. Second, its author and principal adherents held the same isolationist sentiments that had threatened the nation's international role and the future of the Republican party. Those were the very issues that had caused Eisenhower to seek the presidency. Third, and probably most important, he felt that the amendment would limit his actions and those of subsequent presidents to a dangerous degree. He was particularly anxious not to have the administration's disarmament efforts prematurely foreclosed.

Although Secretary of State Dulles did not want to have such a broad statutory limit placed on his own perogatives, he encouraged the debate on the Bricker amendment. His equivocation was no more helpful to a public understanding of the issue than the president's silence. But Eisenhower was relying on both Dulles and Attorney General Brownell to evaluate every nuance of the proposed amendment. After consulting with professors of law and constitutional history, Brownell pointed out that state review of federal executive agreements would undermine the keystone of the Constitution: the supremacy of the federal government over state governments. That was the very point Eisenhower stressed when speaking with the amendment's advocates. (Among the latter were his brother Edgar and other officials of the American Bar Association.) Privately, the president thought these zealots were motivated more by fear (and past hatred of FDR) than by constitutional concerns. Eisenhower assured the Brickerites of his scrupulous intentions in the conduct of foreign policy, but his promise converted none of them.

Following the advice of several members of his cabinet that outright opposition to the Bricker amendment would be most unwise, the president agreed that some kind of statement by Congress was needed to reassure the public. He therefore encouraged his assistants to work with Bricker and other senators to rephrase the measure. If such a change was made, the president would not have to express absolute opposition to the amendment, thereby losing important support for his domestic policies. Bricker, he said, was as important an adviser as Dulles and Brownell were. Nevertheless, the senator remained obdurate. Eisenhower then asked majority leader Knowland to convince his Republican colleagues that the prolonged debate was impeding consideration of the administration's programs, but the Californian supported Bricker's position. Finally, Eisenhower found a steadfast ally in Senator Walter George, Democrat of Georgia, a member (and soon to be chairman) of the powerful Foreign Relations Committee. In May 1954, George sponsored a resolution that removed the state review clause from the amendment. Bricker's adherents were numerous enough to defeat that attempt to emasculate their measure, and they were strong enough to pass a substitute proposal requiring the president to submit international agreements for approval within sixty days after they were concluded.

Although the administration's conduct of foreign policy served increasingly to undercut his support, Bricker continued to introduce his constitutional amendment at each subsequent session of Congress; and Eisenhower continued to talk with him about the issues it raised. But by 1956, it was obvious that the president was letting him down gently. Some embittered proponents hoped that Dulles and Brownell would be replaced after the election that year, but Senator Bricker pointed to the real killer of his dream: "Dwight Eisenhower—nobody else."[12]

During the same years as the debate over the Bricker amendment, another controversial issue also raised serious constitutional and political questions. Following the Republicans' victory in 1952, Joseph R. McCarthy became chairman of the Senate Committee on Government Operations. In continuing his hunt for subversives within the executive branch, he seemed to ignore the fact that a president and administration of his own party was now in office. Those of his colleagues who had considered McCarthy a convenient weapon to drive the Democrats from power, were now unable to check or even redirect his continuing crusade.

Perhaps hoping to head off McCarthy, Eisenhower told the new Congress that maintenance of internal security was clearly the responsibility of the executive branch of government. He immediately issued orders to the Justice Department calling for vigilant surveillance of personnel and of classified information; these orders emphasized prevention not punishment. Rather than support congressional proposals to outlaw the American Communist party, Attorney General Brownell preferred to secure greater jurisdiction for the Federal Bureau of Investigation and for federal judicial officers.

The administration's moderate beginnings, however, were soon blemished by two highly publicized incidents.

The first of these was the Rosenberg case. In 1951, Julius and Ethel Rosenberg had been sentenced to death for passing secret information on the production of atomic bombs to agents of Communist countries. In January 1953, when their lawyers asked the new president for clemency, Eisenhower had not had time to decide on a pardons policy nor had he appointed an assistant to oversee that responsibility. He therefore relied entirely on Herbert Brownell to brief him on the matter. The attorney general argued that every legal, judicial, and procedural facility had been made available to the couple during the course of their trial. The jury, moreover, had expressed no doubts about their guilt. At a meeting of the cabinet, Brownell asserted that there was additional evidence against the Rosenbergs that had not been presented at the trial.

In deciding not to grant clemency to the Rosenbergs, the president's primary concern was what he called the effect of their actions. Their crime, he declared in a statement to the nation, "far excelled that of the taking of the life of another citizen; it involves the deliberate betrayal of the entire nation and could very well result in the death of many, many thousands of innocent citizens. By their act these two individuals have in fact betrayed the cause of freedom for which free men are fighting and dying [in Korea] at this very hour."[13] When the Rosenbergs were executed four months later, he expanded this statement to include responsibility for the deaths of millions of innocent people. Eisenhower's reasoning was consistent with his wartime decision not to stay the execution of Private Slovik during the Battle of the Bulge. (Subsequently, the president commuted death sentences and granted pardons in cases involving much smaller consequences.) But his position on the Rosenbergs' appeal helped sustain the very fear-mongers he loathed.

The impact of the Rosenberg affair had hardly receded when a second controversy arose over Eisenhower's judgment on internal security matters. In November 1953, Admiral Lewis Strauss, the president's appointee as chairman of the Atomic Energy Commission (AEC), presented Defense Secretary Wilson with a startling report. In it Strauss charged that J. Robert Oppenheimer, one of the scientists who had developed the atomic bomb, had associated with Communists while having access to classified information on nuclear weapons. Wilson was greatly agitated as he informed the president of Strauss's assertion. The president, however, doubted that Oppenheimer was guilty of treasonable activities. He personally admired the scientist and especially had approved of his writings favoring the use of atomic energy for peaceful purposes.

Because the Oppenheimer question was wholly within executive jurisdiction, the president directed Wilson to take Strauss's report to the attorney general and also asked the AEC to investigate the matter in closed hearings. Strauss later assured Eisenhower that the commissioners agreed that there were sufficient grounds for doubting Oppenheimer's discretion. The president, therefore, ordered a "blank wall" be placed between the scientist and all classified information until the charge could be verified or dismissed. In his news conference, Eisenhower defended the AEC's evaluation but would make no comment on its effectiveness. When one reporter asked if he thought the nation was more secure now that the "wall" had been erected, the president told him to take his question to the AEC. Eisenhower would not say that the Oppenheimer case confirmed charges that the internal security of the United States was in jeopardy, but Senator McCarthy did so with unmistakable inferences.

In keeping with his personal code against a president publicly denigrating anyone, Eisenhower refused to discuss the senator's actions at his news conferences. In remarks to his White House assistants, however, he likened McCarthy to Adolph Hitler—a man drunk with power, demanding unquestioning loyalty no matter how he acted. But Eisenhower reserved special condemnation for those who had praised and publicized the man's demagoguery. Those same promoters, he complained in a letter to a newspaper publisher, were now "the loudest in their demands that I be the one to cut him down to size."[14] Recalling the career of Huey Long of Louisiana, Eisenhower decided that anything he might do to McCarthy would serve only to increase that man's notoriety and make him a hero to those who admired the underdog.

Instead, however, the president enhanced McCarthy's impact by remaining aloof: Eisenhower's silence was mistaken for timidity or quiet approval. His only notable expression of reproof in 1953 came while the senator's adherents were purging libraries and harrassing educators at home and abroad. "Don't join the book burners," he told a college audience. "Don't be afraid to go in your library and read every book. . . . How will we defeat communism unless we know what it is?" The people's right to have access to any book, he said, is unquestioned, "or it isn't America."[15] Shortly afterwards, he also asserted that teachers should be loyal citizens, "enjoying true freedom of thought, untrammeled by the inroads of political fashion or expediency."[16] He named no names in his speeches or press conferences, but in response to a reporter's question, he said that current Senate investigations threatened the very values they were supposed to be defending.

Eisenhower's self-restraint proved inadequate in restraining his own men. In November, Brownell told a small, private meeting that President Truman had harbored a Communist among his top advisers. When the accusation made newspaper headlines, members of the press corps asked the president to comment. Eisenhower admitted that he had read the attorney general's speech before it was delivered. He implied that he thought Brownell had evidence to substantiate his charge, but he did not offer any explanation for the fact that the attorney general had not first presented his case to the proper judicial authorities. The frailty of the president's remarks further aroused public doubts about his own position.

The president's obliquities and ambiguities may be accounted for by recalling his strong conviction about the separation of powers. However McCarthy behaved, he was nevertheless a United States senator and the duly elected spokesman for the people of his state. While the legislature's power to investigate should be used with restraint, Eisenhower believed it would be constitutionally dangerous for the executive branch to try to limit those investigations. Moreover, only the Senate could handle one of its members. If the president tried to do so without the cooperation of McCarthy's supporters in that chamber, he would jeopardize the chances for adoption of the administration's legislative proposals. Such an intrusion would deepen the division among Republicans. Eisenhower therefore urged Republican legislators to seek an early end to McCarthy's probes on the grounds that sufficient information had already been accumulated and that an executive review of internal security was proceeding. (In fact, McCarthy never submitted any of his committee material to the Justice Department, and Brownell did not ask for it.)

Unimpressed by executive assurances, McCarthy stepped up his attack, charging that the State Department and Central Intelligence Agency had delayed development of the hydrogen bomb. The senator's request for pertinent executive documents raised the question of "executive privilege." As Eisenhower well knew from his peacetime military assignments, congressmen were sometimes meanly motivated and insatiable in their demands for information from the executive branch. Once when he was chief of staff, Eisenhower had ordered reluctant subordinates to give historians access to military records, but that instance did not involve the constitutional question. Subsequent congressional attacks on Truman's use of executive powers had prompted legal experts to examine past practices. Any president, they concluded, could properly deny access to executive documents and could determine exceptions to that rule. One of the men who had participated in those studies was William Rogers, now Eisenhower's deputy attorney general.

But the senator from Wisconsin was not to be disposed of so easily. During the first months of 1954, his investigations touched on several of the president's personal concerns. In an attack on the United States Army, McCarthy alleged that high-ranking officers had coddled Communists. After grilling General Ralph Zwicker, one of Eisenhower's former associates, McCarthy then dismissed him from the hearings with the comment that he was not fit to wear his uniform. Secretary of the Army Ted Stevens was also summoned to answer the senator's accusations.

"I am not going to have my people browbeaten,"[17] the president exclaimed to his White House assistants. If McCarthy insulted any executive official, he ordered, that person should get up and leave the committee room. Vice President Nixon tried to mediate the tense situation by arranging for Stevens to endure the senator's abuse in private, but the concession merely seemed to encourage McCarthy. In March, when a confrontation between the two branches of government seemed likely, Eisenhower asked Brownell to prepare a statement for the time "when I may find it necessary to take action"[18] to defend the executive branch against legislative intimidation.

On the basis of several Justice Department briefs, Eisenhower answered McCarthy's request by refusing to submit documents relating to national security matters, and he also ordered department chiefs to deny such access. He was reluctant to raise public alarm over an apparent constitutional confrontation, however, and therefore explained his directive as an effort to keep the committee's investigation on track by preventing it from wandering into extraneous topics. Once again, McCarthy prepared to take another step. But forewarned that one of the senator's men would accuse the nation's church organizations of Communist leanings, Eisenhower quickly headed off the attack by issuing a refutation of the outrageous charge.

Finally, by mid summer of 1954, a congressional election year, a handful of apprehensive Republican senators concluded that they must curb McCarthy's proceedings. In July, Ralph Flanders of Vermont called for the Senate to censure him. While McCarthy stood by muttering obscenities, Arthur Watkins of Utah conducted the indictment with dignity and fairness. Five months later—after the election—a sufficient number of Republicans joined with Democrats to pass a mild censure resolution. Pleased that the legislators had properly disposed of their own business, Eisenhower acceded to his aides' suggestion and made public his letter of thanks to Watkins.

The president could justifiably conclude that events had finally confirmed the wisdom of his detachment in the McCarthy controversy, but members of both parties questioned his perception of the political consequences. Flanders and Watkins evidently had acted only after party chairman Leonard Hall warned them that the McCarthy affair would harm the chances of Republican candidates in November. But many Republicans, Eisenhower noted, remained unconvinced that the senator was a political detriment.

The ongoing Bricker and McCarthy controversies enabled the president to underscore his advice to party leaders to overhaul the Republican image. Anachronistic dogmas and negative dialectics should be abandoned, he argued. The party should take to the middle ground, the only terrain for dealing with problems of vast proportions. That middle way, however, was not a refuge for timidity or indifference; the true radical was the man who battled the extremism of both Right and Left. Republicans were forearmed for that struggle, Eisenhower believed, because they were more united on economic principles than their opponents. The Democrats clung to the rhetoric of the depression years, he claimed, and offered paternalistic security instead of new opportunities. But it was access to opportunity, Eisenhower concluded, that would appeal to young Americans, new voters looking to the future. This reasoning led him to expect the Republican party to attract every voter under the age of thirty-five.

The president was willing both to encourage Republicans to modernize their image and to set an example which they could follow. But he did not want to use his office for partisan advantage. He confessed to Dewey that nothing had so shocked his sense of propriety as Truman's barnstorming campaign in 1948. Quite apart from consideration of his own prestige or popularity, Eisenhower wanted to retain bipartisan support for his programs; that support would be seriously jeopardized if he publicly sniped at the opposition. When scattered off-year elections went to the Democrats in November 1953, Eisenhower had coolly remarked: "I have lost skirmishes before."[19] But the next year, the pleas of Leonard Hall and other party leaders caused him to reconsider his stand. During the course of the 1954 campaign, he traveled some twenty thousand miles and made 204 speeches in ninety-five cities.

Eisenhower concentrated his public remarks on the notable improvement in national affairs after two years of his administration. The anguish and disruption of the war in Korea had been ended; the national budget had been reduced by $10 billion and Americans retained almost that much because of a tax cut. The myth that prosperity could come only with war was dissolving with increases in every economic index; the only declines, happily, were in unemployment and labor strikes. The nearest the president came to partisanship was his prediction that there would be a kind of Cold War stalemate in Congress if the Democrats won control. The prospect of running the government under such circumstances, he said, would be most frustrating. As for outright endorsements, Eisenhower appeared to be less than enthusiastic about some of his party's candidates and made only passing reference to Old Guard Republicans standing for election.

To his aides, the president predicted that his party would win or lose control of the Eighty-fourth Congress by a slim margin. When the votes were counted, the Democrats had added twenty-nine seats in the House and had transformed their two-vote minority in the Senate into a two-vote majority. Across the nation, Republicans were rejected in many instances by margins of less than two percent, even in areas that had been party strongholds before 1952.

Bitterly, Old Guard Republicans blamed the losses on Eisenhower. His administration had not sustained traditional Republican principles, they said, nor had it successfully sold its own policies to the nation. In private remarks, the president turned their criticism back on them. Republicans would have to realize, he argued, that they could not survive unless they became a party of "progressive moderates" and proved to people that they were not controlled by proselytizers of the extreme Right. During the next two years, besides "keeping this world at peace," Eisenhower's only purpose would be "to build up a strong progressive Republican Party in this country." "If the Right Wing wants a fight," he swore, "they're going to get it." If the party did not reflect progressive views, or if it still thought that it could nominate a right-winger for the presidency, he promised, "I'll go up and down this country campaigning against them."[20]

Although political commentators reported that Eisenhower was considering forming a third party, he later denied that rumor. What was needed, he said, was a "commonsense party." But in 1954, he made no effort to purge those he described as right-wing extremists. Perhaps he thought he could convert the irreconcilables just as he had persuaded some of his more reasonable opponents. Or perhaps he thought that the defeat of Bricker, McCarthy, and their adherents had effectively chastened the party's membership. Before the election, he had asserted that Republicans could enhance their congressional majority by running on the executive and legislative accomplishments of his administration. But the administration's policies designed to encourage "partnership" were either invisible to the public or had been largely discredited by the Democrats as "giveaways" to special interests. In the legislation it proposed, the Republican Congress seemed continually to want to take a step backward, and the president did not encourage his congressional lieutenants to do more than gently modify a particular bill to his approach. However substantial the economic gains recorded—or assured—by the new administration, its first two years had not been sufficiently impressive in the political sense. The president would not abandon his scrupulous regard for the separation of powers; but if he was to fulfill his purpose in seeking the office, he would have to reconsider his initial assumption that he could restore the proper balance to the nation's government in the course of a single term.

4

★★★★★

THE WEAPONS OF PEACE

In formulating a domestic program and dealing with party politics at the start of his administration Eisenhower was on unfamiliar ground. But in his role as the nation's chief diplomat, he drew on earlier experience and on some long-held convictions. In general, his response to international affairs was based on three tenets. The first of these defined the nature of what he invariably called "international communism." He viewed the continuing Cold War as an encounter between those who considered man to be created in the image of God and those who considered him a mere instrument of the state. "To my mind," the president declared at the end of his first year in office, "it is the struggle of the ages."[1]

The death of Stalin on April 11, 1953, necessitated a reassessment of relations with the Soviet Union, but a change in leadership did not fundamentally alter the Communist system. That structure, Eisenhower believed, had no foundation other than materialism. Employing the rhetoric that was common during the 1950s, he concluded that "atheistic communism" would not attack the "free world" militarily because such an action would risk its own extinction. Instead, the Russians (and their apparent ideological partners, the Chinese) would concentrate their efforts on undermining the security of other nations. That could be done not only by armed subversion, but also by destroying a nation's economic stability.

Like the sermon of an old fashioned preacher, if Eisenhower's first proposition was esteemed as truth, then his second was undoubtedly true as well. The second of his principles involved collective security. In meeting the threat of international communism, the "free world" had to share its superiority in arms and resources. But it had something even better than material strength: it had a moral cause. This gave the anti-Communist effort the sanctity of a crusade, far greater than the one that had succeeded in World War II. By its very nature, the crusade produced a dichotomy. All those who joined, no matter how diverse their practices, were—by definition—freedom-loving nations. All those who did not participate gave comfort, if not aid, to the enemies of freedom. There could be no neutral in "the struggle of the ages" and no indulgence in selfish nationalism.

The part that Eisenhower saw the United States as playing in collective security was actually a continuation of the role and the sense of mission outlined by Woodrow Wilson, although he ascribed its modern origins to Republican William McKinley. American might and American abundance would be extended to other nations like a shield of freedom. Some, like Great Britain, warranted special assistance. In theory, at least, a country must want to preserve free institutions before aid would be extended, but the United States would never try to convert other nations to its own ways. "Any nation's right to a form of government and an economic system of its own choosing is *inalienable*," Eisenhower asserted. "Any nation's attempt to dictate to other nations their form of government is *indefensible*."[2] He did not consider giving arms and money as a means of persuasion, but as stewardship and as evidence of the shield.

The third general purpose of Eisenhower's foreign policy was not to practice war but to wage peace. The opportunity to influence people to work for peace was, in one of his favorite expressions, "a fascinating business." At home, he taught the lesson of spiritual unity and solicited bipartisan support for the international assistance programs that he pointedly described as "mutual security." In his dealings with America's allies abroad, he was again the honest pedagogue, promoting by the quality of his behavior a sense of trust in America. Many critics maintained that the peace he waged was a *pax americana*. Anxious to avoid that implication, Eisenhower advocated the settlement of international differences by the United Nations whenever possible. But the effectiveness of that organization ultimately depended on the strength of its chief advocate. Therefore, American leadership in the quest for peace appeared to turn on the question of the president's use of military force.

Eisenhower, the professional soldier, was in many ways the least militaristic of any of the American presidents. While he employed military allusions in speeches and press conferences, those remarks were offered as lessons in human behavior and were not sheer hubris. He knew that many citizens had voted for him because he was a military man, but he remained particularly sensitive to the traditional antipathy toward things military. ("No, no! No more generals, no more generals!" Senator Taft had shouted during a White House discussion of presidential appointments.)[3] Eisenhower selected several former wartime colleagues to assist him in the White House, but he also went to great lengths to bolster civilian participation in military matters.

One of his first actions as president was to enlarge Truman's National Security Council (NSC) by adding to its membership the secretary of the treasury and the director of the Bureau of the Budget. Thus, economic consequences of security decisions were always in the forefront of the council's deliberations. Treasury Secretary Humphrey often pleased the men from the Pentagon by finding categories into which their defense requests could be placed without arousing congressional opposition. But just as frequently he wrecked their recommendations with a few words. "George," Eisenhower would ask, "what would all this do to the budget?" "It'll mean a deficit, Mr. President."[4] That terse response usually settled the matter.

The NSC was also subjected to White House staff procedures by the appointment of Robert Cutler and later Gordon Gray as its secretariat. These men had been Eisenhower's associates in wartime and postwar defense policy assignments; he trusted them and knew they were capable and conscientious. Cutler and Gray were included in the NSC inner circle along with Generals Andrew Goodpaster and Walter Bedell Smith, two former military aides now in mufti as presidential assistants. Eisenhower relied on these four men when sudden foreign crises called for an immediate decision rather than a full-scale council discussion.

While the president privately scorned congressmen who thought that they were experts on military affairs, he admonished the Defense Department's military staff not to indulge in interservice rivalries that could adversely influence the legislators. Supervision of the military by knowledgeable civilian authorities, he believed, was highly desirable. For example, by his orders, American troops accused of crimes against civilians in foreign countries were to be tried by the civil courts of those nations. Referring to the celebrated

Girard case of 1957, he was privately disgusted by army officials who seemed bent on making a national hero out of "a man who shot a woman in the back at something like ten to fifteen yards distance."[5]

Many army men were certain that the president was biased against his own service branch. He was, to be sure, notably curt with those who expected special consideration simply because he was a former General of the Army, and he frequently deflated their expectations for increasing the size and jurisdiction of that branch. This apparent hostility may actually have been an effort to avoid any appearance of favoritism. Similarly, he chose members of the other services to be chairmen of the Joint Chiefs of Staff. Of the men successively appointed to that post, Admiral Arthur Radford and Air Force General Nathan Twining were outspoken advocates of using armed force to secure advantageous positions in foreign affairs. Well aware that military men were habitually over-confident when pressing their plans, Eisenhower probably assessed their advice more critically than a civilian president would have done. Moreover, if they asserted their opinions publicly, he would order the secretary of defense to reprimand them. In several instances, high-ranking staff officers found it necessary to resign after making public remarks critical of policies discussed by the NSC.

Eisenhower viewed the nation's arsenal of weapons with remarkable equanimity. Reasoning that a nation, like a soldier, ought to "trust God and keep your powder dry," he believed that there was no mutual antagonism between "a nation's faith in God and her determination to defend herself against attack." Defenselessness was no virtue, he argued. "In my own conviction the purpose for which weapons are developed is the determining factor as to whether their possession is good or evil."[6]

During his first weeks in office, Eisenhower advised Americans that no amount of force could give absolute security or wholly obliterate risk. He regarded the growing enchantment with weaponry —whether by industrialists seeking government contracts or by military chiefs building their own empire—as a tendency with grave consequences for America. Instead of responding to these pressure groups, he directed that weapons be ordered and distributed according to two objective considerations: first, with new and superior arms, a smaller number of fighting units were to assume greater responsibilities; second, the duplication of equipment among the several services was to be eliminated. These guidelines would also, of course, ensure great savings in production and maintenance costs.

The administration's policy of enlarging the impact of the nation's military force while reducing its manpower was quickly labeled the "new look" by the media (a term popular in the world of women's fashions) and was summarized somewhat simplistically by both admirers and critics as promising "more bang for the buck." Some observers were surprised that a former infantry commander would pare down the size of field forces; other citizens welcomed the policy because it meant that fewer men would be drafted.

The president did not like the slick implications of the label the "new look." Very little would be changed, he insisted. Some new weapons had undoubtedly altered past reliance upon ground forces, but conventional weapons, he said, were still the mainstay of each armed service branch. Furthermore, Eisenhower did not depend wholly on the self-interested recommendations of the military chiefs; he personally scrutinized and evaluated each new weapon idea. When the navy urged construction of an atomic-powered aircraft carrier, he preferred to see the concept tested first in a much less expensive cruiser. Indeed, he chose to publicize the voyages of an atomic-powered merchant vessel in order to emphasize the peaceful uses of such energy. Similarly, he approved of a short-term missile program so that results could be gauged before further investments were made in any long-range plans. In other instances, he simply rejected weapons proposals as unnecessary or too expensive or both.

Eisenhower's views on the development and use of atomic and nuclear bombs were the topics of greatest interest to the nation and to the rest of the world. His critics assumed that a military man would be dangerously enamored of these vastly destructive devices. In fact, he was far less impressed by them than many would-be strategists of the Cold War. Their sole value, as he saw it, was to enable the United States to fulfill its commitments without bankrupting the nation economically. But it was a grave error, he advised his countrymen, to assume that the bomb alone was an effective way of winning wars or maintaining peace. Because of their overwhelming power, he warned, nuclear weapons could not be confined to military targets. And because most combat situations were of small magnitude, the bombs were useless in tactical operations. To be sure, he would include nuclear weapons on the list of options whenever a military response was formulated, but he would carefully weigh international consequences as well. Because Eisenhower believed that the only real deterrent was an enemy's fear of retaliation, he empowered the Strategic Air Command (SAC) to use nuclear weapons only in a retaliatory (or second) strike. The

United States would never call up a first attack, Eisenhower announced, because the humanitarian beliefs of Americans, and their respect for the opinions of all mankind, would never permit it.

Since the end of World War II, the very existence of a stockpile of atomic and nuclear bombs had become one of the most disturbing questions of the presidency. Eisenhower was neither awed nor frightened by those reserves, and he depended on the level-headed advice of men who were technical experts, not politicians. Periodically, Admiral Lewis Strauss, chairman of the AEC, would meet with him alone and inform him orally of the current number of bombs in the nation's stockpile; in response the president would tell Strauss how many should be made during the coming year. Both men agreed that the size of these weapons should be determined strictly by military need, not by sheer killing power, and that tests of the new models should be held to a minimum. In 1954, when radioactive fallout from an American nuclear test explosion injured some Japanese fishermen in the Pacific, widespread protest prompted newsmen to question the president about it. Eisenhower's response was curt: his primary responsibility, he said, was the defense of the United States. Consistent with his reasoning in the Slovik and Rosenberg cases, he implied that a few deaths were regretable, but the development of nuclear bombs was a grim necessity to prevent millions of deaths from a future enemy attack.

Although he would not order a unilateral suspension of testing, Eisenhower was a tireless advocate of disarmament. He instructed Strauss to keep the nation in the forefront of atomic research and development, but he also urged Strauss to direct his main efforts toward finding technological bases for a disarmament policy. In addition to choosing scientists to keep him informed of nuclear technology, the president appointed Nelson Rockefeller as his special adviser on disarmament and sent former Minnesota governor Harold Stassen to be his spokesman at various international disarmament conferences. Those meetings proved to be both continuous and continuously stalemated, but because there was no acceptable alternative to disarmament, the president instructed Stassen to persist in his efforts.

Like every other "weapon" at his disposal, science was to be directed toward the requirements of a peaceful world. Soon after the inauguration, a specially chosen group of scientists, economists, and military men conducted a top-secret evaluation called Project Solarium; they estimated that continuation of the arms race with the Soviet Union could, in the foreseeable future, exhaust the human and economic resources of both nations. Disarmament was therefore not only a humanistic ideal, it was an international necessity.

The president first revealed his own thoughts on the subject when he addressed a meeting of newspaper editors, three months after he took office. Expressing the cost of the arms race in everyday terms, he offered a shocking example: the price of one heavy bomber would pay for a modern school building in each of more than thirty cities or two power plants in two large communities, or would fully equip two hospitals, or build fifty miles of concrete highway, or pay for half a million bushels of wheat. "Every gun made, every warship that is launched, every rocket fired signifies, in the final sense, a theft from those who hunger and are not fed, those who are cold and are not clothed. This world in arms is not spending money alone. It is spending the sweat of its laborers, the genius of its scientists, the hopes of its children."[7]

Eisenhower asked rhetorically what the Soviet Union would be willing to do if the United States was willing to set limits on military and strategic materials production. A few months later, the Russians successfully tested a hydrogen bomb. Rather than being discouraged by that reply, Eisenhower thought it made his disarmament proposals all the more relevant. In December 1953, he took his case to the General Assembly of the United Nations. Referring to recent events, he observed that there was a new international language— that of atomic warfare—but that there was also a "new avenue of peace." "It is not enough to take this weapon out of the hands of the soldiers," Eisenhower said. "It must be put into the hands of those who will know how to strip its military casing and adapt it to the arts of peace." He pledged that if the United Nations would establish an international atomic energy agency to oversee production and storage of fissionable material, the United States was determined to "devote its entire heart and mind to find the way by which the miraculous inventiveness of man shall not be dedicated to his death, but consecrated to his life."[8]

The General Assembly delegates gave the president's speech an ovation that moved him deeply, but the response at home to his "Atoms for Peace" proposal was decidedly mixed. If the plan was anything more than glittering rhetoric, several commentators said, then it was merely visionary. Some Democrats denounced it as a subterfuge for giving private corporations control of a public energy source. Republican supporters of McCarthy and Bricker were alarmed by the direction in which the president seemed to be moving. In addition, Eisenhower publicly indicated that he favored alteration of the McMahon Act of 1946 so that American atomic technology could be shared with other nations. He did not, however, reveal his hope that specific information could be made available to British scientists. As a further demonstration of America's intentions, the administration worked for and secured passage of the 1954 Atomic Energy Act. In effect, that measure established a partnership between government and private capital for the peaceful development of atomic energy and its application to problems of power and transportation. Nevertheless, congressional politics and Cold War issues prevented the president from making further progress with his "Atoms for Peace" proposal. Instead, he appointed former Nebraska Governor Val Petersen to direct plans for national civilian defense. Like the issues of stockpiling and testing nuclear weapons, the very existence of a civil defense program aroused widespread apprehension and resentment. By the end of the 1950s, those feelings took the form of organized public protests, but Eisenhower continued to promote the program until he left office.

Preparedness called for calmness, the president believed, not demagoguery. Accordingly, he did not address the nation or the Congress about international problems with undue frequency. Apart from the democratic obligation to inform and explain, he felt that the actual conduct of foreign relations was properly the business of a handful of leaders in the executive and legislative branches. Within that framework, some aspects of diplomacy were perforce clandestine.

The president knew from his military experience that superior intelligence was a weapon of immense power. Information gathered by "G-2," the intelligence unit of every command, played an essential role in any combat action: with it, disadvantageous battles could be avoided and unavoidable ones could be won. Eisenhower, therefore, regarded the agents of the CIA as "my G-2 boys." Although the public knew little of the CIA's existence, in 1953 and 1954 a few congressional Democrats did raise objections to it on the grounds that in a democracy no part of government should be beyond legislative scrutiny.

When these critics demanded a public accounting of the agency's operations, the president refused to permit it. He told inquiring newsmen that the CIA was acting under his personal supervision, thus implying that it was also guided by his sense of propriety. Eisenhower talked to Herbert Hoover in 1954 about a possible reorganization of the agency but both men were leery of possible interference by Senator McCarthy, whose wide net of suspicions had already touched that mysterious organization. In 1956, the president agreed to the idea of examination of CIA financial records by a committee of persons not connected with any branch of the government. But if that study was ever made, its findings were not available for congressional scrutiny.

The head of the CIA was Allen Dulles, younger brother of the secretary of state and, therefore, something more than just another presidential adviser. In NSC meetings, he not only contributed details of reports from his agency's operatives, but participated in the discussion of all options. Although the president did not make a special point of secrecy unless national security was involved, he was sometimes irritated by reported "leaks" in the State Department. In order to insure the secrecy of his own directives, therefore, Eisenhower relied on several personal emissaries. Among the men he dispatched to trouble spots around the world were two sons of former presidents, Herbert Hoover, Jr., and Quentin Roosevelt, and two former wartime associates, Robert Murphy and Walter Bedell Smith.

While he clearly understood the military advantages of weaponry, Eisenhower considered diplomacy to be the first line of national defense and the most practical alternative to war. "Now war is a political act," he lectured the press corps at the end of his first two years in office, "so politics—that is, world politics—are just as important in making your decisions as is the character of the weapon you use."[9] He had, of course, acquired an extensive personal knowledge of the military aspects of world politics during his career. But just as he relied on legal and legislative experts in domestic affairs, he had someone advise him on the limits and possibilities of diplomacy, one who also represented his views with undoubted authority. That man was the secretary of state.

Secretary of State John Foster Dulles's role was the single most controversial issue of the Eisenhower years, and it remains the most difficult topic in sorting out Eisenhower's presidency. When the Democrats demanded to know, "Who's in charge?" they especially referred to the administration's foreign policy. It did Eisenhower no good to publicize (in greater detail than any of his predecessors or successors) his working procedure with his secretary of state. Those descriptions merely provoked further disbelief and never succeeded in answering the critics' persistent questions of why Dulles was chosen and why he was kept on as secretary of state for six years. Misunderstandings began with appearances. Dulles looked like an effigy on a medieval tomb and spoke with an excrutiating slowness and solemnity. To many who watched him at work, he seemed a mixture of Puritan presbyter and Wall Street lawyer, as hypocritical, devious, and ruthless as the men of wealth and power with whom he associated in the worlds of finance and politics. Others concluded that he was a human chameleon, changing his color smoothly to match the shade of the main chance: first as diplomatic lieutenant to Dean Acheson, Truman's controversial secretary of state; then as the Republicans' leading critic of the Truman–Acheson foreign policy; then as Dewey's adviser and choice for secretary of state; and at last switching quickly from the Taft camp to support Eisenhower just before the 1952 convention.

In contrast to those impressions, the president spoke of Dulles in the highest terms: he was "the most valuable man in foreign affairs that I have ever known."[10] When newsmen asked who Dulles's successor would be, Eisenhower used a figure of speech that revealed how profound that association had been: "You don't try to hold a wedding until the other man has at least left the house."[11] The basis for their intimate partnership was threefold. First, Dulles had been a diplomat for as long as Eisenhower had been a soldier; he had been personally familiar with the international problems faced by the United States for more than forty eventful years. Second, he was a veritable encyclopedia of the conditions, options, and precedents of American diplomacy during the twentieth century, and he was an ideal staff officer because he could respond immediately to any question with accuracy and examples. Moreover, Dulles was a man of such extraordinary self-confidence and dedication that, according to Hagerty, he reminded Eisenhower of what Cromwell's Roundheads must have been like, of everything that was admirable about those soldiers. Indeed, Dulles's righteousness matched Eisenhower's own certainties, and neither obstacles nor criticism daunted either of them. Second, what others saw as Dulles's duplicity, Eisenhower counted as skill. At the conference table, the secretary would acquiesce only when there was an advantage in doing so, but he would not initiate a move that might weaken his leverage or show his hand. With such tactics he gauged the strengths and weaknesses of both friends and foes and would predict their likely responses. Third, Dulles's pessimism and rigidity were useful as a yardstick against which Eisenhower could measure his own evaluation, express his optimism, and demonstrate the flexibility of his response.

Secretary Dulles was also an indifferent administrator who complained that he had to spend too much time settling intramural jealousies and testifying before Congress. Yet he appointed under-secretaries of such high caliber that they could act in his place while he was traveling around the globe. In addition, he was ever ready to answer the questions of the press and to explain policy to legislators. By so doing, he was obviously trying to avoid Acheson's fate. Apparently he meant to mollify the McCarthyites by appointing strong anti-Communists to lesser posts in the department, but the behavior of those assistants seemed to undermine morale at State and belied the administration's promise to retain career officers. Eisenhower, however, was disturbed mainly by their failure to obey Dulles's directives. Nevertheless, of greater importance, as far as the president was concerned, was the secretary's ability to secure highly qualified field officers. In the case of Charles Bohlen's nomination as ambassador to the Soviet Union, Dulles's quiet assurances proved decisive in winning confirmation over the objections of leading Senate Republicans.

In accordance with his concept of staff administration, Eisenhower did not tell Dulles how to conduct his public relations. The secretary called his own press conferences and easily captured the headlines with such apocalyptic phrases as the "liberation of enslaved peoples," "agonizing reappraisal," "the brink of war," and "massive retaliation." While the rhetoric may have pleased some, it also seemed to undermine general confidence in his diplomacy. Many observers wondered whether his doomsday statements reflected the president's outlook, and whether they would prevail as policy in time of crisis. Although Dulles's hard-line pronouncements did reflect Eisenhower's attitudes, the president was somewhat annoyed by what he once called the secretary's lapses into "smart aleck" journalese. On occasion he had to urge Dulles to clarify his language to confirm that he was referring to options and alternatives rather than to policy.

Because Eisenhower did not publicly contradict his subordinate, however, critics insisted that the president was really being manipulated by Dulles. That allegation was strengthened by other reports. Eisenhower often exchanged notes and whispered asides with the secretary during cabinet meetings and international conferences, and he would sometimes look disturbed by Dulles's presentations in executive meetings. Yet these gestures may well have been demonstrations of the president's confidence in the secretary's analyses and of his total concentration on the problem being discussed. If Eisenhower sometimes seemed indifferent to what Dulles was saying, it was because he was already totally familiar with the secretary's views. Indeed, the two men conferred several times each day, and sometimes exchanged hourly cables when Dulles was overseas. As a result, the subordinate came to know his chief's values and priorities so precisely that he never accidentally violated them.

Although Dulles regarded other presidential advisers with suspicion and asserted that he was the administration's only "secretary of peace," he never overstepped his relationship with the president. At the outset, there was an understandable period of adjustment between the two. They spoke in public and in private with deep respect for each other's principles, but they differed on the best way to express them. Even after many years of working with Dulles, Eisenhower still questioned the secretary's practice of behaving like "a sort of international prosecuting attorney"[12] in dealing with the Soviet Union. In one instance, he calmed the secretary in the midst of a tirade by gently joking, "You *are* a militant Presbyterian, aren't you?"[13] In his later accounts of conversations with the secretary, Eisenhower implied that he frequently had to remind Dulles about two very important subjects. The first was military force and the consequences of its use. The second was the high cost of international commitments. Perhaps it was those lessons that the president had in mind when he told an aide that there was one man who knew more about foreign policy than the secretary of state, and then jerked his thumb back at his own chest.

The president drew upon his own experience and his own reasoning in dealing with Korea, the first foreign policy problem his administration had to face. Several weeks before he took office, Eisenhower left New York in secrecy and flew across the Pacific to South Korea. There, he interviewed officers and enlisted men (including his son John, who was serving in a G-2 unit) and examined the blasted terrain of the battle front. The war was unwinnable, he concluded, because United Nations troops could not pursue the enemy into its own strongholds across the border without the risk of sparking a Communist Chinese retaliation and a full-scale war. Although he had not liked General MacArthur's suggestion that the United States should drop atomic bombs to drive back the North Koreans, he instructed Dulles to use neutral channels to inform the enemy that if they did not withdraw to the prewar border, allied forces would "just go and crack them."[14] The phrase may have been purposely ambiguous, but any threats by a military man with atomic bombs at his disposal carried unquestioned weight.

A few months after his inauguration, the president accepted

arrangements for a truce in Korea to end the war that had drained American men, resources, and morale for three years. "The war is over," he mused privately, "and I hope my son will be coming home soon."[15] Mindful that some Americans would leap to happy conclusions about the cease-fire just as they had about his campaign pledge, he cautioned his countrymen: "We have won an armistice on a single battleground—not peace in the world. We may not now relax our guard or cease our quest."[16] A few months later, Eisenhower candidly informed congressional leaders that if the Communists renewed the fighting in South Korea, the United States would hit them with everything it had. But, he said, he preferred to employ other "weapons." At his request, Congress appropriated $200 million to begin economic reconstruction of that devastated nation. On his orders, several hundred American troops were assigned to instruct the republic's armed forces so that it could conduct pursuit-and-strike operations in the event of another invasion from the north. The government of South Korea—like that of Spain, another recipient of U.S. economic and military aid—was a veritable police state under the absolute rule of one man, President Syngman Rhee. Irascible and demanding, Rhee seemed more a detriment to American policy than an ally. But like Chiang Kai-shek on Formosa, he was a useful surrogate for full-scale United States presence.

Having devised that kind of commitment in the Far East, the president then applied it to the Middle East during the same period. In 1953, British Foreign Minister Anthony Eden, whose friendship with Eisenhower dated from the war years, came to the White House to seek American support of his country's continued military control of Egypt. Because of the implications of colonialism, the president did not agree. Indeed, he publicly announced that the United States would support a fair settlement of the issues, acceptable to both sides, thereby encouraging Egyptian leaders to hold fast to their demand for the expulsion of the British. But Eisenhower did assist British interests in the same region by intervening indirectly in Iran.

According to CIA reports, the ineffective administration of Premier Mohammed Mossadeq threatened to make that nation a pawn of Communist power. Furthermore, his erratic course jeopardized the security of Anglo-American oil corporations in the region. After clandestine American military assistance was extended to the ruling Shah of Iran, Mossadeq was driven from office. Later, American military instructors were sent to help the Shah build up his armed forces. In 1954, after Communist influences were removed and the political situation was stabilized, the United States sponsored an agreement for collective security in the Middle East in the form of a five-nation pact. It was signed in 1955 at Baghdad, the capital of Iran.

The indirect intervention in Iran may be viewed as an effort to prevent another situation like that in South Korea—that is, to stabilize a legitimate government and to provide aid to strengthen local resistance to communism. To be sure, American economic interests were also thereby secured. Moreover, many critics found no difference between intervention and outright aggression. Just when the Baghdad Pact was being formulated as the model of American policy in the Middle East, a third question of intervention developed much closer to home. According to the CIA, the legitimate Guatemalan government of Jacabo Arbenz y Guzman was decidedly Communist in its composition and policies. When that government announced a program of land reform, the American-owned United Fruit Company, which virtually controlled the nation's agricultural economy, confirmed those intelligence reports. Some Guatemalans opposed the government and its policies, the report noted, but opposition forces lacked effective means to overthrow Arbenz.

The Eisenhower administration had not yet formulated a complete foreign policy for Latin America when the Guatemalan developments emerged early in 1954. Unofficially, the president encouraged private American investment in the region as a more desirable form of economic and social assistance than outright federal spending. As a result, corporations became an extension of the State Department and exercised a certain political influence on that continent. Although previous presidential corollaries to the Monroe Doctrine seemed applicable in the case of Guatemala, Eisenhower was anxious to build his policy within the framework of the Organization of American States (OAS).

When American intelligence revealed that Arbenz was receiving shipments of arms from Communist nations, Eisenhower directed Dulles to secure an OAS resolution condemning the trade as outside interference in the hemisphere. Although the measure was duly adopted, the organization had no way of stopping the shipments. The propinquity of Guatemala, and the extent of American investments, seemed to call for U.S. intervention, but the problem involved two traditions of American foreign policy. One was that of de facto recognition. After its own war of independence, the United States had been a de facto government and thereafter had readily extended recognition to other de facto governments trying to attain independence. Eisenhower recalled vividly, however, that Woodrow Wilson had found it necessary to abandon that tradition when he judged the revolutionary cadre in control of Mexico to be unrepresentative of the Mexican people. Similarly, Eisenhower decided that Arbenz's rule did not represent the democratic principles of his own people and was, therefore, not a legitimate government. And so the president ordered American naval forces to patrol the waters off Guatemala and to search vessels suspected of carrying arms shipments, thus shattering a second tradition.

Search and seizure of American ships by the British had led to the War of 1812; now the tables were turned and the British angrily objected to Eisenhower's use of that same policy. In private, the president remarked that he had already been "too damn good" to them in the Middle East. "Let's give them a lesson,"[17] he said. After Eden and Churchill talked with the president, Great Britain merely abstained from a Security Council vote upholding the OAS and, in effect, American actions in Guatemala.

Eisenhower considered presenting the Guatemalan situation to Congress as a matter of Communist influences in the hemisphere, but Dulles pointed out that a formal congressional response would be seen as a blatant example of American intervention. Moreover, any overt action taken would constitute an encouragement of rebellion and would undermine the administration's professions of noninterference. Relying on assurances from his department's intelligence agents, the secretary of state pointed out that a handful of American aircraft (but no bombers) would be sufficient to enable the antigovernment forces to overthrow Arbenz. The plan was an inexpensive way to end Communist rule and protect American investments at the same time. Eisenhower approved, and the plan quickly succeeded. After Arbenz fell, Vice President Nixon visited Guatemala and reported that the people there were relieved to be rid of both communism and a corrupt, incompetent administration.

Eisenhower told the American people that communism's first foothold in the hemisphere had been halted by an uprising of freedom-loving Guatemalans. Soon afterwards, the OAS encouraged the United States to sell several fighter planes to Costa Rica and Nicaragua in order to "stabilize" the governments of those Central American nations. The Guatemalan episode was little noticed by most Americans at the time, but in retrospect it assumed ominous significance. It was the first time that the CIA went beyond its job of gathering and analyzing information and took up a new role as the maker of events. It was also an early example of what came to be known as the credibility gap, demonstrating the distance between official acts and official explanations.

Important as Guatemala was in retrospect, however, the Eisenhower administration faced two much more important tests of its foreign policy that same year, both in the Far East. By 1951, the example of the Chinese Communist revolution had spread into Indochina and found fertile ground in the independence movements of Laos, Cambodia, and Vietnam—all French colonies. Observing that the United States was willing to bolster British interests around the world although officially opposed to colonialism, France asked for American aid in its military efforts to check the Communist-supplied guerrillas in Southeast Asia.

Eisenhower had first studied the military problem facing the French forces in Vietnam while he was at NATO's Paris headquarters. Because of the jungle terrain and the nature of guerrilla tactics, conventional armies were at a great disadvantage; France's reliance upon fortress enclaves in the interior seemed to be an ineffective way to conquer areas held by the enemy. Yet potential Communist control of an independent Vietnam was no less threatening to the "free world," in Eisenhower's view, than such an influence in Korea or Guatemala. Eisenhower and Dulles used the image of falling dominoes to illustrate their belief that the crisis in Indochina could eventually endanger British and American economic and strategic positions in the western Pacific.

In discussions with his NSC advisers, the president rejected the military's idea that air strikes would be effective enough to bring victory in a ground war. Moreover, he told the French, "I'm not going to make my country just another Hesse to hire out mercenaries for you people."[18] Dulles asked the French what they would do if the United States gave them two atomic bombs. It was not an offer but merely a characteristic ploy to measure intentions. Eisenhower would not, of course, permit control of those weapons to leave his hands; he may also have regarded their use in Vietnam as no more desirable than in Korea. Moreover, the question was moot because the French refused to declare that independence would follow the success of its armed efforts against the Communist guerrillas. Eisenhower decided that American assistance could not support what he considered weak leadership in the government of France, and he informed them that Congress would not authorize any aid without the guarantee of independence. The president explored with the British the alternative of collective action to assist the French, but

Churchill was unable to obtain his cabinet's approval of military participation.

The only possible action that remained was to work for a negotiated peace. But American confidence in the outcome of the Geneva conference, which opened in January 1954, was undermined by the presence there of delegates from China. After the French army was overwhelmed at Dien Bien Phu in May, France had to bargain for a settlement as the defeated power. Any anti-Communist nation that supported France, Dulles reasoned, would now share its disadvantageous position. When the Communist delegates demanded that their opponents renounce the use of collective intervention, the secretary of state left the conference. As he feared, the French ultimately agreed to a division of Vietnam, with the northern portion controlled by Communist Vietnamese. A provision calling for free elections as a prerequisite to future reunification was, in Dulles's opinion, an empty assurance: American intelligence informed him that the Communists would be certain to win those elections. As a result, he advised Eisenhower that if the United States approved the Geneva accords, we would have to assume all of France's former burdens in Indochina when those accords gave way to Communist control.

In an attempt to find some other alternative for holding back the spread of communism in Southeast Asia, the president redesigned his Korean policy to fit South Vietnam. Finding no strongman like Syngman Rhee, the United States supported Ngo Dinh Diem, a Catholic in the primarily Buddhist society, whose police-state rule secured neither unity nor efficiency. Before these facts about Diem's rule were apparent, however, Congress appropriated $400 million in aid and sent military technicians to South Vietnam to act as advisers. The United States also promoted formation of the Southeast Asia Treaty Organization (SEATO) for concerting international mutual-defense policies in the region.

As late as 1957, the president was still publicly describing Diem as a "staunch patriot" who had shown "great courage and statesmanship in the development of his country and government, with a very great respect for free institutions."[19] The dubiousness of America's involvement caused several congressional Democrats to warn that the presence of advisers in South Vietnam eventually might lead to full-scale military intervention. But the president assured them that those advisers would, in fact, make further U.S. actions unnecessary by enabling the South Vietnamese themselves to hold back Communist aggression.

A far more visible test of the administration's international commitments developed late in 1954 when China began bombarding the small islands adjoining Chiang Kai-shek's stronghold on Formosa. Public reaction in the United States was greatly influenced by the current arguments of the Republican "China lobby" and advocates of the Bricker amendment. Eisenhower's press conference remark that any Chinese invasion would have to run over the American Fifth Fleet, stationed in Formosan waters, aroused further apprehension. Publicly, he said only that the United States would support Chiang's morale but actually he hoped to preserve the generalissimo's forces for possible use in the event of further Communist aggression either in Korea or in Vietnam. At a meeting of the NSC, the Joint Chiefs of Staff argued that the Formosan crisis called for armed intervention. The president reminded them of the possible chain of events: if force was used at all, the United States must be prepared to employ whatever was necessary—including nuclear weapons—to bring victory; and if the intervention was pressed to that point, the Chinese might well call on their ideological partners in the Soviet Union for aid. He was also aware that any decision to intervene would affect the pending congressional elections. (Indeed, the Formosan crisis may have contributed to the Republicans' loss of their majorities in Congress.) When several American airmen were captured after their planes had been forced down over China, Senator Knowland, now the minority leader, joined with McCarthy in calling for a blockade of the mainland. Instead, Eisenhower offered Chiang a defense arrangement and dispatched aircraft carriers to strengthen the Fifth Fleet.

When the new Congress assembled in January 1955, the president asked the members for a statement in support of his actions. (In order to avoid giving the impression that war was imminent, he decided not to deliver the message in person.) After conferences were held between legislators and the White House staff, a declaration was passed by a unanimous vote in both houses. The Formosa Resolution, as it was called by the media, supported the president's use of military forces whenever he judged them needed. Armed with this new weapon, Eisenhower informed the Chinese through neutral channels that American power would be used to stop any aggression against Formosa.

Within a month, Chinese leaders agreed to a cease-fire and approved of negotiations for the return of the American airmen. Only at the point did the president discuss his reasoning in public. "I feel that the Korean conflict started," he told reporters, "because of our failing to make clear that we would defend this small nation."[20] In order to avoid repeating that mistake in Formosa, the president was asked, was he ready to use nuclear weapons? "Now, in any combat where these things can be used on strictly military targets for strictly military purposes," he replied, "I see no reason why they shouldn't be used just exactly as you would use a bullet or anything else."[21]

Thus, the Formosan crisis had emphasized the destructive alternatives available to the United States, but Eisenhower preferred to concentrate on the constructive side of his administration's foreign policy. Just after Congress had equipped him with the Formosa Resolution, changing conditions on the other side of the world gave him an opportunity to demonstrate that preference. Beginning late in 1954, the Soviet Union seemingly adopted a new attitude. Premier Nikolai Bulganin and party Chairman Nikita Khrushchev, the new leaders, made a series of friendly gestures—first toward neutralist India, then toward the renegade Communists of Yugoslavia, and most notably toward the new capitalist nation, the Federal Republic of Germany. To underscore their reasonableness, the Soviets also agreed to a treaty recognizing the independence of Austria and withdrew their occupation forces from that country.

Dulles had regarded the Austrian treaty as the *sine qua non* for a meeting at the "summit"—that is, a conference of the heads of state of the four major powers. Anthony Eden, Churchill's successor as prime minister, urged that the time had never been more propitious for such a meeting, but Dulles remained pessimistic. Geneva, the proposed site, was associated with the disreputable Vietnam settlement, he argued. Furthermore, he predicted, the Soviets would use the summit as a forum for propaganda. He warned the president that their real intent was better indicated by the recently formed Warsaw Pact, which would facilitate their military operations in Eastern Europe. Eisenhower, however, did not think that the agreement constituted any substantial danger to NATO. Although members of his own party were brandishing copies of the newly published record of the Yalta Conference of 1945—the meeting at which Roosevelt allegedly betrayed the peoples of Eastern Europe—the president refused to permit a new chance for peace to be jeopardized by past mistakes. He said that he was ready to "pick up and go from any place to Timbuktu to the North Pole to do something about this question of peace."[22] This conference would be no latter day Tilsit, he noted, referring to the historic meeting between Napoleon and Alexander I; Eisenhower sought and received congressional leaders' approval of the trip to Geneva. Any dangers or disappointments involved in the summit meeting, he reasoned, were preferable to an aimless drift toward conflict.

In mid July 1955, as he prepared to fly to Europe, the president assured his countrymen that the nation's hopes were strengthened by alertness, caution, wisdom, and faith.

> By caution I mean: a prudent guard against fatuous expec-
> tations that a world . . . can be miraculously cured by a
> single meeting. I mean a stern determination that we shall
> not be reckless and witless, relaxing our posture merely
> because [of] a smiling face and a soft voice. By wisdom
> . . . I mean also a persevering resolution to explore every
> decent avenue toward a lasting and just peace, no matter
> how many and bitter our disappointments.[23]

His words referred to Republican criticism of Yalta, of course, but his purpose was to emphasize that summit conferences, properly conducted, could be a valuable tool in the quest for peace. In closing his remarks, he asked all Americans to pray for peace that Sunday.

Upon arriving in Geneva, the president declared that on this trip he brought something much more powerful than the armed might that had accompanied him when he had arrived on the Continent eleven years before: this time he brought "the good will of America—the great hopes of America—the aspirations of America for peace."[24] Abandoning the State Department's suggestion that he remain socially austere, he sought out his wartime associate, Marshall Gregory Zhukov, who was now the Russian minister of defense. Zhukov was cordial but seemed tense and acted as if he had been coached to make certain points about Soviet intentions. Even Premier Bulganin seemed as if he was under instructions, but Eisenhower was determined to deal with issues rather than personalities. In an opening statement, he told the assembled leaders that they could create "a new spirit." "It is time," he said pointedly, "that all curtains, whether of guns or laws or regulations, should begin to come down."[25]

Turning to speak directly to the Russians, he proposed that the two nations should open their skies to aerial inspection, exchange charts of all military facilities, and agree on rules for conducting surveillance flights. As if to emphasize his words, outside there was a clap of thunder and the lights in the hall went out momentarily. Bulganin responded by saying that the Soviet Union would consider the idea, but after the session adjourned, Communist party Chairman Nikita Khrushchev came up to the president, shaking his head. "That is a very bad idea," he said. "Who are you trying to fool? . . . It is nothing more than a spy system . . . a very transparent espionage device. . . . You could hardly expect us to take this seriously . . . we'll have none of it." It was then, Eisenhower later remarked, "that we knew who the hell was boss" in the Kremlin.[26]

Although the Russians subsequently agreed to an October meeting of foreign ministers, they were angered by the president's references to international communism and satellite peoples. When they rejected every suggestion for reunification of East and West Germany, Dulles urged Eisenhower to leave the conference as a gesture of protest. But the president thought that something more could be salvaged from the stalemate. The Russians, he noted, were just as interested in public relations as the Western powers. With that in mind, he offered to accept their draft of a conference statement if they would support free elections in any future unification of Germany. That harmless transaction was nothing more serious than a gesture of encouragement for future negotiations on the subject.

When he returned to the United States, the president pronounced the meeting at Geneva a good one on the whole. Although noting a tangible "new friendliness" among the leaders of the four nations, he advised Americans not to be discouraged if proposals, approaches, and beliefs were not immediately adopted by all sides. The press, however, played down his cautionary words and instead transformed the phrase he had used before the meeting into "the spirit of Geneva," using it to describe the conference's accomplishment. British and French leaders contributed to that gloss by calling Geneva the basis for detente with the Communists. Whether or not the meeting had restored American confidence in the fruitfulness of summit diplomacy, it certainly rebounded in Eisenhower's favor: within a week after Geneva, his rating in the public opinion polls rose above 80 percent approval, the highest level of his entire presidency.

Eisenhower was deeply moved by these expressions of good will and satisfied that his efforts had sustained the new friendliness in the world. Even though the Russians had used Geneva as a propaganda forum, just as Dulles had predicted, they obviously were ready to continue negotiations. But the president took no further unilateral steps to implement his "open skies" proposal, and American embassies were advised to remain vigilant. Perhaps he was concerned about the way the NATO allies would respond, or perhaps he meant to avoid any charge that his proposal was a bribe to elicit Soviet concessions on Germany or disarmament. Geneva, he reminded his countrymen, was only a spark that had to be fanned into flame by further negotiations. Until then, he would not gauge the success of his foreign policy initiative.

5

★★★★★

HIS OWN COURSE

Dwight Eisenhower may have intended his bold gesture at the Geneva summit to be a heartening and useful legacy to his successor in the White House. Following his election in 1952, he had assumed that four years would be sufficient for his administration to restore responsibility to the government and a sense of confidence to the nation. During that period, he had also intended to bolster the ideals and record of the Republican party and emphasized that he would have his fill of things political. When he returned from Geneva, however, the antics of the Eighty-fourth Congress reminded him that the continuation of his purposes and emphases was by no means certain.

In January 1955, after the president presented his recommendations to the new Congress, the Democrats, now in control, examined them in the light of partisan advantage. As Eisenhower saw it, Senate majority leader Lyndon Johnson meant for his followers to construct a legislative record that the party could use as a springboard from which to regain the White House in 1956. Among the recommendations carried over from the Republican Congress were creation of a soil bank for agricultural staples and funding for construction of the interstate highway system and for water resources development in the Upper Colorado Basin. The opposition was able to delay consideration of these measures, but it was still too rent by factions to turn them around completely. Instead, the Democrats concentrated on enlarging housing and school construction programs, far in excess of administration recommendations.

Ambition and opportunity made strange bedfellows on the floor of the Eighty-fourth Congress. A combination of pork-barrelers and federal waterpower advocates tried unsuccessfully to reverse the administration's resources "partnership" policy by authorizing the enormous, multipurpose federal dam on the Snake River that the Republicans had rejected two years before. A combination of economizers and conservationists blocked approval of the series of federal dams on the Upper Colorado River which the Eisenhower administration strongly supported. The Democrats also threw out partisan lassos, hoping to catch a cabinet member or two. They excoriated the secretary of the interior as "Giveaway McKay" and called for the resignation of Secretary of Agriculture Benson. When Air Force Secretary Harold Talbott resigned after being charged with a minor conflict of interest, their appetite was whetted. Finally, just as the president was preparing to go to Geneva, they directed public attention to what they claimed was HEW Secretary Hobby's "criminal" mismanagement of the distribution of a new polio vaccine.

Eisenhower defended the integrity of his cabinet officers without exception. At the same time, he also had to defend himself when a Senate subcommittee looking into the TVA demanded testimony from the White House. The investigation of the Dixon-Yates contract which was conducted by Alabama's senator, Lester Hill, seemed to lead to the president's own staff. Initially, Eisenhower instructed former budget director Dodge to tell Hill's committee everything he could. That did not satisfy the senators, however, and Hill asked for relevant White House files. Although the documents would have shown nothing more than the administration's strong desire to supplement federal control of the TVA with private management, Eisenhower invoked executive privilege. The files, he said, were honeycombed with staff memoranda and procedural materials representing conflicting views considered before the decision was made. "If any commander is going to get the free unprejudiced opinion of his subordinates," the general indirectly lectured the senators, "he had better protect what they have to say to him on a confidential basis."[1]

In the president's mind, in the thoughts of most Republicans and many Americans, the continuing conflicts between the executive and legislative branches was central to the question of whether he would seek a second term. A few days after the party's setback in the 1954 congressional elections, his associates began urging him to be a candidate for a second term. Although Eisenhower resented their desire to commit him, he agreed that the revitalization of the party was still being obstructed by its reactionary wing. But those on the far Right, he told a political adviser, generated so little political strength in the country that they could not even elect "a man who was committed to giving away $20 gold pieces to every citizen of the United States for each day of the calendar year."[2] That faction, he felt, was not the most important problem facing the Republican party. What it needed primarily was a younger man who could handle the increasingly severe and complex problems facing a president. If the party depended on Eisenhower's candidacy, its vital structure could collapse if he should die or become disabled. These were his thoughts on the subject during the summer of 1955.

Above all else, Eisenhower believed that the Republican party must make itself strong enough to regain control of Congress. Assisting its members in that task was a matter quite apart from his own decision about running for reelection. In September, he urged Republicans to remember the spiritual basis for their cause and to live by ideals, by an honest philosophy. They should be conservative in everything basic to the American system, he explained, yet dynamic in applying that conservatism to the problems of the day. Democrats ridiculed his search for the right descriptive phrase (dynamic conservatism, moderate progressivism, modern Republicanism), but Eisenhower thought no slogan could convey the fact that his was "the party of progress."[3]

The president's fellow Republicans were far more interested in his reelection plans than in his definitions. In Denver, he made oblique references to a new team taking over, spoke of the help he could give the party after he left the White House, and reminded them that men were frail and mortal. Then, choosing a nautical analogy, he cautioned, "You never pin your flag so tightly to one mast that if a ship sinks you cannot rip it off and nail it to another."[4] When these words hit the headlines, speculation ran high within both political parties. Was he implying that his health was so bad that the "ship" might sink? Or was this a trial balloon to test his popular support? His health, the president confided to his brother Milton, was quite beside the point. "I think that if I thought the end of my days would come even before I returned to Washington, I would probably be even more emphatic and insistent in supporting the things in which I believe than I am under the more normal uncertainties of life."[5] Publicly, Eisenhower would say only that he would wait to see whether the world situation overrode personal considerations. In the meantime, he asked close associates to make a preliminary evaluation of the party's strength. The inference that he might let down his friends provoked him to plead: "I've given all of my adult life to the country. What more must I do?"[6] Such outbursts merely convinced some close observers that Eisenhower was putting on an act to conceal his decision to run again.

The contentious Eighty-fourth Congress was late in adjourning, and after all the noise-making, it had enacted just four of the dozen major measures the president had asked for. Only one of these pleased him: it would enable the chief executive to call up military reserve units for emergencies proclaimed by him. Dejected by the behavior of congressmen and other politicians, he headed for Colorado in September for a belated working vacation. The change of scene did not improve his mood. He was frequently irritable, impatient, and resented every demand on his privacy. His physician, Dr. Paul Snyder, had never seen his temper so unrestrained. That temper must have been especially provoked by two messages he received that month. One was a letter from Russian Premier Bulganin flatly rejecting the "open skies" proposal. The second was Harold Stassen's report from the disarmament meeting in London, indicating that the Russian and American delegates could not even agree on an agenda. While the public was still riding the high hopes of Geneva, therefore, the president was faced with the fact that his carefully prepared efforts had in no way altered Soviet intransigeance and distrust. He refused to be discouraged. The Russians' behavior merely reminded him that the United States could not let down its efforts in the slightest.

Because the security of the United States required precise and immediate knowledge of Soviet weapon sites, Eisenhower had to find an alternative to the "open skies" plan. It was at about this time that the CIA urged him to approve use of an aircraft newly developed by American technologists—the U-2. A heavily instrumented, fast, and high-flying plane, the U-2 could make sharp, close-up photographs from great altitudes without danger of being spotted or intercepted. The president considered it a modern extension of traditional G-2 (intelligence) activities and expected that the men who would pilot the aircraft would be motivated by "a high degree of patriotism, a swashbuckling bravado, and certain material inducements" (a $30,000 salary).[7] He therefore agreed to U-2 flights over the Soviet Union and ordered the CIA to show him in advance what areas would be covered, along with weather reports and other pertinent information. He would specifically approve a limited schedule of flights, but subsequent limited schedules would be approved only after the same procedures were followed in each instance. He had a final comment, however, for the intelligence agents: "Some day one of these machines is going to be caught," he predicted, "and then we will have a storm."[8]

Burdened by deep disappointments and serious decisions on national and international problems, Eisenhower plunged into a heavy schedule at his Colorado headquarters. He occasionally interrupted his paperwork to fish in mountain streams and give outdoor barbecue parties for friends and newsmen. Ending one hectic week with twenty-seven holes of golf, he ate some hamburgers heaped with onions, declined a cocktail, and then shared a roast lamb dinner with his family and close friends. That was on September 23. At 2:30 the next morning, his restlessness woke Mamie, and he complained of indigestion pains. She called Dr. Snyder who ordered him taken to the nearby army hospital for diagnosis. While he was placed in an oxygen tent, a specialist arrived and determined that the president had had a heart attack (coronary thrombosis).

Over the weekend, a news blackout was clamped on the hospital, but on Monday, September 26, press secretary Hagerty obeyed instructions that the president had given him at the beginning of his tenure. Recalling the constitutional impasse created when Woodrow Wilson was paralyzed by a stroke in 1919, Eisenhower had ordered Hagerty to keep the public and his staff fully informed of his condition in any such emergency. In an effort to provide complete information (and to prove that the president's physical machinery was functioning), Hagerty even reported details of bowel movements. (Told of that fact weeks later, Eisenhower grimaced but agreed that it had been necessary.) Hagerty released the doctors' reports daily, mindful that the announcements were being read in the Kremlin and Peking as well as at home. The news of the president's coronary stunned Americans. Remembering the sudden death of Franklin Roosevelt ten years before, many watched the hospital bulletins anxiously. The stock market slumped alarmingly that first Monday and recovered no faster than the patient himself.

The White House staff was scattered on vacation and business when the news reached Washington. After the cabinet and the president's advisers were quickly assembled, Secretary Dulles proposed that Sherman Adams was the proper liaison man to go to Denver while the vice president remained in the capital. Nixon seconded the idea and subsequently presided at the meetings of cabinet and National Security Council just as he did whenever the president was out of town. No bills needed attention and there were no significant stirrings from abroad. Any talk of Nixon handling such matters stopped when Attorney General Bownell declared that in terms of the Constitution, Eisenhower was not incompetent to act. Several Old Guard Republicans in Congress later grumbled that the vice president had let the White House clique take over, but in fact Nixon was anxious to perform the tasks his associates agreed he should handle and hoped his performance would not seem politically motivated. His work during the emergency earned high commendation from his colleagues in the executive branch.

After two weeks, the president was taken out of the oxygen tent. Looking pale and thin, he nevertheless flashed the famous grin and showed off the dressing robe given to him by the press corps. It bore the words "Much better, thanks." He was full of questions and wanted to get to work immediately. At first, Adams and Hagerty screened out any news that they thought might upset him and his family confined their conversation to amiable topics, but the screening arrangement was not needed for very long. On October 2, the president recorded an official message on film; on the tenth, he replied to Bulganin's recent letter; on the twenty-second, he wrote the vice president to say that Dulles had his permission to use discretionary authority in negotiations at the forthcoming foreign ministers' conference.

Shortly after his sixty-fifth birthday, Eisenhower was walking and making self-deprecating cracks about getting to be a "big boy" now. He returned to Washington on November 11 and told the large welcoming crowd at the airport that his doctors had given him a parole if not a pardon. He would have to ease himself back into his duties, he said, not bulldoze his way into them. Recuperating at the Gettysburg farm, he experienced the usual postcoronary depression, even referring to himself once as an old dodo, but generally he kept busy with official business. A flight to Camp David for a meeting with the cabinet on November 22, two months after the heart attack, marked his return to active work schedules.

During the last weeks of 1955, Dwight Eisenhower underwent what was for him the agonizing process of decision. The procedure he followed illustrates precisely the method he used in making every major decision of his career. It began with self-confidence. He could, he believed, "delicately" but firmly control the 1956 Republican National Convention so that it would nominate his kind of man. But who would that be? For years he had urged party leaders to groom some young successor to replace him. He had not tried to groom anyone himself; that was not his way. He wondered whether Vice President Nixon could be elected. Dewey's chances might be better, but there was little likelihood that he intended to be a candidate again. The president toyed with the idea of a George Humphrey–Milton Eisenhower ticket, but neither one had a political following. Yet "strictly political men like Knowland" could not be elected either, and in any case Eisenhower thought that the California senator "would be impossible."[9] That left only Earl Warren, but the president did not think there was a chance that the chief justice would leave the Court.

By the beginning of the new year, Eisenhower was considering two sets of arguments. The first came from Republican National Committee chairman Leonard Hall. The party, Hall claimed, could win neither the presidency nor control of Congress without him. Eisenhower grumbled about that, perhaps because it reminded him that he had failed to strengthen the party as much as he had hoped to. Afterwards, he remarked enigmatically to Hagerty: "I don't want to run again. . . . I'm not so sure I will not do it. . . . I don't want to, but I may have to."[10] Was it to be 1952 all over again? Lucius Clay, one of the principal influences in that earlier episode, reminded the president that he still needed to live an active, dutiful life, just as he had recommended four years before. John Eisenhower, on the other hand, believed that the president could act as an elder statesman if he retired. He could see his policies carried out by a successor satisfactory to him and could continue to lead the "free world" as much as it could be led. The president's son did not say who the successor might be, how he could be elected, or exactly what kind of leadership a private citizen could wield.

As usual, President Eisenhower paid more attention to oral arguments than to position papers. In mid January, he held a dinner meeting of his closest advisers. During the ensuing discussion, most of them emphasized that the policies so admirably begun at home and abroad remained unfinished. The administration's foreign policy, its bolstering of world peace, Secretary Dulles argued, would end if Eisenhower left the presidency. The Russians, he was sure, would take advantage of that absence to renew their international aggressions. In that connection, Hagerty reminded his boss that no one else could so effectively command the attention of the world news media. At the president's request, his brother Milton summarized the consensus of the meeting, adding two observations of his own on topics he knew weighed on Eisenhower's mind. As for the summons to duty, Milton thought that the president had already fulfilled every duty that could be fairly expected of him. And realistically, Milton noted, there was just as much chance that the president would face serious setbacks in a second term as there was chance that he would be able to enhance his influence. When the presentation concluded, the president merely thanked his guests and said no more about the subject that evening.

In the course of yet another month of deliberation, Eisenhower considered the real possibility that Old Guard Republican dissidents would split the party convention, allowing the Democrats to regain complete control of national policies. As had happened four years before, Eisenhower received very substantial support in the virtually uncontested New Hampshire primary that month. Once again, his spirit buoyed by evidence of public approval, Eisenhower emerged from the decision-making ordeal in a distinctly pugnacious mood. He had had earlier doubts about being the first "lame duck" president under the provisions of the newly adopted Twenty-second Amendment to the Constitution, which limited a president to two terms, and wondered how much influence he really would have. "I might be a duck," he decided, "but I [will] not be sitting and I [will] not be lame."[11]

In February, he went to Secretary Humphrey's Georgia plantation for some golf and quail shooting. When his mood suddenly brightened one day, Hagerty guessed what his decision would be. Playfully, Eisenhower asked his wife what he should do. "It's your decision," Mamie answered. "I'm not going to have anything to do with it." Relenting, he said, "Well, I've made up my mind. I am going to run again." Characteristically, he had no second thoughts, but reportedly he told one of his aides, "You'll never know how close I came to saying no."[12] The illness had been a challenge to prove himself and the period of recuperation had given him the opportunity to fully reassess his initial intentions. As he explained to Sherman Adams, "You know, if it hadn't been for that heart attack, I doubt if I would have been a candidate again."[13]

Dwight Eisenhower was even more indispensable to the Republican party in 1956 than he had been in 1952. He had no real competitors in terms of political backing or popularity among voters; moreover, none of his lieutenants or closest advisers could match his purposeful approach to domestic and foreign policies. He had never been comfortable with the idea that he (or anyone else) was indispensable, but he recognized that his attributes fitted the needs of the nation and the people. His desire to finish the substantial work already begun was understandably stronger than his initial hope of restoring an equilibrium in government and in national purpose. On that basis alone, he probably would have been a candidate for reelection even if the party leaders had not claimed that he was their only hope. As in 1952, his decision to run was based ultimately on his own convictions rather than on associates' arguments.

In contrast to his grimly reticent mood of four years earlier, the president was obviously delighted with his decision. He restrained his exuberance, of course, and let it out bit by bit as was his style. On February 27, he kept a poker face when he greeted newsmen at his customary press conference. He began his remarks by mentioning the current Red Cross drive, the pending visit of the president of Italy, and the need for congressional approval of the Upper Colorado River project. Then, in what was surely his most tantalizing use of "Eisenhower syntax," he began: "Now, my next announcement involves something more personal, but I think it will be of interest to you. . . . I have promised this body [an answer to the question of my running for a second term]. . . . Now, I have reached a decision . . . there were so many factors. . . . Some full explanation. . . . Moreover, I would not allow. . . . So for both reasons . . . I don't know . . . I am asking. . . . And my answer within the limits I have so sketchily observed, but which I will explain in detail tonight so as to get the story out in one continuous narrative, my answer will be positive, that is, affirmative."[14]

After the announcement was published, public speculation turned immediately and insatiably to the identity of his running mate. Once again, Eisenhower pointed out that there were several young, able members of his administration who could qualify for the vice presidency, but he did not offer a list of names either to the press or to party leaders. It was his hope that the delegates to the national convention would feel free to make their own choice. For that reason, he was greatly upset by questions about his opinions of possible candidates and especially by questions about Richard Nixon's future. Eisenhower had nothing but praise for the vice president, of course; Nixon had fulfilled the expanded role that Eisenhower had created of that formerly slight job. When pundits claimed that the president really wanted someone else as a running mate, he angrily told newsmen that anyone attempting to drive a wedge between himself and Nixon would have as much chance as if they tried to divide him from any one of his brothers. He was still testy about the allegation years later when he told an interviewer: "If I had not wanted him as a running mate I would have said

'Dick, I just don't want you this time.' You see, that would be the soldier's way."[15]

The president expected Nixon to make up his own mind about candidacy and to "chart out his own course"[16] just as he himself had done. He would do nothing to affect the vice president's future until that decision was made, but he suggested that Nixon might well enhance his executive qualifications if he took a cabinet post. Eisenhower may have had the Interior Department in mind; that post was available and the president was noticeably slow in filling it. Defense Secretary Wilson had indicated his intention of leaving the cabinet; Eisenhower thought that office too was a very likely possibility for Nixon. The vice president, however, feared that some of the White House staff, together with some party leaders, were trying to shuffle him to the sidelines, and he therefore regarded Eisenhower's suggestion as a nudge in the wrong direction. For that reason he quickly informed his chief that he wanted to run for the vice presidency again. Pleased and relieved that a decision had been finally made, Eisenhower ushered him out to tell newsmen.

There was one last disturbance of the president's political scenario. Harold Stassen, whom the Eisenhower aides agreed was a brilliant but eccentric colleague, asked permission to support Governor Christian Herter of Massachusetts for the vice presidential nomination. Eisenhower allowed his disarmament adviser to do so publicly, but he resented media interpretations of it as his own trial balloon. After Nixon received a large write-in vote in the New Hampshire primary, the president insisted that Stassen speak on behalf of Nixon's nomination at the convention. When Stassen did so, Democrats described the Republicans' meeting as no more than a rubber stamp. These episodes contributed two more awkward incidents to the Eisenhower-Nixon relationship.

The president opened his campaign for reelection by declaring that he would not permit the Democratic Congress to play politics with his proposals. For Eisenhower, that was an unusually outspoken public statement. The charge of partisanship, however, was not entirely accurate. Democrats had supported his recommendations in sixty-nine out of ninety-nine roll call votes taken. For example, it was Democratic support that broke the deadlock and passed the Upper Colorado River project. Although the Interior Department played no part in devising an effective compromise, the president described the bill's passage as an administration victory. He was also gratified by congressional approval of a financing plan for the interstate highway system. A gasoline and users' tax would be the basis for the three-year, $2 billion initial phase of the project, instead of the tolls that Eisenhower initially had favored. Anticipating booms in the heavy construction and trucking industries, Democrats joined Republicans to pass the measure, but the president did not appreciate their collaboration in this instance.

As if to dramatize the need for a Republican Congress, Eisenhower charged the Democrats with outrageous irreponsibility as he vetoed two of their bills. The first would have amended federal regulation of natural gas for the benefit of producers, as he favored, but it was adopted after such arrogant corporate lobbying that he thought Congress should investigate that interference. In the second case, election-minded legislators had turned his request to extend the provisions of the Agricultural Act of 1954 into a renewal of farm subsidies. After vetoing their substitute bill, the president took a step which was unusual for him and explained his action to the nation on radio and television. Thereupon Congress enacted parts of the earlier bill, prompting Eisenhower to remark as he signed the measure that the acreage involved was but a fraction of what could have been saved had Congress acted correctly sooner.

As was his custom, the president endorsed all Republican candidates for election even though some of the most prominent of them held views that could hardly be defined as "modern Republicanism." He personally did very little, however, on their behalf. Instead, Sherman Adams and other White House advisers encouraged several selected men to run for Senate seats. If the margin of control in that chamber was to be as thin in the Eighty-fifth Congress as it had been in the Eighty-third, then the administration needed additional champions. John Sherman Cooper of Kentucky, ambassador to India, was induced to return and run for his former Senate place. Douglas McKay, secretary of the interior, reluctantly agreed to enter the primaries in his home state of Oregon. Because that Senate seat was held by Wayne Morse, the *bête noire* of the Eisenhower administration, a victory by McKay would be doubly important. Unfortunately Oregon Republicans decided that the selection evidenced White House interference. Although McKay won the primary, he subsequently received only minimal assistance from the president or from the party campaign chest and was defeated by Morse in the general election.

Just when Eisenhower was ready to hit the campaign trail himself, he was hospitalized by ileitis, a painful blockage of the intestine, necessitating immediate surgery and weeks of recuperation. Unlike the postcoronary period, however, the president was immediately able to attend to all administrative duties. As if to demonstrate his quick recovery, he flew to Panama in July to discuss the status of the canal and then came home to deliver a rallying speech to the Republican National Convention. On the hustings the president talked about small businesses in Pennsylvania and Ohio, water and power development in the Pacific Northwest, and defense policy in California. He also used several new techniques to reach the voters. The televised question-and-answer sessions seemed somewhat contrived, but they enabled him to display his common sense and graciousness to a far greater extent than was otherwise possible. Later, when international crises curtailed his personal appearances, he issued public letters addressed to representatives of special segments of the population—union members, conservationists, and young voters.

One of the topics he repeatedly touched on that summer was his assertion that Republicans did the work of government better than their opponents. In reply, the Democrats claimed that their Congress had secured more constructive legislation than had the preceding Republican Congress and, indeed, that Democrats had supported the administration more frequently than had some Republicans. They dragged out their 1954 caricature of the president as a lazy, golf-playing boob, totally insulated by his lieutenants. Democratic campaign literature also depicted Richard Nixon succeeding the sick man in the White House. But it was only when the opposition described his foreign policies as militaristic that Eisenhower displayed his anger in public. "Do they think they can make American parents and wives believe that their sons are being shot at? Do they think they can bring Americans to believe that our nation's powerful voice is not daily urging conciliation, mutual understanding, and justice?"[17]

When Adlai Stevenson, again the Democratic presidential nominee, called for an end to the peacetime draft and for unilateral termination of nuclear testing, he shook the president's assessment of his statesmanlike qualities. In reply, Eisenhower branded the proposals as threats to the nation's security. Both the draft and nuclear testing, he insisted, were grim necessities and were unquestionably warranted by the present state of the world. As Eisenhower later described it, the Democrat seemed to be looking down the double barrels of a gun that exploded in his face when Premier Bulganin first endorsed Stevenson's ideas and then ordered the resumption of nuclear testing. The issue, in fact, provided the president with two excellent opportunities. The first was his unqualified support for enfranchising men old enough to be drafted. The second was his public release of a letter to Bulganin in which he chastised the Russian for fishing in the waters of America's internal affairs.

The president was campaigning with unusual energy and outspokenness, not because he was worried about the outcome of the election but because he wanted to win by a substantial margin. But his reelection efforts were virtually relegated to a back seat as the situation in the Middle East worsened during the summer. Continuing disagreements among the nations using the Suez Canal now threatened to erupt into military confrontation. The crisis not only threatened to involve America's NATO allies but also raised the possibility of intervention by the Soviet Union.

The main targets of the Arab nationalism preached by the leader of Egypt's recent revolution, Gamal Abdel Nasser, were British and French military bases on Egyptian soil and foreign influence in its economy. The other target of Nasser's hostility was Egypt's neighbor, Israel. The territorial integrity of the Jewish state had been an object of American concern for a decade. While not abandoning that consideration, Eisenhower did not intend to give Israel special treatment in its belligerent response to Egyptian threats. He told every nation in the area that the United States favored no one nation over any other and that it was unalterably committed to negotiations as the only method of resolving disagreements among them.

After Nasser's government began nationalizing foreign properties as part of his economic program, and after Syrian guerillas conducted raids across Israel's northern borders, there seemed to be no chance for a negotiated settlement in the Middle East. These developments, moreover, seemed to be ominous signs of an Arab renaissance that would endanger the Western powers' vast holdings in oil production and shipping in the region. The United States was further disturbed by reports from the State Department's intelligence agents that Egypt and other Arab nations were buying arms from Communist Czechoslovakia. As a result, when Nasser applied to the World Bank for an American-supported loan to build a gigantic multiple-purpose dam at Aswan on the Nile River, both Republicans and Democrats in Congress were opposed. As Eisenhower later described it, Nasser seemed to be playing each side against the other and at the same time blackmailing both of them.

Economic aid had long been a tenet of American foreign policy. The advantages for American investors were obvious, but its primary purpose was to bolster the political and economic stability of recipient nations so that they would not fall prey to communism, whether internally or externally generated. In the case of the Aswan loan, it would allow the United States to exercise substantial influence in moderating the militant inclinations of Arab nationalists. With those considerations in mind, Eisenhower was personally inclined to assist Egypt at Aswan. Nasser tactfully pledged that he would not seek Russian aid for Aswan if the United States agreed to participate in the World Bank loan. Yet the Communist arms shipments continued, and Egypt chose just that moment to establish diplomatic relations with Communist China.

In the opinion of Secretary Dulles, Nasser had thus compromised his country's neutrality and would not, therefore, feel bound to uphold it even if he was given aid for Aswan. The secretary of state argued that Nasser himself could well be a Communist and claimed that the dam project would dislocate Egyptian economic life during the many years of its construction. Either prospect would have grave consequences. When Dulles recommended that the United States not participate in the loan, the president was surprised. Nevertheless, he approved of the secretary's recommendation because the NSC and congressional leaders also opposed the loan. Personally, however, he thought the decision was too brusque. Instead of anticipating Egypt's behavior, Eisenhower felt it would be far more practical to hold the loan as leverage, while waiting to see how the rapidly changing situation in the Middle East would affect the prospect. Whenever hostility to the loan lessened, at home and abroad, he reasoned, the United States could then extend assistance for the later stages of construction at Aswan. (Indeed, when those changes did take place four years later, the president proposed that such assistance be given.) Secretary Dulles's recommendation, on the other hand, seemed to be a negative form of leverage, aimed at teaching Nasser that his blackmail would not work.

Unfortunately, the United States announced the decision to withdraw from the loan just after Egypt announced that it would accept the loan. Angrily, Nasser asked for and received Russian assistance in building the dam and used the rebuff as a perfect opportunity to nationalize the Suez Canal. Outraged by the move, British Prime Minister Anthony Eden and French Premier Guy Mollet quickly decided on a plan to remove the Egyptian leader from power. In order to prepare international opinion, they described Nasser as a small-time Hitler and implied that there would be no appeasement this time.

Early in 1956, Eden came to the White House to secure Eisenhower's general approval of the idea of allied intervention at Suez. But the president's reaction was that the British had never had much sense about the problems of the Middle East. This new proposal was "a thin scheme that would not work,"[18] he decided. In conversations then and thereafter, he told the prime minister that the United States would do anything to assist the United Nations in relieving tensions in the Middle East, but it would firmly oppose the use of force there—by anyone. As the prospect of a confrontation loomed that summer, the president assured apprehensive Americans that he would take no step that could be interpreted as an act of war.

Eden later claimed that Eisenhower had not made his views at all clear. At the time, however, he was simply unwilling or unable to believe that the United States would desert its old allies when the chips were down. Although he thought that the State Department's men were distinctly anti-British, he apparently counted on Eisenhower's concern for perpetuating the World War II alliance and perhaps depended on the effectiveness of what the British called an "old boy" camaraderie. The prime minister assumed, moreover, that pressure from Jewish-American voters would bring American acquiescence in Anglo-French intervention during that election year. Whether or not that pressure had accounted for earlier American support of Israel, there was certainly no basis for assuming that it would affect the Eisenhower administration's actions. But the possibility of such influence seemed likely enough to fit not only Eden's purposes but those of Israel as well. An Israeli military offensive toward the Suez Canal, timed to coincide with an Anglo-French assault, was part of the Eden-Mollet plan to bring down Nasser, and the French were already sending aircraft to Israel for that purpose.

By July 1956, American intelligence agents had learned of the existence of the intervention plan, but not its details or timetable. Anxiously Eisenhower argued against the idea of intervention in long telephone conversations with Eden—talks which he later referred to as a transatlantic essay contest. Indeed, his efforts proved to be no more effective than a literary conversation. The president then sent Dulles to London to participate in an allied conference concerning use of the Suez Canal. Although American shipping accounted for less than 3 percent of traffic through that waterway,

United States presence was more appropriate at the London conference than it had been at Geneva in 1954. Dulles, however, feared that the talks would result in another Geneva if they led to American participation in any actions that were agreed upon. Such apprehension may have accounted for his behavior at the meeting. Even State Department colleagues were dismayed by his apparent determination to do nothing more helpful than make legal points in the manner of a Wall Street lawyer. The allies thought his words devious, if not dishonest. Eisenhower always appreciated Dulles's concentration on details and may have viewed the secretary's ambiguities as a tactic to counter the deceptions the British and French were employing.

When Nasser announced that international use of the canal would continue under Egyptian operation, Eisenhower was grateful for a break in Middle East tensions. But Britain and France did not abandon their plans for intervention. The president, therefore, gave Eden a friendly piece of advice. The United States would not support the use of force, he repeated; if force was used, however, it must not be resorted to over such a specious matter as the allies' belief that the Egyptians were incapable of operating the canal efficiently. Instead, he cautioned, they should wait until they had a reason that clearly justified their intervention, so that world opinion would support them. He meant, of course, American opinion as well. At a press conference in September, he pointedly remarked that a situation could arise in which the British and French would have no other recourse than to continue to use the canal, even if they had to be "more forceful than merely sailing through it." Whether or not the allies were pleased with the statement, they must have particularly noted the wording of another remark made by the president at that same meeting. Asked if the United States would be involved in any forceful action, he replied: "I am not going to be a party to aggression if it is humanly possible to avoid it or [if] I can detect it before it occurs."[19]

The next month, October 1956, proved to be the most crowded and demanding period of Eisenhower's presidency. It began with the report from American surveillance aircraft that Israel was mobilizing. Because most of the Arab raids on that nation had come from Syria and Jordan to the north, it appeared likely that those countries would be the object of an Israeli strike. No matter what the provocation, a move by Israel would, in Eisenhower's judgment, be an act of aggression. In response, he meant to seek special authority from Congress and secure United Nations support for a blockade. Many Americans would be shocked to see Israel, the symbol of democracy reborn, branded as an aggressor. Would Jewish voters in New York and the heavily populated northeastern states register a protest at the polls? The president did not like the idea that some Americans would place special interests before justice. When Milton Eisenhower observed that a blockade might ruin his chance for reelection, the president glared at him, held his temper, and quietly indicated that the outcome of the election was the thing farthest from his mind.

The president warned both Anthony Eden and Israel's president, David Ben Gurion, that there should be no misinterpretation of public sentiment in the United States. Even if Jewish voters did exert pressure, he asserted, they would not have an iota of influence on the administration's policy in the Middle East. Meanwhile, Eisenhower learned from Robert Murphy, his personal emissary, that the Egyptians were operating the canal competently; there was, therefore, no legal or logical reason for allied intervention. But the president's assessment was obviously of no interest to the British and French commands as they poised their forces to execute a military strike against Egypt.

At that moment, the world's attention was shifted from the Middle East to Eastern Europe. In Poland there was a sudden popular uprising against Russian control. When the same sentiment sparked a rebellion in the nearby Communist satellite of Hungary, the Soviet Union sent in armored forces. Earlier, propaganda broadcasts beamed from Radio Free Europe, together with the rhetoric of Dulles and Nixon, had encouraged the rebels to expect American military assistance. Although President Eisenhower testified publicly that he believed in their cause, in private he sadly concluded that he could do nothing to help them. Any military move would have to be made with the participation of all NATO members, he believed, and would inevitably escalate into a general war. And collective action was not likely in view of allied disarray over Suez. Even if the United States wanted to act alone, its forces could not reach Hungary without violating the neutrality of Austria; and subsequent battles would devastate both that nation and Hungary— developments which would surely be condemned by other European nations. But the most decisive factor in the formation of the president's response was his belief that if Russian was willing to use armed forces to protect its control of Eastern Europe, it would be ready to use nuclear weapons if the United States intervened. Just as he had previously decided that Indochina and Quemoy were not worth the risk, he now concluded that Hungary was not worth a nuclear world war.

Instead of fulfilling the rhetorical declarations of Dulles and Nixon, the president ordered shipments of food and medicine to Hungary, suspended immigration provisions to permit the entry of thousands of Hungarian refugees, and instructed American intelligence agents not to give assurances of armed intervention by the United States. He also dispatched a sternly worded letter to Premier Bulganin pointing out the possible consequences of Russia's actions and urging him to withdraw his forces and submit the matter to the United Nations.

Realistically, Eisenhower recognized that he could not make America's enemies do what he could not get its friends to do. Prime Minister Eden perversely assumed that the Hungarian affair would occupy the attention of the United States and make it more inclined to support the British and French in the Middle East. Apparently remembering the president's cryptic press conference remarks three weeks before, he now dropped a blackout on communications with the White House and State Department. On October 31, British and French aircraft bombed Cairo while Israeli troops crossed over their southeast border into Egypt's Sinai peninsula.

"I just can't believe it," Eisenhower reportedly exclaimed when informed of the attacks. "I can't believe that they would be so stupid as to invite on themselves all the Arab hostility to Israel."[20] The "damn fools" could have been patient a while longer, he said, or could have at least found an acceptable excuse for their intervention. Moreover, their military strength proved indecisive and their strategy was a mess. It had been set so long before that it did not take into account changing conditions of supply; the air strike, therefore, could not be followed up with other actions. "All right, Foster," he told the secretary of state, "you tell 'em that, goddamn it, we're going to apply sanctions, we're going to the United Nations, we're going to do everything that there is so we can stop this thing."[21] The next day, Eisenhower addressed the American people on radio and television. "We cannot and we will not condone armed aggression," he intoned, "no matter who the attacker, and no matter who the victim. We cannot—in the world anymore than in our own nation—subscribe to one law for the weak, another law for the strong; one law for those opposing us, another for those allied with us. There can be only one law—or there will be no peace."[22]

Eisenhower's critics at home and abroad protested that he himself was violating that very principle: he was applying one set of judgments to the uprising in Hungary, they said, and another to the crisis in Egypt, enforcing "one law" against the allies but not applying it to Nasser at all. In a larger sense, Eisenhower was being Wilsonian in his desire to use American neutrality as a lever to force a peaceful resolution of the Suez problem, while at the same time he was adopting the self-interested stance of Republican isolationists in refusing to let America's arsenal be used merely to benefit its friends.

On election day, 1956, the president put the armed forces of the United States on alert and consulted with his innermost circle of national security advisers. CIA director Allen Dulles reported that Russia was not mobilizing along the northern boundaries of the Middle East, and Joint Chiefs of Staff chairman Radford thought it unlikely that the Soviet Union would employ ground troops or missiles anywhere in the region. While Eisenhower did not think that the Soviet Union would choose that moment to make war, he did expect its leaders to watch developments in the Middle East and make the most of their opportunity there. When the president went off to Gettysburg to cast his ballot, he directed Ambassador Henry Cabot Lodge to support a resolution in the United Nations Security Council calling for a cease-fire by all parties involved at Suez. Indignant over the stance taken by the United States, England cast its first veto in that body against the resolution.

Through the blackout of communications with the White House, a letter came from Winston Churchill appealing to the president to use his unique talents to heal the rupture between their two nations. The real enemy of peace was Russia, Churchill wrote; England and the United States must be ready to present a united front against any Communist move. Let the historians argue about the rights and wrongs of Suez, he added. Responding to his old friend's moving plea, Eisenhower agreed that Russia was the true object of allied attention but repeated that the United States would stand by its international principles. Wounded by having to give up the gage they had won (as Eden described it), the British found themselves forced to their knees. Because their nation was on the verge of a financial crisis, any further military operations in the Middle East were out of the question. At just that moment, Treasury Secretary Humphrey pointedly informed the International Monetary Fund that the United States would not approve of a loan to England until the cease-fire resolution was adopted.

"I could really use a bridge game," the president joked to a friend during these tense days of waiting. England's decision to

react "in the manner of the Victorian period," Eisenhower concluded, could be the result of Eden's determination to do something
to enhance his stature at home. "But I don't see the point in getting
into a fight to which there can be no satisfactory end, and in which
the whole world believes you are playing the part of the bully and
you do not even have the firm backing of your entire people."[23]
When Eden accepted the cease-fire resolution on November 6, the
president called him directly, using the recently improved transatlantic telephone. The new connection, he said in possible veiled
reference to the British communications blackout, was very clear.
The ailing Eden resigned three months later and was replaced as
prime minister by Harold Macmillan, another of Eisenhower's British wartime associates. The president's amiable letter of congratu-
lations to the new leader elicited a cool note of thanks. Blood was,
at that moment, thinner than water.

As the Suez crisis was moving toward a resolution, Eisenhower
had little time for politics at home. There was nothing he could
do in the final days before the election, he concluded, that might
change the outcome. He earnestly desired to win with "a comfortable . . . popular plurality." If he did not get one, he would rather
not be elected. "If I could get only 50.1 percent of the vote, then I
would feel that the American people have gone so far away from
my philosophy of government that nothing I could do thereafter
would be of any real help. This I think in spite of the fact that
Stevenson and Kefauver as a combination are the sorriest and
weakest pair that have ever aspired to the highest office in the
land."[24]

Perhaps the most important factor in the president's overwhelming victory at the polls that November was the juxtaposition
of foreign crises with the events at home. "Have you ever been
Nasserized and Stassenized on the same day?"[25] the president
cracked to one of his friends early in the campaign. In July, his
ileitis operation coincided with reports of Communist arms shipments to Egypt; in September, Democrats' cries about his militaristic
foreign policies coincided with his pledge that the United States
would not participate in aggression in the Middle East. In October,
he drew a clear distinction between the crisis in Hungary and that
in Suez. With Secretary Dulles hospitalized at the time of the
Anglo-French-Israeli strike against Egypt, the president was obviously far more "in charge" of diplomatic strategies than his critics
at home and abroad would acknowledge. The manner in which he
thus threaded his way through the pressures and paradoxes of

international crises, using America's neutrality and strength to prevent a general war, was the best argument for his reelection.

Whether or not posterity would regard the events of those tumultuous weeks during the fall of 1956 as the apogee of Dwight Eisenhower's presidency, the American people so judged it. The voters gave him a plurality of 9.5 million votes, three million more than he received in 1952. He also added fifteen electoral votes to his earlier total by taking Louisiana, a feat so incredible that he jokingly likened it to winning in Ethiopia. He was especially pleased by the large support he received in New York and by the fact that he once again carried his native state of Texas. For Republicans the presidential election of 1956 was an achievement comparable to Roosevelt's 1936 victory.

The president's personal satisfaction, however, was mixed with profound disappointment over the inability of the Republican party to secure sufficient support for its congressional candidates. The Democrats were able to increase their control of the Senate by only one seat and of the House by only two seats, but that slim margin meant that the Eisenhower administration would face two more years of contention, obstruction, and measures it could not claim as its own. If he had known that he was going to face another Democratic Congress, the president later remarked, he probably would have refused to run again. The cause which had impelled him to seek reelection, the continuation of his policies, was in no less jeopardy now than it had been before his heart attack. "If they don't approve what I stand for," he told newsmen after the election, "I would not understand why they voted for me."[26] The puzzle was answered, perhaps, when his rating in the Gallup Poll reached the second highest point of his presidency. Referring to Eisenhower's popularity, a reporter asked whether he considered the election a personal victory. The president objected to the implication that the Republican party consisted of nothing more than one personality. Such an interpretation, he wrote to a friend later, belittled the intelligence and judgment of the American people.

If 1956 was the high-water mark of the Eisenhower presidency, it was not because he acted any differently than he had during his first three years in office, but because he moved in two areas in which he was the sole decision-maker: determining his own future and selecting the alternative to war. Until that time, he had had to depend on professional politicians; in 1956 no politicians were needed to establish the record of his presidency. The fact that neither his age nor his past illnesses eroded the quality of his campaign made his effort even more admirable. During those first years he had slowly evolved a policy for America as shield of world peace; in the Suez crisis he quickly assembled the weapons of diplomacy and employed them to immediate effect. The fact that the "aggressors" in that instance were friends and not enemies of the United States made that response all the more impressive. During the remainder of his presidency, he would never again have two comparable tasks offering such striking opportunities to chart his own course.

chuckled over a propaganda film shown at his wartime headquarters because it portrayed Negro soldiers carrying rifles in combat, a sight he professed he had never seen in real life.

Yet Eisenhower did not share his associates' prejudgments and stereotypes; he believed that a man should be given fair chance to improve himself and use whatever abilities he had. A sense of tolerance was the source of his experiment with integrating several army units near the end of the war. When friends and colleagues criticized that attempt, he concluded that he was comparatively liberal on the subject of race. At the war's end, however, he discovered that attitudes considered liberal by the military were viewed by many citizens as reactionary. During the Truman administration, civil rights became a major plank in the Democratic party platform, after the president ordered the desegregation of the armed forces. As army chief of staff, Eisenhower told a congressional committee that he did not think discrimination could be rectified quickly or in a wholesale manner. Although civil rights organizations branded him a bigot for his statement, he was not opposed to equal treatment but did oppose its establishment by federal coercion. Neither laws, nor legal decisions, nor imprisonment could change men's emotions, he believed. While he considered the elimination of prejudice a matter of long-term education, he viewed racial injustice as a denial of everything that America stood for. During the 1952 campaign, he also objected to the Democrats' claim that they were the exclusive champions of Negro civil rights, but he did not address the subject himself except in the terms of harmony and gradualism, terms he had employed in his 1949 speeches.

As he entered the presidency, Eisenhower intended his administration to continue to act in those civil rights areas where the federal government had clear constitutional jurisdiction. Herbert Brownell, Jr., newly appointed attorney general, confirmed the president's hope that such an unquestionably proper and humane policy would also restore the Reublican party's historic role as the steward of Negro rights. In his first message to Congress in February 1953, therefore, Eisenhower directed attention to racial discrimination as a national, not just a regional problem, one which should be subjected to "the power of fact, fully publicized, of persuasion, honestly pressed, and of conscience, justly aroused."[1] In order to underscore his determination that progress be made in every federal branch, he ordered the desegregation of facilities in federal offices and on military bases. Looking toward the immediate future, he also urged fellow Republicans to rededicate themselves to the cause of racial justice "so that no man of any color or creed will *ever* be able to cry 'This is not a free land.' "[2]

The president's initial efforts were criticized by some as superficial and impotent, and by others as politically divisive and socially disruptive. When Governor James F. Byrnes of South Carolina objected to the administration's continued use of Truman's Fair Employment Practices Commission, Eisenhower replied that such a device was far more desirable than legislative fiat or executive force. Neither he nor Brownell expected that the Republican Eighty-third Congress would be able to set aside more pressing problems to take the initiative on civil rights laws. When they could get to it, however, the attorney general advised the lawmakers that segregation in interstate transportation was a likely area for their consideration. The second alternative, the use of force, did not appeal to Eisenhower; he well knew that armed power could conquer and subjugate an enemy but could never be the basis for justice in a democracy.

Satisfied with calling attention to the need for progress in civil rights and setting an example by executive procedure, Eisenhower did not return to the subject until a year later when he spoke to a convention of the National Association for the Advancement of Colored People (NAACP). Ideals, he told them, echoing his speeches as university president, could not be attained by mere gestures; the efforts that they were making for change through constitutional means would ultimately make better men of all citizens. Two months after he expressed those banalities, a great bull lurched into his orderly school room. In the case of *Brown* v. *Board of Education of Topeka*, all nine justices of the Supreme Court of the United States voted to reverse the doctrine of separate-but-equal school systems that had been upheld by their predecessors almost sixty years before. The man who delivered the decision was Earl Warren, nominated eight months earlier as chief justice by Dwight Eisenhower.

The clouds of bitterness engendered by the actions of the Warren Court have concealed facts concerning the relationship between the two men. And unfortunately another decade still must pass before essential documents covering that relationship become available to scholars. The testimony now accessible is ambiguous. Eisenhower had known Warren slightly since 1948, when the California governor was on the Republican ticket as Thomas E. Dewey's running mate, and was impressed with his record as a talented executive who won support from both parties. In 1952, Warren

107

had played a helpful but not decisive role at the Republican National Convention. Eisenhower's men therefore approached him not out of any obligation but out of respect for his national stature. Clay had seriously considered recommending him as secretary of the interior. As an old friend, Brownell asked him if he would take a federal appointment. Warren indicated that he would be interested in the chief justiceship but in no other job. Brownell promised that he would be considered for the first vacancy on the Court and Eisenhower called Warren later to say that they would discuss an appointment whenever a vacancy occurred. As it happened, the first opening was caused by the death of Fred M. Vinson, the chief justice.

Years afterward, Eisenhower said that he had considered only two men for the job. The first was Secretary of State John Foster Dulles. That choice would, of course, deprive the administration of Dulles's contribution to foreign policy. At sixty-five, moreover, Dulles was just beyond the age that the president thought practical if a justice was to remain on the court long enough to wield any influence. The secretary was honored to have this evidence of Eisenhower's high regard, but he preferred to hold the diplomatic post. Pleased with that decision, Eisenhower then turned to Warren, who was just sixty-two. He did so because of Brownell's promise. "While I had not made the promise," the president told a disgruntled Republican leader years later, "I just felt that I couldn't turn him down. That was the sole reason that appointment was made and it's one of the two biggest mistakes I made in my administration."[3] (The latter phrase echoed a remark ascribed to several other presidents. Asked if they had made any mistakes during their tenure, the joke ran, they had replied: "Yes, and both of them are sitting on the Supreme Court.")

At the time of the appointment, however, Eisenhower expressed no such regret. Indeed, writing in answer to the objections of a political conservative, he described Warren as a man who represented the kind of thinking needed on the Court and one who would be able to overcome the factionalism that had frequently produced single-vote margins in the decisions of the Vinson Court. He also sent words of admiration for Warren to his own older brother Edgar, who had criticized the appointment, and to his younger brother Milton, who had praised it. To the latter he swore that if the Republican-controlled Senate did not confirm Warren, he would form an independent party. Old Guard senators threatened to test his resolve by delaying the confirmation for many weeks.

Brownell told Eisenhower ahead of time that the *Brown* decision would probably sustain the Negro plaintiff; if it did, the administration would have a better basis for its recommendations to Congress. Eager to tie his department to the case, Brownell acted as *amicus curiae* (friend of the court) during the final months of argument. With the president's approval and the cabinet's knowledge, he also assigned to his deputy, William Rogers, the task of making a special effort to encourage southern officials to comply with school desegregation. Nevertheless, when the *Brown* decision was announced in May 1954, Eisenhower was disappointed. The court had assumed for the executive branch an impossibly vast responsibility, he felt, and had wrongfully taken the federal government into the lives of millions of American families. He judged that in view of the deeply held traditions of thousands of American communities, the decision had actually set back progress in integration by fifteen years. "It is all very well to talk about school integration," he reportedly said to his staff, "—you may also be talking about social *dis*integration. . . . We can't have *perfection* in these moral questions. All we can do is keep a goal and keep it high. And the fellow who tells me that you can do these things by *force* is just plain nuts."[4]

Eisenhower's objections to the 1954 decision did not indicate any antipathy toward the equal treatment of Negroes; instead they revealed his paramount interest in adequately implementing the Court's orders. Instead of offering any plan for integration, the Supreme Court said nothing about procedure. Brownell duly conveyed to the justices the president's private solicitude for southern attitudes, a view shared by some of its members. Several months later, when the court issued guidelines for integration "with all deliberate speed," their phrase precisely expressed the president's own conception of a proper pace. He was, moreover, pleased that their decision was unanimous and took it as evidence that Warren was indeed bringing harmony to the high bench. The day after the *Brown* judgment, the president demonstrated his own adherence to the supreme law of the land by ordering the District of Columbia Commission to make the capital's schools models of integration.

In keeping with his regard for the proper separation of powers, Eisenhower issued no public statements about the *Brown* case, about school integration, or about his own opinions on civil rights subjects. The same week that the Court announced its decision, he chose to indicate his approval with an oblique axiom in a speech delivered at a United Negro College Fund luncheon: "Everything that the Constitution accords to me, I must defend for others—or else finally there will be nobody left to defend me."[5] Responding to reports of widespread public objection to the decision, he merely quoted a statement issued by his erstwhile critic Governor Byrnes: "Let's be calm and let's be reasonable and let's look this thing in the face."[6] At his press conference, Eisenhower denied that Warren had acted out of partisan motives and added that in that election year southern voters would have to judge for themselves whether "I have got any sense or have not." His own opinion of the *Brown* decision was irrelevant, he said. "The Supreme Court has spoken, and I am sworn to uphold the constitutional processes in this country; and I will obey."[7]

If the president hoped that this dutiful response would set the tone for all Americans, he was to be disappointed. During the months that followed, public debates raged over what would be the proper, possible, and desirable means of securing civil rights for Negro citizens. Eisenhower welcomed nationwide discussion, but he was also disturbed by the way this issue disrupted the national unity he had sought to promote. In private, he would speak to neither advocates of resistance to the law nor to zealots of immediate compliance with it. The members of his White House staff did not even welcome internal references to the subject. Although they provided the president with expertise in domestic economic problems and foreign policy, they were woefully backward in their understanding of the civil rights issue. Like their chief, they distrusted pressure groups in general and Negro organizations in particular. The latter, they felt, tended to overdramatize single incidents of racial injustice and to demand a disproportionate amount of attention and assistance. Even in reminiscences years later, several of these aides were reticent to discuss civil rights, a subject which by then had become an extremely sore point among Eisenhower's partisans. While making a few bland comments, however, one of them habitually used the term "black boys" and "blackamoors."

E. Frederick Morrow, a special assistant in foreign affairs, was the only, in his words, "black man" in the Eisenhower White House. He did not claim to be an expert on the subject of race, but he was appalled to find that his colleagues were unaware of such basic realities as the high unemployment rate among Negroes. As civil rights became an increasingly hot topic, his associates regarded him warily, believing that he was a spokesman for Negro pressure groups. One of the most important of Morrow's superiors, Jerry Persons, ultimately refused to discuss the subject with him. Persons, a Georgian whose brother had been a governor of Alabama, told him: "Fred, I would appreciate it if you would never approach me or come to me with anything involving civil rights. This thing has almost split my family in two, because of my relationships with the administration and its stand on civil rights. It would save both of us a lot of heartache if you would always discuss any matter in this area with somebody else, including the President himself, rather than with me." Once in the Oval Office, Morrow tried to explain that Negroes were increasingly sensitive to such phrases as "you people," one of the president's favorite circumlocutions. "Oh, Fred," Eisenhower responded, "you're an alarmist."[8]

Eisenhower and Brownell agreed that unless federal statutory authority was enlarged in the area of civil rights, the only possible action would be executive use of police power; that cure, they thought, would be worse than the disease. As the Democratic Eighty-fourth Congress debated the issue during 1955, the president became increasingly impatient with what he considered ill-conceived efforts to implement the *Brown* decision. Democrats, led by Negro Congressman Adam Clayton Powell, Jr., of New York, pinned desegregation riders to a school construction bill and a mutual security appropriation. When Powell asserted that the administration was reneging on its self-proclaimed solicitude for Negro rights, the president announced that there would be no backward steps in what he described as the progress being made. Eisenhower privately regarded Powell as an out-and-out demagogue and at first refused to talk with him. When the congressman later declared that he would support the president for reelection, Eisenhower thanked him, just as he thanked anyone who made such a pledge.

Late in 1955, a hundred members of Congress representing southern states signed a manifesto calling for a reversal of the *Brown* decision. Public sentiment was further aroused by a successful bus boycott in Montgomery, Alabama, led by Reverend Martin Luther King, Jr., and by the University of Georgia in rejecting the enrollment of Autherine Lucy, a Negro student. When questioned about these evidences of increasing tension over civil rights throughout the nation, Eisenhower preferred to cite statistics showing increases in school desegregation and the rescinding of segregation statutes by some southern courts. He still refused to say anything at all about the Supreme Court's decision, and his public reticence and reportedly irritable private remarks led to the widespread assumption that he too thought the decision was wrong.

111

(Later, he would admit that he thought it had been made too quickly and would opine that any citizen had the right to disagree with the Court.) He insisted that he was not angry with the ruling, but he said nothing in public to allay speculation about his real views. That speculation doubtlessly contributed to the prevailing mood of hostility and defiance, especially in the South.

Eisenhower may have originally planned to cap his single term in the presidency with an edifying gesture in domestic matters like the one he would make in foreign policy at Geneva. That possibility, together with the heart attack, may explain why he waited until 1956 to recommend that Congress enact a civil rights bill. Just as he had waited out the fever of McCarthyism until Congress was ready to deal with what he believed was its own jurisdiction, so he waited out the public debate over civil rights. By the end of 1955, he concluded that Americans would now be more receptive to a legislative solution than they had been to the Supreme Court's order. In that manner, he could also regain executive initiative for progress in civil rights. Because he believed that the Supreme Court's mandate covered the subject of school integration sufficiently, Eisenhower centered his request for legislation on the subject of voting rights. Although several members of his cabinet advised him to avoid making any civil rights recommendations at all, he nevertheless instructed Brownell to draft some basic provisions. Revealing his own distrust of extremism, he needlessly warned the attorney general not to act as if he were "another [Charles] Sumner."[9] As written by the attorney general, the administration's proposals would authorize federal district courts to insure citizens' access to the polls and would set up a bipartisan commission to look into instances of economic discrimination against Negroes. These recommendations hardly met the demands of the growing civil rights movement, but at the same time they were enough to alarm advocates of the *status quo* in the South.

Liaison between the White House and Republican leaders in Congress evidently was not very effective in passing a civil rights bill. The president blamed the Democratic majority for the subsequent impasse; they killed his bill, he recalled years later, and then proceeded to kill their own version of it. In retrospect, neither party seemed overly anxious to take up the controversial issue in an election year. Eisenhower himself had little to say on the subject during his campaign that summer. Told that Negroes were registering as Republicans in greater numbers than ever before, he merely replied that he was working for the interests of all Americans and that any citizen was welcome under the umbrella. Referring to increasing hostility toward integration in the South, newsmen asked him what means the executive branch would use to enforce the Supreme Court's desegregation order. Eisenhower replied that he did not intend to settle things by a great show of force or by arbitrary action.

A few days after that statement was publicized, the governor of Texas tested the president's resolve. Allan Shivers was a Democrat who had supported the Republican ticket in 1952 amid much fanfare. He now declared that the integration of a school in one small town in his state could not be permitted because it would create civil disorder, and he ostentatiously dispatched Texas Rangers to the community to halt integration. If Eisenhower was angered by this clear defiance of federal law by a man he liked personally and respected as a state executive, he concealed his feelings behind the bland remark that state officials were simply trying to grapple with complex problems. But, he added, if any authorities—federal or local—employed force, then the nation would be in trouble.

The overwhelming vote Eisenhower received that November indicated that he had great support from Negroes and from white southerners, in spite of the *Brown* decision and his recommendations for civil rights legislation. Encouraged by his electoral mandate, he resubmitted his civil rights proposals at the outset of his second term in February 1957. Instead of quieting down, however, the national debate was increasing alarmingly. The FBI reported to the White House on the formation of White Citizens' Councils in the South, a somewhat more respectable version of the Ku Klux Klan. The FBI obviously considered these groups less menacing, however, than Black Muslim organizations in the North, allegedly conducting sessions in weapons training. With these developments in mind, Eisenhower urged Congress to take up his recommendations with a deep respect for law and justice. Ultimately, he emphasized, rectification for violations of any citizen's right to vote should rest with the federal courts. The traditions of "Jim Crow" and all-white juries constituted impediments to securing justice, he acknowledged, but he did not think that correcting those abuses was, at present, within the jurisdiction of the federal government. The abuses were, however, proper objects of examination by his proposed Civil Rights Commission, whose findings should lead to further legislation. As a third recommendation, he called for the establishment of a Civil Rights Division in the Department of Justice; it would be charged with bringing voting cases to the courts and seeing them through to resolution.

When Brownell presented his department's plan for the enforcement of federal integration orders to attorneys general from southern states, they reminded him of the variety of political obstacles to local cooperation. Their unenthusiastic response caused him to conclude that some southern officials were more willing to be involved in a nuclear war than in integration. Indeed, he became a target of assault himself. Because the pending legislation would enlarge Justice's jurisdiction, he was publicly accused of empire-building; unknown persons poured kerosene on the lawn of his home and sent threatening letters to his family. Yet Brownell refused to exceed the administration's directive to work within present jurisdictions even when confronted with evidence of racial violence. He had opposed antilynching legislation as an unwise, drastic, and possibly unconstitutional redistribution of federal-state authority. When Emmett Till, a Mississippi Negro, was lynched, Brownell's lieutenants urged him to bring the FBI into the case. He argued, however, that the bureau's jurisdiction extended only to criminal acts as defined by federal law and not to civil rights violations on the state and local level. The Till tragedy at least served to underscore the administration's call for greater statutory authority.

The eight-month congressional debate over the civil rights bill was also an ordeal for the Democratic leadership. At the outset, they warned Republicans that all other legislation sought by the administration would be delayed and possibly lost if the bill was pushed. Eventually, majority leader Lyndon Johnson abandoned his earlier antagonism to the measure and tried to mollify urban Democrats who wanted sweeping federal actions, while convincing southern members that votes for the bill would not jeopardize their seats in the next election. The twists and turns Johnson had to make puzzled Eisenhower. Expecting what he privately referred to as "pseudo-liberals" to conspire with segregationists on a "sham" bill, the president turned to minority leader Knowland to head off a southern filibuster. But by August, it was Johnson who had earned the president's thanks by removing obstacles to bipartisan support of the bill.

As the wrangling continued into the summer months, Eisenhower complained to Brownell that the bill was being enlarged by so many amendments that they threatened to destroy the broad base of support he thought essential to passage. The president was ready to approve of some of these amendments, but he thought that personal assurances could replace others and answer many doubts. Addressing those who shared his abhorrence of governmental coercion, for example, he promised that in this bill the administration was not seeking authority to use the military in enforcing civil rights. On one important amendment proposed by Democrats, however, he refused to budge: a provision that would require a jury trial in cases involving civil rights violations. Citing the opinion of former Chief Justice William Howard Taft, he insisted that putting a jury trial between a court order and its enforcement was tantamount to welcoming anarchy. Although the federal government had the power to bring court action in at least forty other fields, a jury trial was not required in any of them.

Early in September 1957, President Eisenhower signed the Civil Rights Act, the first such legislation since Reconstruction. The White House was deluged with mail both from integrationists and from segregationists urging him to veto it. Liberals thought it too weak without the jury trial provision; reactionaries called it a monstrous example of governmental tyranny. Eisenhower thought that the language of the bill was too broad and that some details were extraneous, but he was very gratified that his three original recommendations were at the heart of the measure. In place of executive compulsion, it upheld the paramountcy of the judicial process in enforcing federal civil rights laws. At the same time, it enhanced the prospect for future executive action and initiated a study of topics for further civil rights legislation. Eisenhower believed that the bill was so obviously proper that it would quiet apprehensions on both sides of the issue. Hopefully, Deputy Attorney General Rogers called for a cooling-off period in the nationwide debate.

By the end of September, however, a sequence of events profoundly shocked and confused the nation, undermining public confidence in Eisenhower's leadership. He had described his administration's civil rights policy as "a very moderate thing, done in all decency and in a simple attempt to study the matter, see where Federal responsibilities lie, and to move in strict accordance with the Supreme Court decision and no faster and no further."[10] But his version of "all deliberate speed" satisfied neither integrationists nor segregationists. In particular, many citizens wanted to know how the administration would enforce civil rights for Negroes. The president did not repeat his earlier public responses to that question. In a private letter to Governor Byrnes, however, Eisenhower declared that he had no intention of persecuting any citizen. But, he added, federal law would be used to protect the rights of all because state law could not adequately do so.

The day after he wrote that private letter, the president gave exactly the opposite impression in a public speech. At a conference of governors in Williamsburg, Virginia, he warned that the federal government could become a Frankenstein monster if the states acquiesced in its dictates by inaction or parsimony. "I believe deeply in States' rights," he said. "But it is idle to champion States' rights without upholding States' responsibilities as well."[11] He was not referring to civil rights when he uttered these words, but they were readily interpreted that way, especially in the South. The only thing Eisenhower recalled about his speech was that it was "very banal and colorless," and its message as obvious as "a lecture on the virtues of sunlight."[12]

Unfortunately, the president did not publicly explain how his belief in individual free will led him to believe in the supremacy of federal law. Instead, he confined such reflections to his private correspondence. "Laws are rarely effective," he wrote to a friend, "unless they represent the will of the majority." The failure of the Prohibition amendment was the best example of that. "When emotions are deeply stirred, logic and reason must operate gradually and with consideration for human feelings or we will have a resultant disaster rather than human advancement. . . ." Precisely because of that cause-and-effect relationship, federal authority was essential: "There must be respect for the Constitution—which means the Supreme Court's interpretation of the Constitution—or we shall have chaos."[13]

Eisenhower was not comfortable with the implications of resistance to civil rights law. During the campaign of 1956, he had rejected a newsman's theoretical question about it by saying: "I can't imagine any set of circumstances that would ever induce me to send Federal troops . . . into any area to enforce the orders of a Federal court, because I believe that common sense of America will never require it."[14] A year later, however, as he prepared to sign the Civil Rights Act, he knew precisely what circumstances would warrant use of federal force: there would be no arrests or punishments by federal officers, he informed a concerned southerner, unless voting rights were violated after a federal judge had ordered all interference to halt. In public remarks during the congressional debate, he asserted that voting rights was a matter distinctly separate from school integration. Some Americans noticed that enforcement of school integration was not included in the new jurisdiction given to the Justice Department by the Civil Rights Act. They remembered too the president's passive response to Governor Shiver's defiance a year before, and the president's clarion call for states to reject federal domination issued just three months before he signed the Civil Rights Act. Those were certainly the observations made by Orval Faubus, governor of Arkansas.

A populist Democrat and a moderate on the subject of integration, Faubus had been hailed by the national press in 1956 for devising a seven-year, voluntary desegregation plan for his state. The federal district court had approved it and ordered that the first phase would begin in September 1957 with the all-white Central High School in Little Rock, the state capital. As the time approached, however, members of segregationist organizations in and beyond the state pressed Faubus to seek a delay in the execution of the court order. When he indicated that he did not share their extreme views, they warned him that violence was inevitable. As a compromise, therefore, the governor asked the court for a few months' delay. When the district court replied with an order for immediate compliance, Faubus called up a state unit of the National Guard and instructed it to prevent any action that might provoke civil disorder.

Learning that Attorney General Brownell was acting as *amicus curiae* to the district court, Arkansas officials assumed that the federal government was preparing to make an example of Little Rock. Faubus charged that his telephone was being tapped and claimed that he was about to be arrested; Eisenhower personally issued a curt denial of both accusations. Against this backdrop of mutual distrust, a meeting was arranged between the two men. Arkansas Congressman Brooks Hays, another moderate on integration, urged the governor to ask for an appointment to see the president at Newport, Rhode Island, where he was taking a late summer working vacation. Faubus was very reluctant to do so. Although Brownell advised against the meeting, Eisenhower did not want to close the door against a state governor. At the same time, he did not want to appear to be interfering in a state's affairs either. As a solution to the dilemma, Sherman Adams investigated the governor's attitudes and, through Hays, informed him what he must say after the meeting at Newport. Adams frequently employed the same technique when granting access to the president, but as Faubus saw it, it was an overbearing and distasteful demand. Preconditions, however, were better than continued uncertainty, so the governor agreed to the arrangements. When he and Hays arrived in Newport, they were understandably apprehensive.

On September 14, the governor was alone with the president for fifteen minutes. Faubus later claimed that Eisenhower was angry with him at first, not for calling out the National Guard, but for giving them the wrong orders. In a diary entry written three weeks after the meeting, Eisenhower remembered his words thus: "So I suggested to him that he go home and . . . change their orders to say that having been assured that there was no attempt to do anything except obey the courts and that the Federal government was not trying to do anything that had not been already agreed to by the School Board and directed by the courts; that he should tell the Guard to continue to preserve order but to allow the Negro children to attend Central High School."[15] At that point in the conversation Hays and Adams joined them, and some time later Brownell and Hagerty came in. As the discussion continued, Faubus insisted that he was a patriotic American and summarized the progress his state had already made in integration. Eisenhower, he thought, was duly impressed. The governor then explained that he was seeking a delay in compliance only as a cooling-off period. Eisenhower, according to Faubus's later account, then asked Brownell if he could obtain a postponement of compliance with the court's order. When the attorney general replied that such an action was legally impossible, Faubus thought that he was lying, although he did not make that accusation until after he had left the meeting. (What Brownell may have said was that an *amicus curiae* had no such authority.)

The meeting lasted for two hours. As it wore on, Faubus thought that the president seemed restless and guessed, uncharitably, that Eisenhower was anxious to get back to the golf course. Far from being bored, however, the president was anxious that the session proceed with care: "I did not want to see any Governor humiliated."[16] There would be no test of strength, he reminded his visitors, because if it came to that, there could be only one outcome. The governor, Eisenhower later recalled, duly acknowledged that federal law was supreme. Without referring specifically to any contingencies, Eisenhower promised to give federal assistance if the governor requested it. After the meeting was over, Adams and Hays drafted a statement, which Faubus signed. It described the session as a free give-and-take, and the governor, it said, indicated his *desire* to comply with the court order. At the same time, the president's staff composed a statement for Eisenhower to issue, one which said that the governor had indicated his *intention* "to respect the decisions of the . . . District Court and to give his full coopera- tion in carrying out his responsibility in respect to these decisions." The president's announcement concluded: "I recognize the ines- capable responsibility resting upon the Governor to preserve law and order in his state."[17] The governor's statement, however, said nothing about his own recognition of such responsibility.

When Faubus returned to his hotel room, he was angry with everyone and complained that he had been treated like an ignorant country boy. In retrospect, he may have felt that the president's assistants had contrived to make the official statement look as if it was a pledge by the governor. Having misjudged Eisenhower as ill-informed and indifferent, Faubus returned to Little Rock. There, he made further efforts to delay school integration, and, instead of changing the National Guard's orders, he withdrew the unit from the school area. Eisenhower assumed that Faubus would replace it with a cease-and-desist order to any persons interfering with the integration. When none was issued, the president concluded that the governor was not keeping his promise to comply with the court and to uphold law and order. The reason for such obstinacy, he thought, was Faubus's upcoming reelection campaign.

On September 19, Brownell informed the president orally that several acts of Congress and decisions of the federal courts clearly confirmed the chief executive's power and duty to act whenever a governor did not carry out his own responsibilities in instances of civil disorder. (This resumé of relevant authorities was not spelled out in writing until three weeks later.) But Brownell also pointed out that neither federal marshals nor court officers were present in Little Rock in sufficient strength to handle civil violence. Eisen- hower remarked that he was loath to send in troops because their very presence might cause violence to spread. The president's refer- ence to troops did not necessarily mean that he decided on that occasion that he would have to use them. Sherman Adams thought that Faubus was looking for a way out of his mistake and urged the president to wait. Four days later, on September 23, nine Negro students appears at Central High School and were turned away by a howling mob of local citizens and segregationists from other states. Orval Faubus was not in Little Rock that day; he was in Georgia attending a southern governors' conference.

Eisenhower was greatly angered by the governor's apparent perfidy and by the failure of local authorities to prevent the inci- dent. A White House assistant present at the Georgia conference afterwards worked to get Faubus to sign a resolution supporting compliance, but the governor refused. Learning that the size and vehemence of the mob at Little Rock was increasing, Eisenhower made his decision with state officials behind a communications blackout that was eerily similar to the one employed by the British before the strike on Egypt. Although there were several legal precedents to choose from, he used Section 333, Title 10, of the Federal Statutes, a law specifically covering attempts to interfere with the execution of federal orders. No doubt the president thereby meant to emphasize that this was a matter of civil disorder and not a question of civil rights. Military arrangements were, of course, based on his professional knowledge. A contingent of regular army paratroopers, the 101st Airborne, was dispatched to Little Rock in sufficient strength so that they would not be challenged and no violence would occur. (The Bonus Army rout of 1932 was very much in the president's mind at that moment.) Eisenhower also nationalized the Arkansas National Guard but did not use them because, as he later explained, "I did not want to have brothers fighting up against brothers and families divided. . . ."[18]

That same day, September 24, he went on nationwide radio and television to recount that a disorderly mob—including outside agitators—had violently opposed the federal court's orders. Because neither state nor local authorities had dispersed the crowd, the president's responsibility was inescapable. Personal opinions about the court's decisions, he repeated, had no bearing on the matter of enforcement. In conclusion, he lamented the way in which the disorder in Arkansas had damaged the nation's image in the eyes of the world and had bolstered Communist propaganda efforts. The next day Americans saw shocking photographs of troops carrying bayonets in an American city. (The bayonets were soon removed from the rifles, but some newspapers tellingly juxtaposed these pictures with others showing the president playing golf at Newport.)

In retrospect, it is difficult to understand the manner of Eisenhower's actions at Little Rock. In every domestic policy he had practiced deliberation and restraint, advocated states' responsibility, encouraged governors to act, and abhorred federal—especially executive—interference in controversies best settled by the parties directly involved. Why had he not communicated with or publicly appealed to the citizens and authorities of Little Rock? Why did he not wait until events provided an overwhelmingly convincing reason for intervention (as he had urged Britain and France to do at Suez) or until the southern governors at the Georgia meeting induced Faubus to return to his capital city and take charge? Why did Eisenhower so precipitously employ troops in such overwhelming strength and in so dramatic an appearance instead of waiting to see if the mob would resist? A few citizens felt that the president had not done enough. Impatient integrationists muttered that he had not used the civil disorder as an occasion to clearly demonstrate that opposition to segregation anywhere would be firmly handled. Others, however, considered the use of a full regiment of armed troops to be excessive. Two years before, in another context, Eisenhower had said, "Now you don't send in bombs to restore order when a riot occurs. You get police people to restore order."[19] As much as he disliked the phrase "police action" when applied to the Korean War, he was engaging in just such an operation by using troops at Little Rock.

The reasons behind Eisenhower's actions may be personal in nature. Just weeks after passage of his administration's brave legislation, the president saw his great hope for ending the divisive civil rights debate shattered by one man's political ambitions. A single incident had destroyed his four-year effort to restore power to state and local governments and to demonstrate trust in the common sense of the citizenry as an alternative to the intrusion of federal government.

Questions raised by the way in which the president acted unfortunately served to detract from his purpose. His public and private explanations of that purpose carried none of the contradictions that had characterized his statements on the *Brown* decision and on civil rights legislation. When Senator Richard Russell of Georgia, a frequent supporter of the administration's policies, compared the intervention at Little Rock to Hitler's use of storm troopers, Eisenhower replied that there was no similarity between that tyranny and fulfillment of the constitutional duty to carry out the decisions of a federal court. The courts, he told a news conference, were the people's bulwarks and shield against autocratic government; his decision, he told a southern friend in private correspondence, was solely a question of supporting the judicial branch of government which, in the last analysis, was what protected each citizen against capricious actions by government. The necessity of using troops to that end had been a saddening experience for Eisenhower because he believed that coercion could not be a basis for the American system.

Years later, Brownell claimed that Eisenhower's actions at Little Rock proved for all time that the federal government would enforce the right of Negroes to enroll in schools on the same standing as anyone else. But in the immediate aftermath, the president did nothing to alter segregationists' assumptions that Little Rock was the temporary impulse of a military man, directed against a weak governor. They certainly did not conclude that it was a permanent policy. And thereafter, the administration's version of deliberate speed lagged significantly. Eisenhower called for businessmen, religious leaders, and civil rights organizations to exhort their fellow citizens on the subject and commended those who did. But he did not follow up his address to the nation explaining why he sent troops into Little Rock with an exhortation of his own. Public attention consequently focused on other events. When Brownell resigned as attorney general a month after Little Rock, southern officials gave a collective sigh of relief. Faubus was certain that the attorney general had been fired for misrepresenting the limits of federal authority, but in fact Brownell had submitted his resignation before the crisis and had stayed on until it had passed.

Because neither the governor nor local authorities reestablished order in Little Rock, the army paratroopers were kept on duty until the end of the school term in May 1958. Faubus, reelected by an overwhelming vote, closed all of the high schools the following September. The president did not intervene, however, in that instance or in similarly defiant closings of public schools in several other states because no specific federal court orders had been issued and thus violated. Privately, he was angered by officials who were undermining the concept of state responsibility; publicly, he said only that they should consider the damage their policy of closing schools inflicted on their own citizens. He was encouraged when local police and firemen dispersed a segregationist mob at Little Rock and when the Supreme Court ordered the high schools there reopened.

Within a year after sending in federal troops, the Eisenhower administration had returned to its stance of noninterference. The president rejected the idea of a White House conference with southern governors lest it undermine their ultimate responsibility for establishing and protecting civil rights within their own states. Similarly, when his staff proposed that he meet with several prominent Negroes, Eisenhower criticized the idea because it violated his desire—on any issue—to avoid discussions with only one side. Hoping to make the meeting appear as a natural follow-up, he agreed, but only after first addressing a conference of Negro educators. To the disappointment of both white and black civil rights advocates, the White House meeting lasted only forty-five minutes. The senior man, A. Philip Randolph of the railroad porters' union, used fifteen of those minutes to explain that unless the appeals of his fellow moderates were heard, radicals would takeover the civil rights movement. The president's men thought Randolph was exaggerating. In reply, William Rogers, who had succeeded Brownell as attorney general, defended the administration's record in civil rights. Another of the Negro visitors, Rev. Martin Luther King, Jr., was disappointed to see that the president was made visibly uncomfortable by the discussion. At no time during the session did Eisenhower interject his customary adversarial questions. After it was over, he told newsmen that he was pleased with the meeting because nothing extreme had been proposed. But Negro commentators confirmed Randolph's warning when they described the meeting as a surrender to the government's policy of inertia.

If "inertia" was the proper word, it should have been preceded by "contrived." Although some White House staff members worked to keep the subject of civil rights on the cabinet's agenda and found the president ready to have it discussed there, Sherman Adams decided that there was not enough new information for any presentation to or discussion by that body. Adams also stunned his colleagues by announcing that the administration would propose no legislative recommendations on civil rights to the next session of Congress. The only time the cabinet discussed the subject in 1958 was when it considered how Republican candidates should answer questions on civil rights during the political campaign that fall. For the rest of the time, White House aides maintained a scrupulous distance from the newly established Civil Rights Commission. Not surprisingly, the president complained that he could not find good men to serve on it.

Early in 1959, after further school closings were followed by bombings of Negro property in the South, Eisenhower raised the subject of a second civil rights act. In conference with Republican congressional leaders, Attorney General Rogers presented proposals that would extend the Justice Department's jurisdiction to cases involving bombings, personal violence, and the destruction of voting records. Vice President Nixon spoke in support of these recommendations and described them as a necessary expansion of federal power. Because they would deter instead of punish, he thought that Republicans would endorse them. At the conclusion of the meeting, Eisenhower commented that these proposals were, like those of the 1957 bill, moderate in purpose and in no way divisive.

A few weeks later, he told Ralph McGill, a liberal southern newspaper publisher, that he hoped extremists would gravitate toward the center, following the course of his administration.[20]

When he presented his recommendations to the Eighty-sixth Congress (which was controlled by Democrats) in February 1959, he urged the lawmakers to confine themselves to those topics that the Civil Rights Commission had examined and reported on: the use of federal warrants in instances where court orders were obstructed; federal inspection of district voting records; and federal authority to enter cases involving bombings. But he was once again irritated when Democrats introduced several additional topics for consideration—equal employment opportunities and equal treatment in federal housing and public accommodations. These proposals, he said, were not the proper way to advance the cause of civil rights. Eisenhower felt that equal employment should first be scrutinized by the commission, and he thought that an equal accommodations law would probably be held unconstitutional.

As he had done three years before, Eisenhower again cast doubts on his own limited recommendations by making lame, ambiguous public remarks. He said that he, like many other citizens, had very little faith in the ability of statutory law to change the human heart or eliminate prejudice. Such changes could come about in a democracy only by the mobilizing force of public opinion. As he made that observation, sit-ins by Negroes at public eating places in the South were, in fact, mobilizing public opposition to civil rights. The president had no personal objection to these tactics as long as they were not violent, but he thought the subject of equal accommodations was far less significant than the need for protecting voting rights.

The Congress did not act on the administration's civil rights recommendations for the very good reason that the next year was an election year. In the campaign of 1960, some Republican candidates welcomed, indeed solicited, the support of those who had opposed civil rights progress starting with the *Brown* decision. As they had in 1956, die-hard segregationists used the political circumstances as an opportunity to defy federal court orders. When the school year began in September 1960, local authorities in New Orleans, Louisiana, prepared to turn away five Negroes from enrollment in an all-white school. Anxious to avoid an outbreak of violence before election day, Attorney General Rogers warned the state's governor that he would use his full powers if there was any interference with integration in New Orleans. No confrontation occurred, but the incident revealed that the administration's stand at Little Rock had accomplished nothing: the federal government faced the possibility of many Little Rocks in the future.

The Civil Rights Act of 1960 was passed and signed shortly after the Democrats won the presidential election in November. Eisenhower was pleased to see that in its final form it was practical, proper, and procedural. In his last message to Congress, he sounded a Wilsonian note by urging the legislators to continue their pioneering efforts in civil rights not only because discrimination was morally wrong but also because its impact was world-wide. Unfortunately, that seemed to confirm his critics' contention that he was interested in civil rights only insofar as it enhanced the nation's image abroad.

This judgment unjustly denigrated the administration's record: two bills establishing the machinery to protect voting rights and Negro lives and property. The on-going developments in civil rights unquestionably called for additional ways to end racial discrimination and violence, but Eisenhower did not alter his deliberate pace nor abandon his adherence to the center line on that subject any more than he did on his economic and international policies. In civil rights, as in all other areas, he believed that proper procedure was the soundest foundation for any substantive accomplishment. Perhaps the greatest weaknesses in his approach to civil rights were, first, his hope that extremists would readily "gravitate toward the center line" laid out by his administration and, second, his overestimation of the public's understanding—that is, their "common sense" as he called it. Evidently, he assumed that these developments would relieve the federal government of some of its constitutional responsibility for protecting individual rights.

In the last analysis, Dwight Eisenhower foresaw the basic problem of the federal government guaranteeing civil rights when he decried the burden placed on the executive branch by the Supreme Court's decision in the *Brown* case. Thereafter, his every appeal to the public to understand that the judiciary was the basis for law and order perversely raised the question of executive enforcement. It is impossible to know whether the president's restrained exhortations headed off other confrontations. As far as most Americans could see, the intervention at Little Rock was his answer. It was unmistakably clear, but it was not the kind of lesson Eisenhower wanted to teach.

7

★★★★★

NO SECOND CHANCE

The divisive wrangling over civil rights was but one note in a mounting cacaphony of criticism directed against President Eisenhower as he began his second term in the White House. Initial expectations, raised by his handling of Geneva, his own candidacy, and the Suez crisis, had produced public speculation about a "new Eisenhower"—a tougher, bolder, more expansive leader in the best tradition of the office. His associates noted that he seemed far more interested in his work and far more ready to do battle as he renewed his efforts to set the nation on a proper path at home and abroad. Less than six months into the new term, however, a series of controversies and crises transformed the president's work into a veritable Job's job.

Acknowledging that he had enjoyed a productive working relationship with the preceding Democratic Congress, Eisenhower told legislative leaders of both parties that he would do his best to get along with the Eighty-fifth Congress. If, for example, they wanted to increase spending, he hoped that they would come to him first and talk things over, practically and in mutual trust. But the possibility of such an accord was shattered at the outset when the administration presented its budget for fiscal 1958. The total requested was $70 billion—$10 billion over the administration's earlier estimate. Moreover, 65 percent of it was earmarked for national security, including weapons, overseas aid, and intelligence operations.

What had become of the Republicans' commitment to "fiscal responsibility?" Some of the party's Old Guard described the budget as a reversion to New Deal spending. Minority leader Knowland reportedly considered resigning his post to avoid working for its passage. Newly proclaimed "modern" Republicans also doubted that they would support it. Even the administration's own members were divided on the question. The same day the budget was read, Treasury Secretary Humphrey issued a warning that government spending of such magnitude, if unchecked, would bring about a hair-curling depression. Such outlays, he said, were unjustified even in a period of economic recession.

Humphrey had first submitted his opinion to the president, but it was not in Eisenhower's nature to censor his cabinet members' statements. No one, however, had consulted Percival Brundage. As director of the Bureau of the Budget, he expected the president to uphold the credibility of his own proposals by issuing a public rebuttal of Humphrey's statement. Instead, Eisenhower told the press corps that a depression like that of the 1930s was not likely because of federal safeguards adopted during and since that time. He went on to admit that there was some fat in the budget. If he had an item veto, for example, he could eliminate such nonessentials as federal support for home mortgages, farm surpluses, and reclamation projects. Further savings could be made, Eisenhower said, by doing away with the thousands of jobs connected with those programs. The military and international aid provisions were, however, irreducible.

The Democrats in Congress viewed these remarks as a gauntlet flung at their feet. They proceeded to enlarge the domestic projects they had favored for years, while hacking away at the administration's "irreducible" items. At first, Eisenhower sourly remarked that if Congress could find something that could be cut from the military portion, he was willing to be educated. But his forbearance with the legislators was exhausted when the Democrats discovered the so-called Gaither Report. This assessment of contingencies in the event of a direct attack on the United States had been compiled by military and economic experts and classified as top secret. Some of its details were "leaked" to legislators, however, including the headline-grabbing estimate that nuclear war could occur within two years. The president had not been pleased with the report, particularly with its authors' readiness to establish a "garrison state" in anticipation of such a crisis. When Senate majority leader Johnson demanded a copy of the document, Eisenhower declined to submit it. Claiming executive privilege, he warned that disclosure would make it impossible in the future to assemble advisers or to retain their trust. If such studies could so easily be "leaked," he swore privately, then no more would be made.

The budget debate was at its peak in May 1957 when Secretary Humphrey announced that he was resigning. He had wished to leave two years before, but had stayed on at the president's request. In accepting the resignation, Eisenhower pointedly described Humphrey's economic views as practically identical with his own, and thereafter he maintained a frank correspondence with Humphrey on national economic questions. But the resignation cast greater doubts on the president's budget policy. Recalling Eisenhower's controversial aloofness during the Battle of the Bulge, newsmen now described the struggle between Congress and the White House as the "battle of the budget."

Eisenhower decided to outflank his opponents by taking a step unusual for him. In May, he made two special broadcasts, appealing to the public for support of his budget and especially of its defense provisions. He began by reminding his audience that no American troops had been killed during the four years of his tenure. But it would be supreme folly, Eisenhower said, to let middle-of-the-road governments fall to what he called the continually probing pressures of communism. With an unusual show of emotion he urged his fellow countrymen to sacrifice their dollars for a peaceful world, so that later they would not have to sacrifice their sons, their homes, and their cities to their own shortsightedness.

Critics immediately denounced what they saw as a Wilsonian fallacy in Eisenhower's speech, pointing out that Congress, not the public, decided on budgets. Other commentators, however, compared the talks to Franklin Roosevelt's "fireside chats" and cited them as evidence of the "new Eisenhower." The volume of mail in support of his appeal was gratifying to the president, but, as the critics said, the Congress demonstrated its own disposition. In August, it approved a budget $4 billion below the administration's recommendation, with the largest cuts directed at international aid. The legislators were unexpectedly assisted in reducing nonproductive outlays when the nation's economic indices slid toward recession that summer. While Republicans grumbled, Democrats found in the budget battle evidence that the popular president was vulnerable to their counterattacks, even in the most important area of his domestic concern—the nation's economy. Political analysts would soon recount the struggle as a textbook example of presidential impotence.

Defeated, in the public's view, at the "battle of the budget" and then at the "battle of Little Rock," the president found no chance to recover before another storm broke. Just two weeks after being criticized for doing too much at Little Rock, Eisenhower was blamed for doing too little in national security, the field he was supposed to know best. In October, the Soviet Union announced that it had fired a missile powerful enough to place a 184-pound sphere (called Sputnik) into orbit around the earth. Some leading Republicans responded to the news with absurd nonchalance: Defense Secretary Wilson called Sputnik a scientific trick. Democratic leaders, however, called it a scientific Pearl Harbor and concluded that the Russians were so far ahead in their missile capacity that they could now attack the United States from outer space.

Earlier in the Cold War, many Americans had believed that Russia was so backward technologically that it had to employ spies to copy American plans and subvert or kidnap scientists from other countries. Sputnik also seemed to offer undeniable evidence that the Communists' school system was providing superior science education. What was to be done? Several of the same critics who, a few years before, had denigrated science as a "sacred cow" now demanded federal support for accelerated science programs in American schools and universities. What had been a question of keeping ahead of the Russians turned now into the more ominous task of catching up with them.

President Eisenhower displayed no personal agitation as he faced his press conference a few days after the launching of Sputnik. The presence of one small ball in the air, he said, did not mean that the United States had been caught napping. He revealed that both the army and navy were developing intermediate-range ballistic missiles. Russia's claim that the American first line of defense, the SAC, was now outmoded was, Eisenhower noted, nothing more than propaganda; it was a long way, he said, from weapons testing to actual military readiness. He emphasized the nonmilitary nature of missile development by the United States and noted that American scientists themselves were not alarmed and had not asked for an increase in their budget beyond the $5 billion already assigned to missile projects.

Urged by his anxious advisers to enlarge upon these explanations, Eisenhower made two televised addresses to the nation. In the first, he pointed out that earth satellites in themselves had no direct, present effect on the security of the United States. The Russians, he admitted, were ahead in the development of some types of missiles, but "as of today, the overall military strength of the free world is distinctly greater than that of the communist countries." In building future defense programs, he declared, it was the responsibility of the United States to see to it that any Soviet advantage was only temporary. After describing in detail the nation's complex early-warning and retaliation systems, the president directed public attention to a higher plane: "What the world needs today even more than a giant leap into outer space, is a giant step toward peace."[1] Addressing his remarks to that same theme in a second telecast, he reminded Americans that their nation enjoyed additional strengths, "the quality of our life, and the vigor of our ideals." To that end, American education must produce "not only Einsteins and Steinmetzes, but Washington and [his personal choice] Emersons as well."[2]

But practical-minded citizens, long assured of their nation's technological superiority, were untouched by rhetoric; the question remained: What was to be done? Eisenhower's answer was to avoid doing anything in hysteria or haste. Rejecting this certain opportunity to obtain congressional appropriations, he argued that unplanned expenditures of federal money, whether for missile projects or for educational crash programs, could not be the basis for long-term policies. Moreover, he believed that the direction of American education was a matter to be determined locally, and he trusted that states and individuals would bolster science teaching and training. Although he called upon his chief scientific adviser, Dr. James Killian, to watch the developments, Eisenhower rejected the suggestion that Killian be authorized to oversee all parts of the nation's missile programs. Taken together, the president's post-Sputnik actions seemed to confirm the Democrats' charges that he was unaware of what was or was not being done and that he was dangerously shortsighted in responding to crises and opportunities.

Just as George Humphrey's resignation had given substance to criticism of the administration's budget six months earlier, now Defense Secretary Wilson's departure from office contributed to the missile controversy. Undoubtedly aware of the low esteem accorded him by White House aides, Wilson had indicated his desire to resign a year before. Because of the awkward timing, his post-Sputnik departure made the president's praise for Wilson's contributions to national defense seem unwarranted. In choosing a successor, Eisenhower did not look for a man who could grasp complex technologies so much as a man who could organize actions on his own initiative and harmonize differing points of view. After considering several of his own staff, former Budget Director Dodge, and one academic president (Franklin Murphy of the University of Kansas), the president took the advice of a well-connected Wall Street investment banker, Sidney Weinberg, and chose Neil McElroy to be the new secretary of defense.

As chairman of Procter and Gamble, McElroy was especially adept in the uses of advertising. Avoiding his predecessor's gaucheries, he also soon impressed the White House men as a quick student, able to grasp the budgetry ramifications of weapons technologies and explain them to the cabinet, to Congress, and to other nations. Recognizing that Americans needed performance, not explanations, in the missile programs, he cut through the wasteful rivalries between the army and the navy and concentrated all efforts on just one project—the Jupiter missile. In making that decision he had the approval of the president and the support of Air Force General Nathan Twining, Radford's successor as chairman of the Joint Chiefs of Staff. The first American satellite, Explorer I, was put into orbit three months after McElroy took over at the Defense Department. The president, however, did not think that achievement was grounds for any great hullabaloo; he considered it to be the certain result of the administration's deliberate policy, avoiding flamboyant crash programs and propaganda stunts.

The budget, civil rights, Little Rock, Sputnik—each crisis served to weaken the stamina of the sixty-eight-year-old chief executive. He had cut short his usual working vacation in September 1957 and cancelled his usual week of rest in November in order to prepare for the Paris meeting of NATO foreign ministers. Later that month, as he was dictating to his secretary, Ann Whitman, Eisenhower suffered a cerebral spasm, or stroke, that affected his speech. It was the third serious illness to affect him in three years. Put to bed, he experienced dizziness and difficulty in moving his legs. Once again, he remembered the crisis caused by Woodrow Wilson's disability. Pounding his fists in frustration on the bedcovers, he swore that he would resign if he could not perform his duties. Within a few days, however, he had recovered so fully that his physicians detected no impairment of his mental or physical facilities. Soon after, he made the trip to Paris—in part to satisfy himself that he was able to stay at his job—but when he returned to Washington, he appeared physically exhausted. Mindful that another stroke could be worse, he drafted an agreement with Vice President Nixon on the constitutionally uncertain matter of presidential disability. The paper authorized the vice president to decide whenever the president could not clearly recognize his own inability to perform his duties and then to take over those duties as acting president. The agreement was, of course, also a demonstration of Eisenhower's confidence in Nixon.

During the first months of 1958, the president showed every sign of vigor and command. He admitted to news correspondents that he found the work of the federal government onerous, demanding, and often confining; but it was always rewarding. He felt confident about the future, he said in a letter to Hagerty, from "my knowledge that the Administration is rich in its possession of men of character, ability and integrity."[3] In order to enhance that resource, Eisenhower continued to rearrange the top echelon of his advisers. He could not hold onto Gabriel Hauge, even with the offer of a cabinet place, but he increased Andrew Goodpaster's responsibilities for strategic policies. By assigning his own son, John Eisenhower, to assist Goodpaster, the president indulged in what he would otherwise have described as nepotism. Perhaps he could be forgiven for wanting to have another Milton at hand whom he could fully trust in that critical area.

Recent appointments to the cabinet—those of Fred Seaton, William Rogers, Robert Anderson, and Neil McElroy—made certain that the "new Eisenhower" was well served. Although the views of these men did not greatly differ from those of their predecessors, each displayed a welcome talent for efficient communication. Avoiding dogmatisms and partisan gaffs, they did not damage or delay support of the administration as their predecessors had done. The successful tenure of Interior Secretary Seaton, the first to become a member of what would be the president's "second team," prompted later commentators to ponder what the administration's history might have been.

Seaton, owner of a chain of Midwestern newspapers, first served as assistant secretary of state and then became Sherman Adams's right-hand man, with special responsibilities for congressional liaison on Interior Department policies. He was, therefore, an excellent choice to succeed Douglas McKay in the cabinet's traditional hot spot. Young, well-connected, and well-informed, Seaton was the very model of Eisenhower's ideal administrator. In 1957 and 1958, he correctly judged the weaknesses of Democratic legislators bent on scuttling the "partnership" water power policy and outflanked their efforts to replace the private contract for construction of three dams in Hell's Canyon with one federally built, multipurpose dam there. He also succeeded in mollifying both resource developers and wilderness preservationists. The issues that had pulled down

McKay never again tarnished the image of the Eisenhower administration or the Republican party.

Administrative renovation was, of course, valuable for the conduct of the presidential office, but it seemed quite irrelevant to the issue of Eisenhower's performance in that office. During the first weeks of 1958, the Gallup Poll showed that the president's popularity had fallen below 60 percent, the lowest point of his tenure. That judgment may have been the cumulative result of the budget, Little Rock, Sputnik, and his illness, or it may simply have reflected the grim statistics of the economic recession. By the end of spring, employment was down 30 percent across the nation, reaching the lowest level since 1941, and manufacturing had fallen by 25 percent. "Eisenhower is my shepherd," ran a widely circulated bit of doggerel, "I am in want. . . . He leadeth me through still factories. He restoreth my doubt in the Republican Party. . . ."[4]

The national economic slump provided the Democrats with their finest prospect in that congressional election year. Senator Lyndon Johnson dramatically rallied his party with his own state of the union address, delivered before the chamber had heard the president's version. The Democrats then called for a series of federal construction projects to increase employment and stimulate business. Eisenhower's message appealed instead to business and labor to devise their own steps to hold down inflation and thus reinvigorate the economy. Federal bureaus could also promote jobs locally. "Let's try to use some common sense," he urged, "and not just get a Sputnik attitude about everything." Any tougher policy, the president believed, would create a controlled economy. Achievement and progress, he said, "cannot be created for our people; they can only be created by our people. Americans would have it no other way."[5]

The president not only opposed an overall federal plan to combat the recession, but he also felt that schemes to appease inflation were as dangerous as those to appease international aggression. When he rejected the Democrats' proposals as inflationary, his opponents accused him of being indifferent to the plight of workers. He was, to be sure, more solicitous of businessmen. He urged citizens to continue to buy—cautiously but confidently. He praised car dealers who set up an "Auto Buy Now" campaign, promising to hold down purchase terms in order to increase sales. But he gave no similar encouragement to labor. Union demands for wage increases, he explained, would merely stimulate inflation. The only recommendation concerning labor he sent to Congress that spring was to authorize the Justice Department to oversee the financial records of union pension and welfare plans.

There was no explosion over the administration's budget recommendations in the 1958 session of the Eighty-fifth Congress, as there had been in 1957. The total expenditures Eisenhower asked for were $2 billion lower this time. That sum would return the nation's accounts to the black for the second time since 1953. The budget for national security, however, was $1.3 billion more than the year before. In an attempt to anticipate opposition to foreign aid, the president inserted exclamations into his 1958 State of the Union message: "This is no give-away! Let's stick to the facts! We cannot afford to have one of our most essential security programs shot down with a slogan!"[6]

Second only to the budget, Eisenhower considered his proposal for the reorganization of the Defense Department to be his administration's main business before the Congress. The new weaponry of modern warfare, he pointed out in a special presentation of the plan, had altered the nature of combat; instant crisis was now the typical situation rather than the exception. It was essential, therefore, that the Defense Department's executives be freed from existing statutory responsibilities to recruit, train, and develop the armed forces. Those tasks were more properly conducted by the professional military staff. By implication, the change would end the tradition of each branch of the military promoting its own interests as they had done to the detriment of the missile program. The most controversial part of the reorganization plan gave the civilian secretary, not the military chiefs, full authority to administer the Defense Department's budget.

Other provisions seemed to constitute a belated response to Sputnik. A new post was to be established—assistant secretary of defense for research and engineering—to coordinate scientific and technical developments with military planning. The prospects for enlarging the National Aeronautic and Space Administration's (NASA) special programs were greatly improved after that agency successfully launched four more earth satellites and announced in 1958 that the United States could send a man to the moon within ten years. At his press conference, the president cautioned that regular defense programs would not be replaced by the moon project and then joked that he was not about to volunteer for the trip himself.

In notable contrast to his hands-off approach to the recession, Eisenhower bent every effort to instruct and mollify Congress about his Defense Department proposals because they were of the utmost urgency. "I don't give a hoot about what my particular successor thinks about my ideas on military organization," he wrote to his former aide, C. D. Jackson, "nor on what means I may have in bringing about a reorganization. . . . If the organization is going to be sound and durable, I must be able to lead, persuade, cajole, and of course to some extent compel. . . ."[7] He would put some details into effect immediately by executive order, but he wanted a statutory basis for the plan in anticipation of the day when the commander-in-chief would not be a man with a military background.

Throughout the ensuing months of the legislative session, the president met frequently with leaders of both parties. He extended special solicitude to Democrats by keeping the talks off-the-record. He also wrote hundreds of letters and delivered speeches to representatives of business and the media. Defense Secretary McElroy exercised his advertising talents in the same way. The president proved to be surprisingly flexible in accepting Democratic modifications of some parts of the reorganization bill. He agreed, for example, to Senator Johnson's insistence that the new assistant secretary for research be a civilian instead of a military man, as Eisenhower initially had wanted.

The loudest opposition to the proposal came from an ominous combination of high-ranking military men and congressional members who were outspoken guardians of the interests of the armed services. These critics charged that the changes sought by the president would make a virtual czar of any defense secretary and enable him to carry off a coup d'etat. They also revived the rumor of a decade before, predicting that the traditional branches would be combined into one force wearing one uniform. Eisenhower refused to discipline the Pentagon officers who made these allegations, but they provoked him to speak out in a press conference. "I don't care who is against this thing. It just happens I have got a little bit more experience in military organization and the direction of unified forces than anyone else in the active list." It was far more important, he believed, "to be able to hit the target than [to] haggle over who makes the weapon or who pulls the trigger."[8] When the Congress approved of the Defense Department reorganization, they reaffirmed the right of the military service chiefs to testify directly before the legislators in order to defend their own views on department policies. Eisenhower happily took his whole loaf, but muttered about the provision that, he said, practically guaranteed future insubordination by Pentagon chiefs.

The Democrats' cooperation with the administration that began with the reorganization bill ended with their approval of Justice Department supervision of union welfare funds. Congress then approved less than half of the remaining presidential recommendations. When he received measures they had passed, Eisenhower described many of them as affronts to the nation's budgetary problems. He vetoed an $800 million appropriation for the West's two favorite federal agencies, the Bureau of Reclamation and the Army Corps of Engineers. Their proposed projects, he emphasized, were parochial and technically dubious. He discovered too late that a proposed Jefferson Memorial Arch for St. Louis would cost $17 million, most of it from federal sources. Although he signed the bill, he warned Interior Secretary Seaton that any further historical memorials must be cleared with him before being sent to Congress. He cut out another "frill," a nuclear-powered icebreaker, even though he was personally interested in international cooperation for exploration of the polar regions. He returned an area redevelopment bill without his signature, calling it an improper intervention into the domain of local and private enterprise. A shortage of classrooms necessitated his approving a school construction aid bill, but he complained that it threatened the traditional local responsibility for education. He did sign an appropriation bill for the administration's interstate highway program, of course, but noted that it violated the tradition of federal-local cost-sharing on a fifty-fifty basis.

The president once again seemed to be a "new Eisenhower" when he vetoed the so-called farm freeze bill. The measure had been designed by Democrats to suspend Agriculture Secretary Benson's farm policy for the duration of the recession. Eisenhower argued that it would, in effect, pile up even larger farm surpluses and delay the transition to sound parity practices. The farm program was too important to manipulate for short-term advantages. "If ever there was an issue that called for intelligence instead of prejudice," he observed, "conviction instead of timidity—that issue is the farm program."[9] He thought that it was vital enough to warrant making another television address. This one seemed to be far more effective than the budget appeals he had made the year before. Mindful of the coming elections, the legislators thereafter passed a bill that strengthened the administration's farm policies. The president thought that Congress had learned its lesson well.

The showpiece of legislation adopted by the Eighty-fifth Congress was the admission of Alaska as the forty-ninth state, the first addition to the Union in thirty-six years. The four-year stalemate

137

over the question of statehood was broken partly because the Democrats were arrayed in greater force, but also because the administration's own men worked to resolve the question. Interior Secretary Seaton convinced the president that the territory was ready for statehood and established close liaison with congressional committees to adjust federal requirements to Alaskan interests. Eisenhower's concern for military installations was satisfied by a provision authorizing the secretary of defense to maintain those bases, and his wish for approval of Hawaiian statehood first was overcome when oil was discovered on Alaska's north slope. The following year, southern opposition to Hawaii's mixed population failed to reappear and the bill admitting the fiftieth state was passed and signed. As the president had predicted, assumptions about the political party alignments of the two new states soon proved to be exaggerations.

Before the Democrats adjourned Congress, they succeeded in wounding President Eisenhower far deeper than any previous criticism had. Early in 1958, a House committee was told that Bernard Goldfine, a Boston clothing manufacturer, had invoked the name of presidential assistant Sherman Adams while seeking favors from the Federal Power Commission. Summoned to testify, Adams listed several gifts—a rug, a vicuña coat, hotel accommodations—received from Goldfine as a family friend. But Adams denied the implication that in return he had used his official influence to help Goldfine. Indeed, Adams had lectured his own staff on the subject of the special integrity of federal regulatory agencies. Angered by the charges, he chose just that time to give a speech criticizing congressional Democrats for failing to support the administration's foreign policy. Was he, some observers wondered, thus launching his own presidential candidacy? To the surprise and delight of the Democrats, a number of Republicans, long resentful of the influence wielded by Adams and his "palace guard" at the White House, supported a continuation of the committee's investigation.

The subject of influence peddling had been the Republican party's own weapon against the Democrats in the 1952 election; thereafter, Eisenhower had proudly referred to the ethical standards of his own team. A few months before the Goldfine case was disclosed, the president had expanded his views before a Republican women's conference. In a government as large as that of the United States, he said, some deviations from the public interest would occur. "But all of us can make certain, by prompt, decisive, and fair corrective action, that public confidence in the integrity of government is maintained."[10] When confronted at his press conference in April by the "palace guard" allegation, the president impatiently explained that his staff did "sort out the things that are interesting to Government and to me and make certain that I get them."[11] When newsmen referred to the charges against Adams, Eisenhower snapped, "I don't want anything more about that."[12]

Because of its potential political impact, the Adams case was kept alive throughout the spring of that congressional election year. The president fumed over newsmen's comparisons of Adams's actions with those of Truman's cronies and with the issue of Nixon's slush fund in 1952. Eisenhower viewed the allegations against his assistant as evidence that his critics simply did not understand the concept of the White House staff system. In June, he opened his press conference with an announcement. The reception of gifts by a public official, he pointed out, did not necessarily mean that bribery was involved. He thought that Sherman Adams had not been "sufficiently alert in making certain that the gifts . . . could be misinterpreted as . . . attempts to influence his political actions." But, the president continued, Adams had admitted that he had been imprudent when he testified before the House committee. His outstanding reputation for honesty, the president reasoned, was a proper basis for determining guilt or innocence, and those qualities remained unaltered by the accusations directed against him. Echoing his conclusions about Patton during the war and about Nixon during the 1952 campaign, Eisenhower closed by saying: "I need him." He would accept no further questions from the press corps on the subject of Sherman Adams. Thereafter, he informed his White House staff that he would maintain his own objectivity until all facts were in. In the meantime, he asked Vice President Nixon to watch the matter and report to him on it from time to time.

Republican leaders anguished over the possible impact the case would have on the elections that year. When an early contest in Maine went against them, the old adage was revised to read: "As Maine goes, so goes Adams." But Adams did not go. Anxiously, Meade Alcorn, the party's national committee chairman, and press secretary Hagerty sought a further explanation from the laconic Adams. "Oh, yes, yes," he told them, "a rug, yeah, well, it's been in the house."[13] Deciding that Adams's resignation was essential to the election of the party's congressional candidates, Senator Knowland and a few others encouraged Hagerty to ask newsmen to plant stories to the effect that Adams would resign in order to avoid embarrassing the president.

Eisenhower did not want to pressure Adams, nor to seem indifferent. "If anything is done," the president told him, "and we make any critical decision, as I have always said, you will have to take the initiative yourself."[14] In late September, Adams went on television to again protest his innocence and then went to the president's vacation quarters at Newport, Rhode Island, to hand in his resignation. Eisenhower was silent at that time, but in subsequent correspondence he deplored the circumstances that had caused it: "The pilloring that was Adams' lot was a sorry display for supposedly civilized, sophisticated, educated human beings."[15]

The vacancy at the top enabled Eisenhower to complete the ranks of his second team by appointing Jerry Persons to be assistant to the president. A former army officer, Persons had been considered for the post in 1953, but antimilitary criticism had destroyed his chances. Evidently Eisenhower was less concerned with that attitude five years later. Informal, light-hearted and always accessible, Persons was a noticeable contrast to the dour Adams, and working relationships among members of the White House staff soon improved. Because of his long service with the president, Persons was no less cautious than Adams about protecting Eisenhower's image and perhaps had even wider responsibilities.

The Adams affair, Eisenhower later wrote, was the saddest thing that happened during his presidency. Yet in retrospect, his own behavior contributed to the outcome. His response to the congressional hearings had hardly been the "prompt decision and fair corrective action" that he had thought necessary to retain public confidence in government. Then, by saying that he needed Adams, Eisenhower was treading near to the concept of the indispensable man, an idea that he did not believe in. The president's customary silence, as public criticism reached a high point, created a vacuum into which Adams's enemies moved decisively. Then, in accepting the resignation, the president appeared to be moved by thoughts of protecting the image of his administration and the safety of his party, although his real reasoning was based on the conviction that Adams would do the honest and proper thing in making his own decision. Finally, at his next press conference when Eisenhower insisted that he had not asked for the resignation, the president denied his own responsibility.

(Regret over the loss of Adams may have prompted Eisenhower to try to make amends after he left the White House. According to Jack Anderson, one of the newspaper columnists who had helped expose the Goldfine case, Eisenhower asked his presidential successors not to prosecute Adams because the man had suffered enough already. Neither Kennedy nor Johnson wished to embarrass Eisenhower, but in fact they did not have to intervene. According to Anderson, Adams later admitted to federal officials that he had accepted money from Goldfine to supplement his salary in order to afford to remain at his White House job. He also agreed to pay the taxes due on this additional income.)[16]

Adams's resignation, coming a few weeks before the congressional elections, shattered Republican confidence. Party chiefs had already been shaken by what seemed to be an exodus from their ranks when Eisenhower's popularity dropped and the recession worsened early in the year. Then when party candidates reached for his coattails, they found no sign of a bold "new Eisenhower." Increasingly absorbed in international affairs, the president relied on chairman Alcorn to hold the party factions together. But the Republicans' most prominent candidates for reelection were Old Guard members. In disgust and desperation, they condemned the administration for betraying Republican principles. Like a hopeful coach, Eisenhower assured party leaders that the American people by now understood that the word *Republican* was "simply another way of saying 'responsible government'—that it means constitutional government—that it means honest, dependable government."[17] He made that statement in May, at the height of the charges against Sherman Adams. Impatiently the president told his associates that he could not afford to let the matter of Adams's "mistakes" render him helpless, even if the party leaders did. Bolstered by the news of a drop in unemployment in August, he urged them to "lead the defeatists away from the wailing wall. Time has proved right this Administration's confidence in the American economy. We are on the upward road."[18]

When the president's own schedule for the campaign was announced, it seemed extremely abbreviated. He would go to only six states, two of them (Kansas and Colorado) merely for personal visits. In three others, there were no contests for Senate seats. The omissions, it turned out, could not be covered by making a few "people-ask-the-president" telecasts. Moreover, these presentations were even more contrived and general than those of two years before. Eisenhower made a noteworthy personal effort only in California where Senator Knowland was seeking the governorship, while the incumbent, Governor Goodwin Knight, was trying to win the Senate seat Knowland had just given up. The president thought that Knowland's election was vitally important to the Republican party's future. In spite of past disagreements between them, he explained in private correspondence, they shared exactly the same philosophy of government. Moreover, only Knowland could save California from what Eisenhower described as radicals, who dominated politics in the neighboring West Coast states of Oregon and Washington.

Perhaps because it was his own last campaign, Eisenhower decided to express those private judgments in public. The Democratic party, he told a large audience in California, was dominated by "political radicals"—that is, by big spenders of governmental money. "Long ago," he recalled, "I found out that, to a political radical, a sound program for America is an invitation for demagogic excess." He had watched, he said, his own proposals "mangled and mushroomed" by Democratic Congresses led by extremists "pushing economic and political goals at odds with American tradition."[19] While innuendo was a familiar weapon in political circles, it was also a form of the very demagoguery that he accused the Democrats of using. The "new Eisenhower" in California sounded very much like the McCarthyites he had disdained four years earlier.

A few days before the election, reports came in to the White House from Republican leaders in key states: they found that the earlier apathy had disappeared from their ranks. But their heightened expectations made the outcome of the voting all the more shocking. In the biggest congressional sweep since 1936, the Democrats increased their control of the Senate by seventeen seats and of the House by forty-nine seats—the latter, a margin not attained even in the New Deal era. They also occupied governorships in thirty-five states and carried Vermont for the first time in over a hundred years. One of the very few Democratic candidates who lost was Congressman Brooks Hays of Arkansas, branded by his connections with the Eisenhower men during the Little Rock crisis. The casualties on the Republican side included Knowland, Knight, Bricker and, ironically, the administration's hero in the McCarthy censure, Watkins of Utah. The only major Republican victory was the election of Nelson Rockefeller as governor of New York. Defeated members of the Old Guard now amended their charge to say that Dwight Eisenhower had first betrayed and now had destroyed the Republican party.

The president walked into the Oval Office the morning after the election, looked at the gloomy faces around him, and said, "Pretty bad, wasn't it?" When Hagerty reminded him that the press corps would certainly have questions about the disaster, the president growled, "You don't have to bring that up. I know what I'm going to say on that. Just skip it." Then he seized upon the subject in a burst of anger. "I'm going to go into that press conference," he swore, "and I am going to relate this Democratic victory to the rising cost of government and how much it's going to be in taxes for every person in the United States."[20] But, as usual, he had calmed down considerably by the time he met with reporters. First, he denied that he had meant that all Democrats were spenders and did not admit that the epithet "radical" was his own choice to describe them. Instead of releasing a broadside against the Democratic members of Congress, he merely promised to fight them as long as God gave him strength. Finally, he withdrew from his earlier prediction of a "cold war" between the executive and legislative branches and reminded his questioners that he had learned to work with Democratic Congresses during the course of several years.

Eisenhower was so dejected by the election results that he held no press conferences for almost five weeks thereafter. He was also genuinely puzzled: in 1956, the voters had given him a margin of over nine million votes, yet just two years later, they almost completely reversed their party support. He could not see anything, he said innocently, that the voters wanted his administration to do differently. Alcorn and Nixon believed that Sputnik, the recession, and Sherman Adams accounted for the great reversal, but Eisenhower preferred to point to the fact that Republicans tended to campaign only during the last weeks before an election, and never between elections. Party leaders, he urged, should reorganize and energize their ranks, getting younger Republicans to serve on congressional committees. The consequences for America, he told them, were nothing less than the survival of freedom.

Eisenhower recovered quickly from the setbacks of 1958. Once again, he looked lean, hard, and relaxed, and obviously enjoyed the best health of his presidential years. He even appeared to be somewhat sorry that the end of his term was approaching. "The home stretch is upon us," he wrote to Hagerty, "but a thoroughbred tries to make his best effort in the last furlong."[21] The administration could count on two new lieutenants in the Eighty-sixth Congress. Senator Everett Dirksen of Illinois had defeated an Eisenhower-moderate Republican for the minority leadership, but he was welcomed as one of the most notable converts to the president's programs. In contrast to his predecessor, Dirksen was a well-informed tactician and a dependable supporter of the administration's proposals. In the House, Joe Martin's sterile obstinacy had been set aside when Republican members chose Charles Halleck of Indiana to replace him as their leader. These new team members would soon earn the administration's gratitude for their role in several legislative struggles.

The president expected an all-out battle with the new Congress. As if to confirm his prediction, they immediately challenged two of his nominations. The first was the selection of Claire Booth Luce as ambassador to Brazil. The nominee's well-known partisanship provoked debate, but the Senate confirmed her in recognition of her earlier work as ambassador to Italy. Soon afterwards, however, she publicly ridiculed Senator Morse. Eisenhower did not think her comment was out of line in view of some of the things Morse had said about him. But the Senate rose to protect its honor, and Luce wisely resigned from her new post.

The Luce farce was merely a prologue to the prolonged, bitter fight over the nomination of former AEC chairman Lewis Strauss to be secretary of commerce. Eisenhower thought that Senate confirmation should have taken no more than a few minutes, in view of the man's excellent service as an adviser to two administrations. But the memory of the Oppenheimer case and Strauss's devious, disdainful answers to the Senate Commerce Committee brought down the vengeance of liberal Democrats, led by Clinton Anderson of New Mexico. The president was disgusted by their inquisition of Strauss; White House aides recalled that Eisenhower lost his temper more frequently during those weeks than any other comparable period. Determined to have Strauss lead the administration's crusade for sound federal economic policies, he promised to use "every influence I can to get Congress to see the light." It was a rare departure from his earlier admonitions about proper executive-legislative relations. "If that's lobbying," he admitted, "I'm guilty. . . ."[22] But phone calls from the White House to various senators were ineffective; the nomination was reported out of committee by a single vote margin and failed on the floor by forty-nine to forty-six. Observing the way in which Senators John Kennedy and Lyndon Johnson completely reversed themselves on the subject, Eisenhower wrote them off as mere politicians. The whole disappointing ordeal reinforced his jaundiced view of politics.

It was in defense of his budget for 1960 that Dwight Eisenhower made his last great effort to sustain his administration's economic policies. It would be one of the bloodiest battles he ever fought, and, while he did not expect complete victory, he was determined not to let "the spenders" win either. Thinking of himself as a tribune of the people's interests, Eisenhower was committed to preventing passage of inflationary legislation. That, in his view, was not only an economic necessity, but a humanitarian goal as well. With righteous purpose, he sent to Congress a budget totaling $77 billion ($3 billion less than the previous year's estimate), including almost $41 billion for defense programs. As Eisenhower saw it, the victorious Democrats were convinced that the recession was still on and they were ready for the pump-priming spending of the 1930s. The crisis caused him to abandon his usual wait-and-see attitude. If they persisted in spending and overrode his vetoes, he warned, he would call a special session to secure tax increases.

Although the Democrats did not resort to new spending programs, predictably they did inflate the administration's proposals. Unable to wean themselves from the pork barrel, as Eisenhower later wrote, the majority of legislators provided the Republicans with welcome ammunition. Maurice Stans, the new budget director, carried out the president's postelection pledge by issuing a price list of Democratic actions, showing that the House had increased the administration's requests by $1.25 billion and the Senate had increased them by almost $2 billion. As he had promised, Eisenhower refused to sign the bills and began returning them with coldly indignant veto messages. One such bill was an appropriation for the Bureau of Reclamation. Congress thereupon trimmed it slightly, but Eisenhower vetoed it a second time. As if to flex their muscles, the Democrats overrode the veto. They did not, however, try the same feat with measures of greater importance, such as a bill to construct a moderate number of classrooms and centers for the elderly. As recommended by the administration, these projects were to be financed on a pay-as-you-go basis. When Congress presented its version, containing increased federal outlays and providing additional units, Eisenhower vetoed it; when the Congress revised it, he vetoed it a second time. As a result of the administration's sustained strategy of defense, the budget as finally passed was not only balanced but would make possible a $1 billion surplus. This accomplishment helped heal the wounds of the 1958 elections. "Out of the jaws of political defeat," Eisenhower wrote in retrospect, "we had snatched at least a partial victory for common sense."[23]

The president had at last tasted the great satisfaction of besting a Democratic Congress, but he did not continue the economic fight. When confronted with a major strike in the steel industry, Eisenhower reverted to his belief in federal—and especially presidential —restraint. In 1954, heeding Brownell's advice, he had decided not to press Congress for modifications of the Taft-Hartley Act. Five years later, at the beginning of 1959, he took up the matter in a special message to Congress. He asked for revisions of Taft-Hartley that would satisfy all parties affected by labor-management disagreements. Recent findings of a committee chaired by Democratic Senator John McClellan of Arkansas had revealed that criminals controlled several major labor unions; citing these findings, Eisenhower also asked for legislation that would prevent the manipulation of unions by gangsters and criminals. Commerce Secretary Weeks urged him to seek a measure that would require secret balloting in union elections, but Eisenhower did not think that such an extension of federal supervision was in the nation's best interests.

The Democrats welcomed the recommendations as an unbounded opportunity to show their traditional solicitude for the working class. When they proposed to increase the minimum wage to $1.25 an hour and to expand unemployment compensation, the president and Labor Secretary Mitchell described the measures as inflationary. That objection especially aroused the ire of union leaders then convening in Miami. Eisenhower, in turn, wondered aloud at his press conference why these men pretended to run their organizations while meeting on the Florida beaches. The United Auto Workers' president, Walter Reuther, returned the thrust by asking why the president pretended to do his work while off on duck shoots with his millionaire friends. Following this caustic exchange and expression of mutual distrust, the steel strike began in July 1959.

President Eisenhower immediately announced that his administration would keep the federal government out of efforts to resolve the strike. It was essential to the idea of a free economy, he explained, that all parties concerned work out their own disagreements. By taking a neutral position, moreover, he could stand in sharp contrast to the Democrat's outspoken support of organized labor. George Meany, president of the newly combined AFL-CIO, suggested that the White House host a conference of steelworker and steel-owner representatives, but Eisenhower declined. It would narrow the span of options, he reasoned. If it succeeded, it would constitute outside pressure on the process of collective bargaining; if it failed, a Truman-like seizure of the industry would be the only recourse left.

Although the Supreme Court had overruled Truman's actions

in 1952, its new majority, appointed by Eisenhower, recently had upheld the authority of the federal government to intervene in such disputes. Nevertheless, the president's thoughts on the subject remained unchanged, untouched by that ruling. As the strike wore on into the fall, Eisenhower consulted with his economic advisers. In private, he briefly contemplated using a different form of federal pressure by releasing steel stockpiles onto the market. The idea, he admitted later, was a poor one. During those months, his personal bias against labor leaders was somewhat tempered by conversations with David MacDonald, head of the steelworkers' union. Confident that MacDonald shared his own middle-of-the-road economic philosophy, the president concluded that the union sincerely wanted to settle the strike; it was the industry's representatives who were unable to understand the details of working conditions on which the dispute rested. Yet the president refused to reveal his feelings to steel owners because even that might be construed as improper pressure.

Increasingly, however, Eisenhower was furious at the lack of progress in negotiations. Not only were the nation's revenues for the following year (in the form of lost taxes) being reduced as the strike continued, but there seemed a good possibility that both sides would indulge in retaliations that would drive up the cost of steel and thus depress the recently recovered national economic indices. On October 9, therefore, the ninety-seventh day of the strike, he directed Attorney General Rogers to seek an injunction against the strikers. It was a sad day for Eisenhower because he had had to resort to federal intervention. It was a sad day for the nation, too, he said. Comparisons with Little Rock were made in the press and in the White House as well.

Before the statutory eighty-day "cooling off" period was over, the strike was settled with an alacrity that suggested that each side had unnecessarily prolonged it to discredit the other. The only benefit derived from the strike, it appeared, was passage of the Landrum-Griffin Act, aimed at curbing racketeers' influence in union organizations; the president pronounced it a "tremendous improvement" over the Taft-Hartley Act.

The president's aloofness during the steel strike exasperated those who had criticized his hands-off attitude during the recession the year before. His posture seemed to be quite a contrast to his fierce stand against "the spenders" during many of those same months of 1959. While the budget fight had undoubtedly weakened his leverage, the strike had strengthened his economic convictions.

147

Even as it was being settled under the aegis of federal action, Eisenhower was lecturing his cabinet. "We must get the Federal Government out of every economic activity," he reiterated. "We can refuse to do things too rapidly. Humanity has evolved for a long time. Suddenly we seem to have a hysterical approach, in health and welfare programs, in grants to the states, in space research. We are going to cure every ill in two or five years—by putting in a lot of money. To my mind this is the wrong attitude." His priorities were exactly what they had been when he first took office: the government must pay its bills, prevent the loss of capital investment, and defeat the pressure groups that made it spend too much. He repeatedly stressed the importance of frugality, economy, simplicity, and efficiency, encouraging his advisers to make them "our watch words."[24]

Eisenhower's economic conservatism may account for the puzzling, uneven pattern of presidential behavior that characterized his second term in office. While he opposed greater government support for education, housing, health care, and the minimum wage, he firmly pressed for federal protection of civil rights. That was the most controversial subject and the one requiring the deepest change in public understanding, but it was the only one in which bold action did not entail large federal expenditures. Similarly, Eisenhower seemed aloof to the point of indifference about federal responses to Sputnik, the recession, and the steel strike, but he fought —both defensively and offensively—to secure a balanced budget and the reorganization of the Defense Department. He was also ready to suspend his impartiality in nominating Strauss and in defending Sherman Adams, but in none of these instances did boldness call for federal spending.

An alternative explanation for Eisenhower's on-again, off-again concern with domestic issues during the second term touches on the matter of his own personal interests. There is no evidence that his age or his health sapped his energies for prolonged periods. But his hopes were undoubtedly deflated by the defeat of his own party and the Democrats' success in controlling Congress. As he himself remarked, everything begins to look political in the last fifteen months of a president's second term. In contrast to the sequence of disappointments in domestic affairs, however, foreign policy offered him far better opportunities for a second chance to fulfill the aims of his presidency. Evidently, by the middle of 1958, his attention and interest were focused in that direction.

8

★★★★★

ONE MAN'S DIPLOMACY

The president had been preoccupied with international affairs as he began his second term in January 1957. His notably brief second inaugural address was almost a sequel to his special broadcast made six months before, at the time of the Hungarian revolt. That fierce uprising, he said now, resembled the great force that had risen to meet the threat of totalitarian aggression during World War II. Once again, men who loved freedom were ready to pledge their lives to that love in the struggle against another enemy, international communism. Once again, the United States should pay the material costs at home and abroad to uphold that force for freedom. If other nations did not prosper, he reasoned, America's prosperity could not survive.

Remembering well the horrendous human cost of World War II, Eisenhower was prepared to relegate to second place his principle domestic aim, a sound economy, in order to prevent another war; his new budget, therefore, would request enormous sums for weapons to meet aggression. But he did not think that the United States could depend exclusively on its armaments to shield freedom in the world. If it did, war would be the certain outcome. The nation should use its material resources to build up the economies of countries threatened by communism. Even if communism could not be entirely eliminated, the president believed that such economic assistance could diminish its influence and turn the world away from its dangers. In the ensuing congressional "battle of the budget," however, legislators of both parties showed little trust in the president's vast experience with the costs of war and peace. But while they withheld approval of portions of his budget, they did rely on his judgment in responding to international crises.

To Eisenhower at this time, the question of the Middle East was even more important than the budget. When he addressed Congress that January, he reminded the members that the real consequence of continued conflict in that region would be Communist intervention. Israel's refusal to withdraw its troops from the Sinai, two months after the cease-fire order went into effect, appeared to be potential grounds for such intervention. For that reason, he privately assured President Ben Gurion that Israel would have use of the Suez Canal if its forces were pulled back. Once that was done, Eisenhower thought that Israel's position in the Arab world was a minor part of the overall problem. The larger situation, he concluded, called for something like the authority and flexibility he had wielded as supreme commander.

He asked Congress, therefore, to extend the concept of the Formosa Resolution of 1955 to the Middle East. With such legislative support, he would be able to dispatch military and economic assistance to prevent a Communist take-over of any nation in that part of the world. In effect, he could modify the Truman Doctrine along the lines of selective application, an idea he had advocated ever since Korea and the 1952 campaign. The Middle East resolution he sought was quickly passed, and the president was pleased when the press labeled it the "Eisenhower Doctrine." It was, he said, an example of bipartisan cooperation at its best. With an eye on proponents of the Bricker Amendment, the White House described the resolution as another instance of proper partnership between the two branches in the conduct of foreign policy.

As it was applied, however, the doctrine proved to be a one-man show. Eisenhower set the stage for that performance when he met with Prime Minister Macmillan in Bermuda in March 1958. The family spat over Suez had been resolved, and the two leaders agreed that the United States would be the keeper of the peace in the Middle East. American forces would use British bases there, and the United States would try to win over Egypt with a $75 million loan to aid in the construction of the Aswan Dam. Nasser proved obdurate, however, and described the Eisenhower Doctrine as blatant interference in the domestic affairs of Arab nations. In April, a tense situation developed in Syria, but the president chose to wait until Congress had adjourned before exercising his authority. By that time, the Syrian problem had receded.

Confirming Eisenhower's warning about the larger significance of the Middle East problem, Nikita Khrushchev called for a summit meeting to consider, among other subjects, the dangerous situation there. In order to test Soviet receptivity to any such discussions, the president countered with the suggestion that scientists from both nations meet first to talk about the peaceful uses of space exploration. The Russians thereupon set off a series of high intensity, "dirty" nuclear bombs and then announced the suspension of further tests, demanded that the United States do likewise, and, as a final way of strengthening their position at the bargaining table, put a 2,900-pound Sputnik into earth orbit.

By the end of the year, Russian agreement to the meeting of scientists at Geneva meant little. Eisenhower surveyed the international scene and concluded on the basis of recent events that the Communists were now using indirect aggression: that is, they were supporting regimes favorable to them with money and arms and bringing down governments that opposed them by the same means. To some observers, of course, the Eisenhower Doctrine was a mirror-image of indirect aggression. But the president preferred to use other tactics before resorting to direct intervention. When, for example, a rebellion broke out in Indonesia early in 1958 against the Communist-supported rule of Achmed Sukarno, the Pentagon sent military advisers to assist the rebels, and the CIA assigned American pilots to fly B-26s to supply them. At a press conference, Eisenhower asserted that the United States was adhering to "careful neutrality and proper deportment all the way through as far as not taking sides where it is none of our business."[1] If there were Americans involved in the conflict, he assured reporters, they were "soldiers of fortune," men who were always found seeking adventure in small wars. Three weeks after he gave that assurance, one of the B-26s was shot down and the American pilot was captured by Sukarno's forces.

Eisenhower's deception was an attempt to protect the security of a clandestine operation, much as his explanation of the Guatemala affair had been. But it gave substance to Nasser's description of the Eisenhower Doctrine as modern-day imperialism. Hoping to remove that stigma, the president lectured reporters at his press conference in May. Like all free countries, he said, the United States must observe the principle of live and let live. "We cannot make ourselves the boss. . . . Whether you use money, whether you use politics, or whether you use power to do it, you can persuade; but if you are going to be an equal, then you have got to act as an equal."[2]

The teacher, nevertheless, found immediate reason for not practicing that admirable principle. Although the United States was supporting clandestine interference in the affairs of several small nations, the president viewed that tactic as a preliminary, or stop-gap, measure rather than as basic policy. His emphasis on the long-range strategic effectiveness of economic assistance was exemplified by the administration's new policy in Latin America. To begin with, an inter-American bank was established to encourage capital investment in that region, and trade restrictions were eased in order to expand markets. The policy, however, was not meant as a one-way street. Just as the federal government encouraged local and private initiative at home, the United States recognized that these nations should solve their own problems. When, for example, Uruguay nationalized some American-owned industries, Eisenhower agreed that its domestic emergency warranted such a step.

While nationalization was, in Eisenhower's view, any country's right as long as adequate compensation was given, antigovernment forces were exploiting the issue in several parts of the hemisphere. Early in 1958, an uprising in Venezuela had overthrown a rightist regime whose power had rested on American control of the country's principle resource—oil. In order to offset anti-American feelings in Latin America, Eisenhower sent Vice President Nixon on an extended tour of several nations in May. After attending the inauguration of the constitutionally elected successor to Argentine dictator Juan Peron, Nixon went on to Peru. When a mob of antigovernment demonstrators accosted him there, Nixon's calmness and fortitude earned Eisenhower's praise.

Although the White House received daily reports from CIA agents in those countries, no one considered cancelling the next stop on the vice president's itinerary: Caracas, Venezuela. But when Nixon and his wife arrived there, a belligerent mob surrounded their car, stoned and spat upon it, and tried to turn it over. Learning of the attack, the president angrily ordered two companies of Marines and paratroopers to a nearby base in the Caribbean. He then informed Venezuelan officials that if they could not protect their guests, the United States would go in and get them out. The Nixons were soon moved out of the reach of further violence and flown back to Washington, D.C. As an expression of admiration for their courage, Eisenhower set a precedent by meeting them at the airport. The Caracas incident, he later insisted, had not impaired American friendships in Latin America. Indeed, Nixon resumed his trip the following month, and Secretary Dulles flew to Brazil to discuss inter-American relations soon afterwards.

Continuing intelligence reports informed Eisenhower that Communists were exploiting, if not creating, internal problems of nations in many parts of the world. The disturbing news, his associates observed, seemed to affect his health. It was, he jokingly explained to newsmen, just that his golf scores were terrible. But he made a more candid remark at his press conference: "I would give aid to anything that I would think would help to weaken the solidarity of the Communist Bloc."[3] As he later recalled, it was at about this same time that he said to his wife, "Maybe I should be digging out my uniforms to see whether they still fit."[4] When the next crisis arose, Eisenhower was well prepared.

The diplomatic resolution of the Suez crisis in early 1957 had not brought a lasting peace to the Middle East. The force of Arab nationalism continued its sweep westward and northeastward. Algeria rose in revolt against French rule, and Egypt joined with Syria to form the United Arab Republic. Although Nasser's ultimate ambitions remained questionable, the United States quickly recognized the UAR. Soon afterwards, however, American intelligence agents reported that Syria was exercising its own brand of nationalism by sending armed agents across the border into neighboring Lebanon. There had been a long tradition of American interest and presence in that half Christian–half Muslim nation, an interest now greatly enhanced by the politics of oil. Lebanese president Camille Chamoun depended on that interest and presence in deciding to remain in power after his term expired. That ambition provided the Syrians with a useful issue in their attempts to bring down his government.

Eisenhower had earlier assured Chamoun that American military assistance would be available, if requested, and that the Pentagon had drawn up a full contingency plan. But intelligence sources estimated that Chamoun could effectively handle the Syrian threat with the American arms he was already receiving. Landing military units, Eisenhower felt, would be resented by many Lebanese, interpreted as foreign interference, and would seem to confirm Communist charges of American imperialism. With that in mind, he told members of the press that the Lebanese government should present its case of Syrian infiltration to the United Nations. The State Department quietly informed Chamoun, however, that the previous assurance of U.S. military assistance would not be withdrawn even if the U.N. assumed responsibility for Lebanon. The governments of Lebanon and the United States shared an additional concern: the suspicion that the British were planning to rescue Lebanon in order to recover their traditional influence in the Middle East.

On July 14, 1958, Chamoun asked for American forces to protect his government from rebel forces within the country and from the external threat posed by the successful revolt in neighboring Iraq. Eisenhower met immediately with the members of the National Security Council. In their discussion, Secretary Dulles reasserted his domino analogy by arguing that the overthrow of Chamoun would endanger the governments of nearby countries. His brother, CIA chief Allen Dulles, did not think that the U.N. could handle the crisis at that stage. The ultimate targets of Arab aggression, it was agreed, would be Iran and the destruction of the Baghdad Pact. A military action was therefore deemed imperative. Remarkably, its possible impact at home and abroad was not discussed. Satisfied with the consensus of the meeting, Eisenhower turned to Chairman Twining of the Joint Chiefs of Staff. "How soon can you start, Nate?" "Fifteen minutes after I get back to the Pentagon," was the reply. "Sure?" "Positive, sir." The president gave his order with typical indirection: "Well, what are we waiting for?"[5]

In a televised broadcast to the nation the next day, Eisenhower explained the reasons for the intervention in Lebanon. American troops were being landed, he said, in order to protect American residents and defend the integrity of a nation threatened by acts of indirect aggression. He described the action as a continuation of the policy that was established when Greece was similarly threatened in 1947 and had been extended by his administration to Iran, Guatemala, and Formosa. It was essential, he said, for the United States to prove to nations everywhere that it would halt any kind of aggression. Although he did not use the phrase "Eisenhower Doctrine," that term appeared in messages of approval sent by Iran, Turkey, and Pakistan.

The military landing went off smoothly. American intelligence reported that the Lebanese population greeted the troops with cheers. But the diplomatic and political repercussions were appalling. The largest question mark was Soviet reaction. In his public remarks, Eisenhower issued a warning that the real danger of war could come if one small nation after another was engulfed by forces of expansionist aggression, supported by the Soviet Union. In private, however, he discounted the likelihood of Communist intervention because none of the nations of the Middle East were Soviet satellites.

The unilateral nature of the intervention raised a second question. Despite his belief in multilateral cooperation through the United Nations or among the Western allies, Eisenhower had consulted none of them. The echo of recent events was uncomfortably obvious. "You are doing a Suez on me,"[6] Prime Minister Macmillan complained facetiously when the president called to tell him that the military operation had begun. But the British did not have to pursue a clandestine plan of their own this time, and they landed their own forces in nearby Jordan. At the U.N., Ambassador Lodge was hard put to explain just how the actions of both nations differed from those which America had vehemently opposed at Suez two years before.

A further flaw in the intervention was the embarrassing fact that Lebanese military leaders had threatened to oppose the landing just as it began. Thus, on first application, the Eisenhower Doctrine appeared to be a potent weapon, but unwelcomed by those it was meant to protect. If it was difficult for the United States to convince the world that indirect aggression had occurred in Lebanon, it was even more difficult to establish that it had suddenly ceased. Nikita Khrushchev made the most out of that anomaly, of course. In reply, Eisenhower reminded him that Russia itself believed that indirect aggression had been a cause of World War II. While the president acknowledged that troops could not win the peace in the Middle East, he rejected a Soviet proposal for a special summit meeting on the conflict. As he prepared to withdraw American units from Lebanon, he urged the United Nations to establish a permanent peace-keeping force that could thereafter assume the responsibility for preemptive action anywhere in the world. In keeping with the concepts of Truman and Roosevelt, Eisenhower also proposed the extension of economic aid to harness the Jordan River. Development of that natural resource, he believed, would obliterate the deserts and the diseases that made nations vulnerable to indirect aggression.

For Eisenhower, the most unsettling consequence of the intervention in Lebanon occurred at home. In Congress, the Democratic leadership demanded a full explanation from the administration of what Arkansas Senator William Fulbright called a mysterious and hazardous adventure. Other members demanded to know whether the action had been undertaken merely to protect Anglo-American oil companies in the Middle East. Republican speeches in defense of the administration's military incursion so disgusted Speaker Rayburn that he cut off further debate. The president had initially planned to ask Congress for its approval if he found it necessary to extend the military force to oil-rich Kuwait and, if necessary, to Iran. There was no likelihood that he would be given that support now.

Already shaken by Sputnik and the recession, Eisenhower's ratings in public opinion polls dropped to a new low. Angered by those who did not support their government once a foreign policy decision had been made, the president showed a flash of anger. When he learned that the Voice of America radio network in Europe was broadcasting dissenting opinions on the Lebanon action, he terminated those programs. The agency, he decided, had no mandate to present anything except approval of the nation's policies. (Eisenhower was well aware of a precedent for his action: Franklin Roosevelt had issued a similar order during the controversy over the "Darlan deal" in World War II.)

Although Democrats refused to see it as such, the president considered the Lebanon action as an important foreign policy accomplishment. The United States had demonstrated its willingness to employ armed force as a shield against even indirect aggression. The selective use of specific military units—and their subsequent prompt withdrawal—admirably demonstrated the restrained use of force and made clear to both friends and foes that there were alternatives to nuclear devastation in the armory of the peacekeeper. But for many Americans, the intervention raised more questions than it answered. Was indirect aggression in the Middle East (or anywhere) so powerful and so dangerous that the use of such force was warranted? If military force had been used there because it was both necessary and a deterrent, how did that differ from Russia's action in Hungary two years before? Moreover, was a bolder "new" Eisenhower looking for conflicts that were less costly and more easily won than Korea and Indochina in order to establish the United States as a protector of freedom? If he was willing to react suddenly, strongly, and unilaterally to stop indirect aggression in politically ambiguous nations like those of the Middle East, what would he do if an avowed Communist regime initiated direct aggression?

In August 1958, that last question became a frightening reality. At the moment when the United States was involved in Lebanon, China began bombarding the islands of Quemoy and Matsu, near the Nationalist sanctuary of Formosa. Chiang Kai-shek had only recently stationed a full third of his entire military force on those tiny islands. (Eisenhower had thought that deployment unwise because of the difficulty of supply, but he made no official objection because he felt it improper to coerce an ally in a decision that was rightfully its own to make.) The concentration of troops made the islands far more important than they had been when the Communists threatened them in 1954. Since that earlier crisis, moreover, American forces in the area had been equipped with tactical nuclear weapons. That fact prompted the administration's critics to assert that local commanders would now contrive a provocation in order to use their new weapons.

Eisenhower drew upon his expertise at indirection when he went into his press conference after the Chinese bombardment began. In order to protect information vital to national security, he told the newsmen that nuclear weapons could not be used by American commanders without the specific authorization of the president. There was one exception to that arrangement, but he professed that he could not remember what it was. His act was all too obvious, and some of those present well knew what that exception was: local commanders could use any means at hand if American units were directly attacked. In fact, Pentagon officials and Chiang himself were virtually hounding the president to approve the use of nuclear weapons. (That information would remain secret until Eisenhower revealed it seven years later.)

The president's own estimate of the crisis was just as chilling as his critics' allegations. He believed that the Chinese Communists would take the islands if they thought that the United States would not intervene. Although the action being tested in Lebanon at that time had not yet been concluded, he was ready to apply the same strategy to the Far East in order to support international confidence in America's willingness to stop aggression anywhere. As always, he felt it essential to accept nothing less than certain victory once those forces were committed to battle. In the initial phase of the operation, he judged, conventional weapons would be sufficient, but victory might require use of nuclear arms. He saw no immediate need for those weapons and so refused to yield to the Pentagon's recommendation. Any future decision would perforce reflect future developments, but it would still be his decision to make.

Secretary Dulles emphasized the first part of the president's assessment when he talked with Prime Minister Macmillan at the outset of the crisis. Intervention could not be a limited operation, he said; it would have to include the decision to use small, "clean," tactical nuclear weapons. Dulles also brought out his favorite concept in that conversation. If the United States did not stop aggression at Quemoy, Formosa would be vulnerable, and if Formosa fell, the Philippines and Japan would be the next Communist targets, along with British Hong Kong. Macmillan was appalled at what he privately described as the most brilliant exposition of "brinkmanship" in the secretary's career. The note of greater candor that Dulles had established with the British at the Paris NATO meeting the previous winter now gave ominous weight to his remarks. Duly alarmed, Winston Churchill privately urged Eisenhower to give Quemoy to the Chinese in order to prevent nuclear confrontation, and Macmillan sent his foreign secretary, Selwyn Lloyd, to call on the president at Newport. Eisenhower merely told Lloyd that he was personally opposed to using tactical nuclear weapons in the crisis. Privately, Eisenhower may have wondered if America's great ally was again ready to embrace the long discredited idea of appeasement.

In a televised speech at the height of the crisis, the president asserted that the United States had not forgotten the lesson of Korea. Quemoy was no more than typical of the security problems occurring everywhere in the world. "Now I assure you," he told a nationwide audience, "that no American boy will be asked by me to fight *just* for Quemoy." He was confident that extremes could be avoided. "There is not going to be any appeasement. I believe that there is not going to be any war. . . . This has not been the first test for us and for the free world. Probably it will not be the last."[7]

The president was neither ambiguous nor euphemistic in the remarks he directed at the Chinese in indirect diplomatic communications. "I told them," he explained years later, "what the hell was going to happen to them if they tried to attack Formosa."[8] But at the same time, he intended to give them a chance to find some position short of striking at that island. Even though the Communists continually threatened to overthrow Chiang, there was as yet no evidence that they were making an all-out effort to do so. (At most, he thought privately, they might erect a blockade; in that event, Chiang would learn the lesson of trying to supply his overextended garrisons.) Nor was there at present any reason to assume that if the Communists did move, Chiang's forces, supported by the United States Fifth Fleet, could not contain them. Therefore, Eisenhower decided not to invoke the authority granted him by Congress in the Formosa Resolution of 1955. Instead, he urged China to renounce the use of force in maintaining its claim to the islands. These were the statements given to Secretary Dulles and released by the State Department on September 4. By the time the NSC met to adjust contingency plans, China's leaders indicated that they were willing to advance the nation's claim to the islands through negotiations. Eisenhower suspected that Russia had pressed its ideological colleague to restore calm so that a summit could take place.

During the six months of the Quemoy-Matsu crisis, events in the Far East had a profound impact at home. Secretary Dulles admitted that mail received at the White House ran four-to-one against American involvement in the conflict. In Congress, several leading Democrats demanded withdrawal of the Fifth Fleet from the vicinity of the islands to avoid provocations initiated by either side. Republican members of the old "China lobby" branded these critics as traitors, but also charged that the president had sold out Chiang Kai-shek. Eisenhower was grateful to have one particular voice rise above these cries: all Americans, Harry Truman asserted, should support their president in any event.

Choosing to reply publicly to a hostile letter from Senator Theodore Francis Green, the octogenarian Democrat from Rhode Island, Eisenhower admonished all of his critics. "I deeply deplore the effect upon hostile forces of a statement that if we became engaged in battle, the United States would be defeated because of disunity at home. If that were believed, it would embolden our enemies and make inevitable the conflict which, I am sure, we both seek to avoid provided it can be avoided consistently with the honor and security of our country."[9] Both he and his successors in the White House would have cause in the future to repeat that admonition.

The president was particularly angry when political candidates made Lebanon and Quemoy issues in the 1958 congressional election campaign. Adlai Stevenson maintained that the sequence of problems at home and abroad could have been avoided if the administration had not waited placidly on golf course fairways, mouthing platitudes until mortal danger was upon the nation, and then angrily called out troops to solve those problems. Even General MacArthur supported Stevenson's critical assessment. But Eisenhower remained unmoved by these comments. When Vice President Nixon contributed to the controversy, however, by publicly criticizing the State Department's disclosure of the amount of mail protesting involvement, the president sent him a coldly worded telegram. There was a distinction between foreign policy and the department's administrative decisions, it pointed out; the latter should not and did not lend themselves to political argument.

In spite of the president's belief that foreign policy issues should not be subjected to partisan debate, his response to the Lebanon and Quemoy-Matsu crises set off a storm of criticism during the campaign. Actions in Lebanon were described by some candidates as an over-reaction, while the response in Quemoy was portrayed as an exercise in "brinkmanship." If those instances were tests of America's resolve to stop aggression, the argument went, who could be sure that a further demonstration of that resolve would not lead to war? The administration's defenders could no longer boast of its record for keeping the nation out of war, as they had in each previous election. Widespread uneasiness about the situation in the Far East undoubtedly contributed to the overwhelming rejection of Republican candidates in the election that November.

The president sounded like a prophet, however, when he warned the nation in his Quemoy address that the crisis was not the last test of freedom's resolve. In December, a month after the electoral setback and a month before the Chinese agreed to negotiations, Nikita Khrushchev, as if confirming Eisenhower's statement, issued an ultimatum: if the United States, England, and France did not relinquish West Berlin by May 1959, the Soviet Union would assist East Germany in retrieving the capital city. Eisenhower's response to the threat was characteristically calm. Drawing on his long wartime and postwar experience, he judged that the Russians were bluffing. West Berlin was still peripheral to their primary national interests; it was therefore unlikely that they would go to war over it. Along with Secretary Dulles and Prime Minister Macmillan, he suspected that the ultimatum was no more than Khrushchev's heavy-handed ploy to secure a summit meeting.

If the Russians did intervene in Berlin, however, the United States was ready to act with military force, ready "to put our whole stack in the pot,"[10] as Eisenhower expressed it privately. Dulles supported a Joint Chiefs' recommendation for the immediate large-scale build up of American units in Europe. General Lauris Norstad, Eisenhower's appointee as head of NATO forces, advised the president that his divisions were ready to move. But Eisenhower did not think that armed engagement over Berlin would rely upon conventional military forces. Indeed, partly for that reason, he continued to reduce the number of American troops on the continent. "We are certainly not going to fight a ground war in Europe," he told his press conference. When asked if nuclear weapons would be used to liberate Berlin, he replied: "Well, I don't know how you could free anything with nuclear weapons."[11]

The slow burning nature of the Berlin crisis enabled Eisenhower to avoid acting impulsively, as he had appeared to do in Lebanon and had seemed ready to do in Quemoy. Still sensitive to the public alarm over those issues, he kept his public references to the German problem in low key and held frequent conversations with congressional leaders. By his own account, these sessions were frank examinations of fears and alternatives, give-and-take exchanges that brought out the best in all participants. While not dismissing the crisis as a bluff, he explained his doubts that Russia would strike first. House Speaker Rayburn nevertheless adamantly opposed any armed response to the Russian ultimatum. Senator Richard Russell of Georgia, however, expressed the same kind of confidence in the commander-in-chief that had produced the congressional resolutions of 1955 and 1957. "You do what you have to, Mr. President, and come to us afterwards,"[12] he said. Years later, Eisenhower would recall the direction of his thinking at that moment: "Possibly we were risking the very fate of civilization on the premise that the Soviets would back down from the deadline when confronted by force. Yet this, to my mind, was not really gambling, for if we were not willing to take this risk, we would be certain to lose."[13]

The president was particularly concerned about the impact that the possibility of nuclear confrontation would have on U.S. relations with its old allies; he felt certain that his wartime associate, de Gaulle, now president of France, would take a hard line against Russia. "He's a proud, stubborn man," Eisenhower commented. "But if the chips are down, he's going to be proud and stubborn on our side."[14] Macmillan of Britain, however, was unwilling to let his nation's forces participate in a possible joint-rescue operation for West Berlin. When the prime minister made a surprise flight to Russia to talk to Khrushchev, Eisenhower wondered what he was up to.

After returning from Moscow, Macmillan came to the White House where he found Eisenhower confident about holding on to West Berlin, yet reasonable about alternatives to the use of force. But the secretary of state, now hospitalized with cancer, seemed to Macmillan just as negative and pessimistic as ever. Dulles objected to a summit as neither wise nor necessary and grumbled about the neglect of military options. Why did the United States spend $40 billion on deterrents, he asked, when it chose to compromise every time the Russians made a threat? "If appeasement and partial surrender are to be our attitude," he told the president, "we had better save our money."[15] When other State Department officials echoed that sentiment in public, the president admonished them. America was in a better position, he said, to use force in Europe than it had been in Asia, but because the potential enemy was much stronger in Europe, the chance of nuclear holocaust was much greater. Therefore, as he had with the Formosa threat, Eisenhower chose to wait in readiness to see what alternatives would develop. (Personally, he favored the idea of a four-power conference to discuss making Berlin into a so-called free city under the jurisdiction of the United Nations.) Once again, the wisdom of his patient judgment was confirmed. Having played out his ultimatum, Khrushchev finally showed his hand in March 1959 by agreeing to a conference of foreign ministers to discuss the Berlin issue. That meeting adjourned on May 27, the day the Russian ultimatum expired, so that the participants could attend the funeral of John Foster Dulles.

For President Eisenhower, it was a day of unspeakable sorrow. The secretary of state had resigned in mid April, when the gravity of his illness made it impossible for him to continue his duties. Loyally, the president had created a special advisory post for him, and the two men had discussed the question of a successor. Both acknowledged the particular abilities of General Alfred Gruenther, but Eisenhower did not think a soldier should hold that high civilian office as long as he himself was in the White House. Several high-level diplomats and other officials with whom the president had worked closely were considered. Only one of them knew everything that had gone on between the department and the White House: Undersecretary Christian Herter. Because Herter was physically disabled to some extent, Eisenhower at first doubted that he could do the traveling involved in the job. After doctors assured him that Herter was up to the effort required, the president announced the appointment, with marked concern for the feelings of John Foster Dulles.

While sharing his predecessor's view of the nation's proper attitude toward its allies and its enemies, Secretary Herter was notably more flexible about details than Dulles had been. Although he had the president's confidence, there was no intimate mutual understanding between them such as Dulles had enjoyed over the course of seven years. The old procedure of daily White House consultations between secretary and president continued, but now each meeting was monitored by at least one of the executive assistants. According to some observers, Dulles had been a veritable "right arm" but Herter was just an emissary. When the new secretary of state reported that the foreign ministers conference on Berlin was showing no signs of progress, the president again acted as his own chief diplomat.

While the Berlin crisis continued, Fred Koslov, a member of the Soviet hierarchy, arrived in the United States on an unofficial visit and met with Vice President Nixon in New York City. When Koslov invited Nixon to visit Moscow in the same unofficial capacity, Herter encouraged the president to have Koslov come to the White House. The amiable Russian assured Eisenhower that Nixon would be given "red carpet" treatment in Moscow, an unmentioned but obvious reference to the vice president's recent reception in South America. Because Nixon would not be going to the summit meeting, Eisenhower decided that this would be an opportunity for him to form his own impression of the Soviet leaders and the Russian people. Nixon would not, however, be speaking in an official diplomatic capacity while he was in Russia. Eisenhower also asked his brother Milton to accompany the Nixons, perhaps to demonstrate his own personal interest. The visit went smoothly in spite of a running debate between the vice president and Khrushchev on the relative merits of their two countries. The Russians may have counted on this frank discussion to secure an invitation for Khrushchev to come to the United States.

The possibility of such a visit had been the subject of conversations between Eisenhower and Dulles late in 1958. The secretary was certain that the Russians would merely exploit it for propaganda purposes and advised the president not to waste the "capital" in his "bank account" of world prestige. But Eisenhower thought that an exchange of visits would be a simple and safe alternative to a summit meeting. He also hoped that the visits would provide him with the opportunity to make one last effort toward international understanding before he left office. Just before Koslov's visit, therefore, he had pursued the possibility in a conversation with another member of the Soviet Presidium, Anastas Mikoyan. The Nixon visit was thus Eisenhower's cautious testing of the idea of an exchange of official visits. In July 1959, the president personally initiated correspondence on the subject directly with Khrushchev and sent Undersecretary of State Robert Murphy to Moscow. Murphy was instructed to offer an invitation only if he was assured that there were signs of progress in the Soviet response to American proposals for the summit agenda, but instead he let the invitation slip out. The Russians accepted it with an alacrity that was most unusual for them. As Eisenhower saw it, Murphy's blunder had committed him to receive Khrushchev without the *quid pro quo* of any Russian commitment on settlement of the Berlin issue. Greatly angered by having his plan thus upset, Eisenhower lectured his assistants on the relationship between tactics and consequences. Had Dulles still been in charge, he felt, such a situation would never have occurred.

Nevertheless, Eisenhower pressed forward into personal diplomacy by abandoning the consideration with which Dulles had been obsessed: the matter of "spending" his prestige. Such conceits, the president decided now, must not detract from the task of discovering a route to peace. "I think any President that refused finally to use the last atom of prestige," he explained to newsmen in August, "or the last atom of his energy . . . to do this discovery if it is possible to discover, then I think he indeed ought to be condemned by the American people."[16]

Just before Khrushchev's arrival in the United States, the president took a quick trip—his first jet flight—to England, France, and West Germany to assure the heads of those countries that no deals would be made with the Russian visitor. After his return, his doubts about the Russians convinced him that the visit should be confined to merely ceremonial exercises. He was in one of his dark moods as he discussed the itinerary with his advisers. Khrushchev, he insisted, should see Americans doing what they ordinarily did in cities and suburbs, on farms and in factories; even traffic jams and the ongoing steel strike could serve notice that the United States was an affluent, mobile, and unregimented society. Moreover, Eisenhower did not want official politeness to be interpreted as a sign of weakness. Many Americans, unaware of their president's private misgivings about the visit, considered the invitation to be an expression of Eisenhower's personal warmth. A few, however, feared that it was a capitulation to the Communists, and some local officials who could not reconcile the event with Cold War propaganda announced that they would not welcome the visitor. So that no provocations might occur, Eisenhower asked Ambassador Lodge to act as guide and veritable bodyguard for Khrushchev during the cross-country segment of his visit.

Never the soul of tact, Nikita Khrushchev arrived in the world's largest turbojet, gave the president a replica of Russia's latest space success, a moon satellite, and delivered remarks that sounded boastful and condescending. As he traveled across the nation, he acted as if he had come to teach Americans instead of learning from them. His presence aroused little more than curiosity, however, and the crowds who watched him being driven into their communities generally stared in silence. Eisenhower praised such restraint as normal under the circumstances and set the tone for his countrymen by behaving with unusually stiff politeness toward his guest.

When Khrushchev returned to Washington, D.C., he was in a remarkably mellow mood, a change that encouraged the president to reconsider his own plans and invite his guest to Camp David. In discussions there, however, Eisenhower had to cut off wrangling between the premier and the vice president and had to endure Khrushchev's belligerency; nevertheless, certain progress was made. Repeatedly, Eisenhower guided the conversations back to the questions of Germany, disarmament, unpaid lend-lease credits, and future cultural exchanges. Khrushchev impulsively issued several more ultimatums, but finally waxed cordial and even exuberant. When he agreed that the president's topics would be included on the summit agenda, however, he said that he did not want the concession publicized. That and other details of his behavior convinced Eisenhower that the Russian was worried about his watchful Kremlin colleagues. At the conclusion of the meeting, an innocuous joint statement was devised and issued. At the White House, press secretary Hagerty gave solemn assurances that no nation's freedom had been surrendered in the talks. Although the president would make no public statement about his impressions of Khrushchev, privately he was relieved to get the visitor out of his hair. Later, he informed his cabinet members that although the Soviets were talking more suavely and politely, there was no reason to assume that they had abandoned their efforts to dominate the world.

Eisenhower and Khrushchev agreed that the president's return visit would be postponed from that winter to the following summer. The interval gave Eisenhower the time he needed to undertake his greatest effort in personal diplomacy. His specific purpose, he announced, was to help end the Cold War stalemate by beginning conversations with the leaders of many nations. In doing so, he meant to show that the United States was not taken in by the Soviet Union's recent cordiality. He also wished to counter the widespread distrust of America's power and motives. In the months remaining to him as president, he explained at his news conference in December,

I decided to make an effort that no President ever was called on before to make. I do feel a compulsion to visit a number of countries and through them hoping to reach many others, and tell them exactly what I believe the United States is trying to do: that our basic aspiration is to search out methods by which peace in the world can be assured with justice for everybody. I want to prove that we are not aggressive, that we seek nobody's territories or possessions; we do not seek to violate anybody else's rights. We are simply trying to be a good partner in this business of searching for peace. . . .[17]

Contemporary observers explained the president's decision as evidence that he had finally freed himself from what they called the negative influence of John Foster Dulles. But Eisenhower's conduct, both as a diplomat and as a decision-maker, in the Lebanon, Quemoy, and Berlin crises showed that he was under no such influence during the last year Dulles was still in office. It may be said with greater accuracy that his decision to be his own diplomat was the natural, gradual outgrowth of the authority delineated by the congressional resolutions of 1955 and 1957. Although there was an Eisenhower Doctrine, Eisenhower was never doctrinnaire about applying it. As always, he searched for alternatives to the use of naked military force; troops, he insisted, could never win peace among equals.

Moreover, Eisenhower and Dulles had discussed the idea of presidential trips before the secretary resigned. Dulles probably viewed them as a better investment of "capital" from the president's "bank account" of prestige than a summit meeting would be. Indeed, because Dulles had been especially concerned during the last months of his life with Communist influence in nations from the Near East to India, Eisenhower now selected precisely that tier of countries to visit on the first of the trips. Instead of abandoning the diplomatic techniques employed during his first term, Eisenhower was adjusting to changing conditions. Apart from the loss of Dulles, he now faced increasing objections at home and new anti-American feelings abroad. Both developments, he believed, were the result of misunderstandings and, as such, could be discussed candidly.

During the course of seven years in office, the president had found no surer weapon for peace than his own abilities. In 1945, after giving up the responsibilities of a soldier, he had assumed the role of a teacher as he talked to Americans about his judgment of war and peace. Now, as the responsibilities of the presidency were coming to an end, he intended to resume that task on a far greater scale. This time, he would talk to a class of world leaders, trusting that the dissemination of understanding would lay the foundation for peace.

9

★★★★★

BEYOND HIS GRASP

Dwight Eisenhower was buoyed by several hopes as he began his last year in the presidency. His response to the Berlin crisis had elicited a surprising expression of Russian receptivity to East-West discussions. His two essays in personal diplomacy overseas had created at least a mood of international amity that might serve as a legacy to the next man in the White House. At home, his stern teachings about federal restraint in fiscal and administrative commitments held the attention of the public if not of the Democratic Congress. Along with many Americans, Eisenhower still read "active" to mean a spending and interfering government. Preventing any such change would be the final service he could render to the Republican party and to the nation, and he looked forward to that last battle "full of drive, enthusiasm, and a desire to attack on all fronts."[1]

Before the end of his final year in office, however, Eisenhower's hopes were overtaken by events. Some of these were developments beyond his control; others were beyond his grasp—that is, they were situations he failed to shape to his own ends. Since the beginning of his second term, the nation's self-congratulatory mood had turned to increasing dissatisfaction in the midst of apparent affluence. As is customary, discontent eventually focused on the party in power. Instead of producing order and new freedom, critics claimed, the administration's policies of self-restraint had only cast the inequities of American life into sharper relief. Problems that had earlier been the subject of jeremiads by a few intellectuals now became everybody's concern in that election year. Did a "power elite" run the nation's economy, unchallenged if not actually assisted by the Republicans? Had the appearance of unity at home and abroad been secured by ignoring realities or by glossing over naked force with rhetoric about "free enterprise" and the "free world"? However adequate gradualism had been during the early 1950s, was it now outdated by new demands and new alignments? And in every case, was man nearing seventy, the oldest president since Andrew Jackson, able to judge these critical issues competently?

Even Eisenhower's military expertise came under fire early in 1960. The defense budget he sent to Congress asked for a total appropriation of over $40 billion, yet he insisted as always that increased mutual security programs and new weaponry outlays should be funded within the principle of fiscal responsibility. Congress responded to the budget request with a double-barreled proposal to cut overseas aid funds and increase expenditures for special weapons. The Joint Chiefs of Staff exercised their recently granted prerogative by testifying that the amount earmarked for defense was too small, and that an additional $1.6 billion would be needed before the end of 1961. Many Americans, already puzzled by the highly technical nature of armaments, were further stunned and confused when Eisenhower cancelled orders for the new B-70 bomber, reduced American forces in Europe by thirty thousand men at the height of the Berlin crisis, and was reportedly going to remove the Sixth Fleet from the Mediterranean.

Unable to grill the president himself, congressional Democrats concentrated their scorn upon Thomas Gates, Jr., the new secretary of defense, when he appeared before their military affairs committees. They derided his assertion that the Soviet Union's lead in bombers was negligible; and when he explained his department's reasoning that American strength was adequate to meet the weapons Russia could build (rather than what it might intend to build), they denounced him as dangerously complaisant. As the election loomed, the cries of a "missile gap" (first heard at the time of Sputnik) were revived, and military experts took issue with the administration's estimates. Their remarks belied the president's earlier confidence that no military officer would discuss his personal views once a decision had been made by superiors. Some critics implied that certain as-yet-unspecified emergencies would require larger supplies of arms. General Maxwell Taylor, former chairman of the Joint Chiefs of Staff, warned that the administration's "uncertain trumpet" echoed the unpreparedness of past times. Eisenhower

170

was distressed not only by Taylor's charges but by his revelation of White House conversations.

Angered by the partisan and professional challenges to his own military competence, the president struggled to conceal his feelings as he answered newsmen's questions in February about the preparedness debate. "I'm always a little bit amazed about this business of catching up," he said. "What you want is enough, a thing that is adequate. A deterrent has no added power, once it has become completely adequate for compelling the respect of any potential opponent. . . . money itself will [not] bring you . . . any quicker development." The nation's massive armaments had kept potential aggressors at bay for seven years and were, he implied, clearly adequate to handle sudden emergencies. The cornerstone of defense, Eisenhower continued, was not spectacular special weapons (a reference to Maxwell Taylor's proposals), it was steady work. Abashed by his opponents' accusations, the president denied that he was trying to thwart the will of Congress. The legislators were sometimes unable to see beyond momentary crises, he said, and unable to keep America's larger international role in view. As for the military experts, the commander-in-chief's understanding exceeded the "parochial viewpoint" of "everybody . . . all over the place" who claimed that "the bosses know nothing" about the subject. He especially resented the partisan criticisms. "If anybody —anybody—believes that I have deliberately misled the American people, I'd like to tell him to his face what I think about him. This is a charge that I think is despicable. . . ." At an earlier news conference he had remarked, "I am obviously running for nothing. . . . I want only my country to be strong, to be safe, and to have a feeling of confidence among its people so that they can go about their business. . . . I have done the best I can, and I am doing it with one idea in mind only—America."[2]

During the early months of 1960, few citizens could fairly doubt the adequacy of Eisenhower's grasp of international affairs, but by mid year another series of shocks greatly damaged his credibility in the public's view. As he prepared for the long-delayed summit meeting in Paris, Americans generally expected that he would handle the Russians effectively. He told the nation that he did not expect the Soviet leaders to abandon their customary bluster and intransigeance, but at least the participants could talk together without becoming mutually abusive. Just as the administration had issued assurances prior to the Geneva meeting in 1955, it now emphasized that the president would not bargain away the West's true interests. In recent months, however, Secretary Herter and Vice President Nixon had delivered hard-line speeches about Communist threats to world peace. Their remarks seemed to cast doubts on the chance for any sincere progress at the summit. Moreover, the United States had marked the stalemate in disarmament talks by announcing that it would resume nuclear testing in the near future.

The Russians were reportedly apprehensive. What would be the impact of Eisenhower's appearance on television during his visit to the Soviet Union later in the summer? What was the real purpose of the Herter-Nixon speeches and the resumption of testing? Just two weeks before the Paris summit meeting was to open, the Russians thought they had the answers when Soviet aircraft brought down an American plane that had been flying over their territory.

The Soviet Union had detected surveillance flights over their country within a year after Eisenhower approved the CIA's U-2 program in late 1955. Russian planes had shot down other flights that came close to the borders of Communist countries, but the U-2 flew too high and too fast for interception. Bulganin nevertheless promised Charles Bohlen, the U.S. ambassador, that sooner or later one of the spy planes would be brought down. But, as Secretary Dulles predicted, the premier did not officially protest the flights because he would then be admitting that Russian planes were incapable of stopping them.

The surveillance program was losing its invisibility at home as well. In September 1958, an American reconnaissance plane had been shot down near the Turkish border. Questioned by the press corps, Eisenhower said only that the flight was part of a program he had personally established a few years before. Several newspapers subsequently learned more details about the U-2 flights but did not print their findings. When the CIA opened its vast new quarters in Langley, Virginia, in 1959, it was clear to the public that the agency's activities had mushroomed. Eisenhower considered making a public announcement about the existence of the reconnaissance flights at about that time. The U-2 aircraft was, in fact, outmoded and had gathered as much information as it could. Disclosure of the flights, he thought, would serve to underscore the need for "open skies" and mutual disarmament. When he asked his national security advisers to discuss termination of the U-2 flights, however, secretaries Herter and Gates argued for their continuation. Each time the president brought up the matter thereafter, the decision was postponed. He therefore decided not to make any announcement himself. (Perhaps this was the second "mistake" Eisenhower later admitted he had made while in the White House.)

The last of a series of U-2 flights which had been already scheduled took off from a U.S. base in Pakistan and was forced down by Soviet aircraft on May 1, 1960. Its electronic instruments were intact, and its pilot, Francis Gary Powers, was alive. Informed only of the fact that a spy plane had been captured, American ambassador Bohlen was stunned at the obtuseness of the CIA's reasoning. They should have realized that dispatching such a flight on that particular date was particularly insulting: May 1 was a traditional day of national patriotic celebration.

The president's initial prediction about the consequences of the reconnaisance flights proved to be accurate. While he discussed the status of ready missiles with his military advisers, the State Department impulsively denied that any American aircraft was missing. At the same time, press secretary Hagerty remembered a cover story that had been decided on in 1955 and independently announced that the craft was really one of NASA's weather research planes. The Russians thereupon exposed both lies by exhibiting a photograph of the downed U-2 and by revealing that the pilot was alive. Surveying the sorry tangle of affairs, Eisenhower said to his son: "We're going to take a beating on this. And I'm the one, rightly, who is going to have to take the brunt."[3]

Rumors spread across Europe that the president, the State Department, and the Pentagon were in a panic. The American public's response to the news, however, was a mixture of pride and dismay. Some thought that the spy program was necessary in dealing with the wily Russians or that it was a clever means of preventing a nuclear Pearl Harbor, launched from behind the screen of the Paris summit meeting. Others were shocked to learn that the U.S. was engaged in peacetime spying, a despicable business which that generation associated with tyrannies. Thinking only of protecting Eisenhower's image, several White House advisers suggested that he point to some subordinate as the man responsible for the flights and then discharge him. The president, of course, would not indulge in such cowardly behavior. Nothing was gained by lying, he believed; moreover, he had to demonstrate that he was fully in charge of the policies of his administration. He admitted, therefore, that he had personally approved of the U-2 program, but he did not disclose the fact that he had cancelled any further flights. Although he placed the nation's armed forces on alert, he did not think that Russia would initiate a war for such a slight cause.

During the tense week following the U-2 incident, Eisenhower's mood darkened but his limited hopes for the Paris summit did not vanish altogether. As Prime Minister Macmillan put it, the president's attendance was even more vital now because he was the only one who could save the situation. As he prepared to go, Eisenhower told Republican senators that he did not expect Khrushchev would threaten or that the American position would be encumbered by the U-2 incident. Indeed, the Russian leader had made no objection when told that the president might leave the meeting early and have Vice President Nixon remain in his stead. But when Eisenhower arrived in Paris, Macmillan and President de Gaulle of France told him that Nikita Khrushchev wanted an American apology for the violation of Soviet territory. Eisenhower replied that further discussion of the U-2 affair would have to be set aside if the conference was to proceed to its business.

Secretary Herter had drafted a truculent speech for him to use at the opening session, but Eisenhower rejected it. When the meeting convened he shook hands with Khrushchev and agreed that the Russian should have the floor first. While Khrushchev's ensuing tirade mounted in vehemence, the president's neck and bald head turned ever darker shades of red. Eisenhower must apologize, must punish the men who had conducted the U-2 program, the Russian demanded. His anger was more than official. The aggressor, he pointed out, was a man who had a few months before acted like his friend and had been given true friendship in return, only to betray it in such a shocking manner. In order to show his own steadfastness by contrast, Khrushchev stated that he was willing to make one more effort to continue discussions.

Eisenhower's reply was calm. He announced that the U-2 flights over Russian territory were now suspended, and then he went on to proposals for the conference. De Gaulle who was presiding as host, returned to the subject at hand by announcing in his opening remarks that Russian spy planes had been passing over France for years. Anxiously, Macmillan suggested a brief adjournment to permit the antagonists to talk alone, but Khrushchev left the hall, returned to his quarters, and repeated his charges to the international press corps.

Visibly depressed, President Eisenhower returned to the American embassy where he was greeted with applause and a steak cookout. In the company of his closest aides, he cursed Khrushchev for his behavior but concluded that it was an act put on to impress the men back at the Kremlin. Herter suggested that an American apology might be exchanged for a Russian promise not to take any unilateral action on the Berlin issue. As always, Eisenhower rejected deals of any kind. He replied that he would not be the only one to apologize for what others besides the United States were doing. Moreover, the matter could not be a proper counterweight in further discussions. Even if the conference continued on that basis, the Kremlin bosses would not carry out agreements made under such circumstances. These considerations were shortly rendered academic: Khrushchev suddenly left Paris. When he reached home, he continued to rage and threatened to use rockets against countries that permitted American air bases on their territory. Once again showing his personal wounds, Khrushchev asserted that the man he had once thought of as a wise statesman was, in fact, not good enough to hold a job higher than superintendent of schools.

The president refreshed himself with a stopover in Lisbon and then returned to Washington. At the airport, two hundred thousand cheering citizens gave him a reception reminiscent of those he had received when he returned home from Europe in 1945. Over the next few days, Eisenhower's rating in the Gallup Poll shot up by 6 percent. Confident that he judged the Russian response correctly, the president cancelled the military alert and addressed the nation. Everything that had happened in the preceding weeks, he said, proved that the Russians had used the U-2 issue to destroy the summit meeting. They had known of the flights for years, Eisenhower asserted; indeed Khrushchev had told Lodge during the premier's visit to America that he periodically read the reports of the CIA director. Yet Khrushchev made no reference to the surveillance program when he met with Eisenhower at Camp David. Soviet hypocrisy was further revealed, the president claimed, by the fact that thousands of Russian spies conducted daily espionage operations in the United States. Nevertheless, Eisenhower thought that diplomatic contact with the Soviet Union must continue and referred to Khrushchev's statement of willingness to make one more effort. But he said that the most desirable solution to the problem of spying would be United Nations supervision of all surveillance programs. The proposal for mutual inspection made at Geneva in 1955 was still open.

In retrospect, Eisenhower's behavior in the aftermath of the U-2 affair was surprisingly rigid. He had not been sanguine about the summit, but he was counting on the meeting to accomplish at least as much—both for the international image of the United States and for the image of his administration at home—as Geneva had five years before. Whether or not he gave political advantage any priority in his reasoning, such an accomplishment would surely bolster Republican chances in the coming election and serve as a legacy to his successor. Moreover, in view of his overwhelming desire to use his personal prestige in search of peace, his adamant rejection of any conciliatory move toward Khrushchev was certainly out of character. He could have made some acceptable gesture, especially after the Russian leader had pointedly referred to his personal respect for the president. The move could have been couched in the terms he had had in mind when considering public disclosure of the U-2 flights six months earlier: i.e., that the incident dramatically underscored the pressing need for disarmament. His conclusion that nothing more could come out of the conference belied his fundamental belief in patient deliberation and his knowledge that the mere passage of time could bring solutions to the fore. Although he was certain that Khrushchev had acted under pressure from the Kremlin, Eisenhower did not practice his favorite preachment about leaving a door open when the other fellow found himself in a corner. Surely he could not justifiably view such a slight gesture as appeasement. Finally, the proposals contained in his speech to Americans after his return from Paris were nothing but warmed-over ideas, long rejected by the Soviet Union.

In July, the president further revealed the rigidity of his thinking when another American plane, an RB-47 flying from England, was shot down by Soviet aircraft near the Arctic Circle. The Russians did nothing more than issue a denunciation, a move that convinced Eisenhower and his advisers that the Russians merely wished to provoke the president to cancel his visit. Ignoring a second chance to make some strikingly imaginative gesture that would give his enormous leverage in the Soviet Union, Eisenhower did indeed cancel his plans. At a press conference soon after the RB-47 was shot down, he was in a noticeably testy mood. Reminded by a questioner that Senator Lyndon Johnson had pledged bipartisan support for the president on his return from Paris and asked if he had consulted with congressional leaders about his decision, Eisenhower replied: "If you know what you want to do, you get it done in a hurry."[4] That, he said, was the soldier's way of doing things.

Instead of going to Russia that summer, the president made a third search-for-peace trip, this one to the Far East. In his memoirs he wrote that he especially looked forward to visiting Japan in order to establish a relationship with the Japanese that would be as strong as the one the United States had with the English. But when Hagerty went to Japan to make arrangements for the visit, he was mobbed by protesters, shouting about the U-2 incident. Objections expressed by some Japanese in the ensuing weeks caused the government in Tokyo regretfully to withdraw its invitation on the grounds that it could not guarantee the president's safety. Therefore, Eisenhower flew to the Philippines and on to Formosa, where he talked with Chiang Kai-shek about the prospect of future wars like the Korean conflict in Southeast Asia. His last stop, in Korea, was overshadowed by the recent resignation of President Rhee, whose regime had been sustained by American aid for a decade.

The continuing deterioration of American prestige after the U-2 incident constituted a national security crisis, as Eisenhower saw it. He took, therefore, the uncharacteristic step of rattling weapons in America's arsenals to arouse attention at home and abroad. A wing of SAC bombers scheduled to be phased out would be retained, he told Congress. He also announced the successful firing of the Polaris submarine-based missile. Then, with the world's attention on him, he went to New York City in August to address the United Nations.

When Nikita Khrushchev indicated that he too would be in New York for the General Assembly's debate on disarmament, many observers wondered whether the two would get together to iron out their differences. Eisenhower's behavior during the preceding months, however, gave no grounds for such an expectation. It was unlikely that he himself would entertain the possibility of a meeting and even more doubtful that his advisers would suggest it to him. Yet he did meet with Marshal Josip Tito of Yugoslavia, Nasser of Egypt, and several leaders of new African nations before addressing the General Assembly. His speech once again showed the Wilsonian cast of his mind on matters of international justice. The United Nations, he said, should conduct a universal plebiscite in which every individual in the world would be given the opportunity freely and secretly to choose whether or not he wanted freedom. The idealism of the suggestion was so obviously undermined by the impossibility of its execution that some listeners wondered whether the president was sincere or senile. Later, Khrushchev gave a demonstration of even greater futility when he harangued the members about American aggression and then took off his shoe and pounded it on the desk with childish anger. That scene may have been provoked in part by his realization that no meeting with the president would take place; it certainly precluded any chance for talks thereafter. In private, Eisenhower called the Russian a liar and was prepared to refute his accusations if necessary before the UN. Secretary Herter, however, advised him to say nothing in public about the incident.

Any possibility of making a gesture toward Khrushchev was finally destroyed by a situation developing just ninety miles from the United States. On the island of Cuba, the tyrannical rule of Fulgencio Batista had been ended by Fidel Castro in 1959. Some prominent Democrats had impulsively described the young revolutionary as a new Bolívar, but Castro's actions soon belied his claim to speak for all Cubans. In a matter of months, he confiscated properties, imprisoned those who did not support his rule, and drove many others to seek refuge in nearby Florida. Although the first CIA reports from the island were maddenly inconclusive, Eisenhower noted, the State Department's intelligence agents revealed that Castro's entourage included Communists.

The president made up his own mind about Castro during his trip to Latin America at the beginning of 1960. The Cuban's lieutenants, he learned, were already in contact with leftist organizations in Panama, the Dominican Republic, and other nations. On returning to the White House, Eisenhower decided that Castro would have to be removed from power much as Arbenz had been displaced in Guatemala six years before—and for the same reasons. More diplomacy was called for in this case, however, because the United States could not appear to violate the spirit of the Organization of American States by exercising old-fashioned Yankee-dollar imperialism. Once again, the CIA offered a solution that it claimed would be effective yet not blatant: secret bases would be established in Guatemala with the assistance of the United Fruit Company; American military advisers would train Cuban exiles at those bases; the trainees would then invade their homeland and be joined by compatriots there in overthrowing the Communist-dominated regime. The president approved of the first two phases of the plan two weeks after he returned from Latin America. Referring to the third part, he warned the CIA that the force must be sufficient to see the invasion through to success because it would not be assisted by direct American intervention. Although still personally interested in the plan, he asked Vice President Nixon to oversee its progress.

Just as anti-American sentiment was gathering force in the wake of the U-2 incident, Castro embarked on an unmistakably belligerent course. The "madman," as Eisenhower referred to him in private, confiscated American properties and intimidated American residents in Cuba. Shortly after the collapse of the Paris summit

178

meeting, Russia announced that it would buy the bulk of the island's economic staple, sugar. Cuba also established trade relations with several other Communist countries in Europe. By the end of August, the CIA reported, large shipments of Communist-made arms were being landed on the island. Members of the National Security Council considered the possibility that Russia was also taking advantage of the situation by constructing a military base there in retaliation for the U-2 incident; the state department's intelligence agents did not think so.

The secret reports were not disclosed, of course, but Eisenhower thought that there was sufficient public evidence to reveal in general the dangerous nature of Cuba's policies. Aiming at world opinion, he therefore invoked the same corollary to the Monroe Doctrine that he had applied to Guatemala in 1954. The United States, he announced, would not permit the establishment of a Communist-dominated government in the hemisphere. He then called the National Security Council into session to examine alternatives to direct intervention. If economic sanctions were applied, he told NSC members, then OAS support would be essential and the cooperation of England, France, and Canada might also be necessary. He did not think that Castro could be provoked into doing anything serious enough to justify an American blockade; such an action would, of course, mean armed confrontation. Eisenhower was visibly relieved when the council agreed on a step far short of that action: the Congress would be asked to end U.S. imports of Cuban sugar.

Although the administration's Cuban policy was still one of moderation, it constituted a far more hypocritical departure from professed principles than did the intervention in Guatemala. In his State of the Union message to Congress in January 1960, Eisenhower had repeated his promise of 1953 and insisted that "the United States has no intention of interfering in the internal affairs of any nation." Glaring rhetorically at Russia he added: "We reject any attempt to impose . . . [a political] system . . . on any other peoples by force or subversion."[5] Now, a year later, as his second term was ending, there was widespread apprehension that the president would use armed intervention in Cuba to eject the Communists.

By this time, Castro had learned of the CIA's clandestine preparations. News of those activities also came to the attention of several Democrats in Congress, who at once demanded that the White House account for $13 million which they alleged had been used to support counterrevolutionary groups in Latin America. In a lengthy reply, Eisenhower asserted executive privilege and ordered his officials not to disclose any information. When he met newsmen at his next press conference, he declared that he would follow his own conscience in administering funds in Latin America. Castro chose that moment to announce that he would limit the number of Americans employed at the United States embassy in Havana. The move was obviously one more step in a calculated sequence leading to demands for the expulsion of all Americans from the island. Recognizing Castro's ultimate purpose, Eisenhower severed diplomatic relations with Cuba early in January 1961. A week later, the training of Cuban exiles in Guatemala was the topic of his last discussion with Allen Dulles and a State Department official. In effect, the administration was preparing to bolster rebellion in another country.

In late 1960, Eisenhower faced two other instances of Communist opportunism. One was Russia's economic and military aid to secessionists in the newly independent Congo. Apart from supporting the efforts of a United Nations mediation force there, the United States did not contemplate direct intervention. In its last months in office, the administration preferred instead to study the desirability of sending American aid to the Volta River project in nearby Ghana.

The other crisis was of greater moment. By April 1959, the Diem regime in South Vietnam had proved to be far less enlightened and able than Eisenhower had hoped. In a little noticed public speech, the president warned of the consequences of a "crumbling process" involving South Vietnam and nearby Laos. Collective action, he said, was the only alternative to "vastly increased outlays of money" and "larger drafts of our youth into the Military Establishment."[6] As the situation deteriorated, however, the president began considering the possibility of unilateral American intervention. Although the number of advisers to South Vietnam had not increased by the end of 1960, they now included top-level analysts who recommended a degree of American intervention that would necessitate the very outlays and drafts Eisenhower had warned against. In his own thoughts, however, the president viewed these recommendations as contingency plans not as commitments.

Eisenhower deeply regretted leaving these international problems to the next man in the White House, no matter who he might be. Greatly concerned with the consequences of both domestic and international policies, he took up the final task of his presidency: helping to ensure that his successor would be someone who would carry out the principles of the Republican administration. Although he privately advised Governor Rockefeller not to be a candidate, Eisenhower declined to play the role of king-maker. Instead, in conferences with party leaders, he pointed to the abilities of several young men, members of his executive team, and promised to fight to help any one of them obtain the nomination. He admitted that he had a personal preference, but he would not disclose it publicly.

In 1956, Eisenhower had told Vice President Nixon that he was the party's best hope for 1960. Two years later, he asked Nixon to say whether or not he would be a candidate for the presidential nomination. Doubtless recalling the embarrassment of 1956, Nixon immediately said that he would be a candidate. Early in 1960, however, Eisenhower contributed to widespread speculation when he listed a dozen men qualified for the presidency and put Nixon's name last. In doing so, Eisenhower merely wished to have the convention consider all available talents, not just the most familiar names. That intent accounted for the disappointment he expressed when Rockefeller rejected the possibility of accepting the vice presidential spot on the ticket. Eisenhower especially resented Rockefeller's inference that the vice presidency was still the dead-end job it had been before 1953.

The president was pleased with Nixon's nomination by the Republican convention that summer. He thought that Nixon was, like himself, basically conservative and dedicated to saving the moral fiber of America from the inroads of paternalism. He was also satisfied with the selection of Ambassador Henry Cabot Lodge as running mate. (Milton Eisenhower reportedly had worked behind the scenes to put Lodge in that slot, perhaps with the president's approval.) Two such professional politicians as Nixon and Lodge could take care of themselves very well, the president told newsmen at his next press conference. In order to express his personal interest in the campaign, however, he commented on Nixon's idea for a single term in office, coached him on phraseology and topics for speeches, sent him lists of speakers, and offered the services of White House staff members. Subsequently, one of these, Jerry Persons, was embarrassed to report that Nixon's headquarters had ignored the president's communications. Indeed, it was generally rumored that neither Nixon nor his managers considered the president an asset to their campaign. As they viewed it, the task of defending Eisenhower's record became especially burdensome after the collapse of the Paris summit meeting and the emergence of international crises in Latin America, Africa, and Southeast Asia. According to one report, an official at Nixon's campaign head-quarters privately remarked that they wanted nothing more from Eisenhower except for him to "handle Khrushchev at the UN and not let things blow up there."[7] For his part, the president intended his address at the UN that summer to help Nixon's campaign.

Just as the campaign got under way, the president unintentionally exasperated the Nixon men in responding to newsmen's questions. After the vice president declared his candidacy, reporters repeatedly asked Eisenhower for instances of Nixon's participation in the administration's policy decisions. In reply, the president simply reminded them that he himself was responsible for specific decisions. In the midst of so many current international problems, of course, Eisenhower's thoughts were not focused on such details of the past. When the question came again, he detected partisan purpose behind it and therefore repeated that the power of making ultimate decisions was the president's job. "We understand that . . ." a newsmagazine correspondent pressed him, "I just wondered if you could give us an example of a major idea of his that you had adopted in that role, as decider and final. . . ." Eisenhower, his patience exhausted, cut him off: "If you give me a week, I might think of one," he said, "I don't remember." Another reporter, recognizing that presidential forbearance was at an end, quickly pronounced the words that traditionally terminated press conferences: "Thank you, Mr. President."[8]

When the statement was printed, Republicans gritted their teeth and Democrats whooped with glee. Eisenhower was angry about getting caught in the newsman's trap, but even angrier about the way his remarks were interpreted. He was still grumbling about it years later when an interviewer reminded him of the incident: "No matter how many jobs I gave [Nixon]," he remembered, ". . . some would doubt that he was doing it on his own."[9] After that press conference gaffe, Eisenhower offered Nixon several friendly campaign suggestions. In one instance, he advised Nixon not to engage in televised debates with the Democratic presidential nominee, Senator John F. Kennedy. The "ins" should never take on the "outs" in a public debate, he argued. Moreover Kennedy would benefit from nationwide television exposure far more than the vice president. Finally, he pointed out that Nixon would not be able to use classified security information in his responses to various issues raised during the debates. In the president's opinion,

Nixon's subsequent performance in the debates with Kennedy confirmed these apprehensions.

Eisenhower was also disappointed that neither of the Republican candidates refuted the Democrats' charge that his administration had dangerously neglected the nation's defense forces or emphasized his fundamental yardstick of fiscal responsibility in dealing with that subject and with the problems of the domestic economy. After waiting impatiently for Nixon to use his help during the campaign, Eisenhower agreed to the vice president's request that he appeal to the independent voters of 1952 and 1956 in several speeches to be given late in the campaign. The president's activity was somewhat curbed by his wife's objections to any more strenuous activity, but it was also limited by his own scruples. In the few speeches he did make, Eisenhower's remarks were hardly those of a "fighting general," as many Republicans hoped they would be. In Chicago, for example, he hailed the "reformation" of the nation under his administration, credited the Republicans in Congress for their part in that achievement, and denounced the negativism of the Democrats.

In July, Eisenhower thought that Nixon's election was "a cinch." Reports from party officials in most states indicated a slight but sound margin of support for their presidential candidate. But by October, the party was in a desperate situation in Illinois and New York. Eisenhower urged Nixon and Lodge to go to New York and to work day and night. He himself made a video tape in support of Governor Rockefeller's reelection efforts. Just a week before the election, however, the president confessed, "I do not know what went wrong."[10] Nixon ran slightly ahead of the other Republicans in the balloting, but was narrowly defeated by Kennedy. Eisenhower was plunged into deep personal despair. His jaundiced view of politics and politicians was further confirmed by reports that voting frauds in Chicago and Texas and Nixon's failure to telephone the wife of imprisoned civil rights leader Martin Luther King, Jr., had deprived the vice president of victory by a margin of a few thousand votes. Eisenhower believed that the outcome was a closed matter, but he instructed Attorney General Rogers to make a report on the disputed returns because the issue would be important in the 1964 contest.

Eisenhower's personal hopes for continuity in foreign and domestic policies lay shattered. "All I've been trying to do for eight years has gone down the drain," he remarked to his son. Perhaps remembering the sober sense of duty that had compelled him to enter politics in 1951, he added: "I might just as well have been having fun."[11] Impulsively, he thought of meeting the vice president on his postelection return to Washington, D.C. John Eisenhower persuaded the president not to go, but went to the airport himself as a more appropriate gesture. When Nixon called, the president concurred in his feelings about voting irregularities, but urged him never to use the words "we were robbed" in public; if he did, the president warned, his political career would be finished.

The vice president had carried most of the states of the Far West, the Great Plains, and the Middle West, in part because of public confidence in Eisenhower's fiscal, farm, and resources policies. But the larger cities of all regions had not been the focus of the administration's programs, and it was the cities that swung every heavily populated state except California to the Democrats. Eisenhower's earlier inroads into the Democratic South were also substantially reduced, perhaps because of his civil rights policies. While Nixon repeatedly thanked Eisenhower for his campaign efforts, some Republicans bitterly blamed the president for the defeat. Because he had done all that had been asked of him, however, he rejected their charges with disdain. Indeed, his participation in the campaign, although limited, might very well have kept some states in the Republican column. Afterwards both Republicans and Democrats agreed that if Eisenhower had been a candidate for reelection, he would have won on popularity alone. The compliment was not appreciated at the White House; it reminded the president of the party's persistent tendency to ride his coattails. "I never went into any battle asking any other fellow to carry my flag," he growled several weeks after the election. "I carried my own flag."[12]

The final months of Eisenhower's presidency were gloomy ones. Burdened by international crises and domestic disappointments, he looked wan and shrunken, and his famous smile appeared less frequently and felicitously than before. He met with John Kennedy in two postelection conversations, finding him much better informed and more responsible than he had seemed as senator and candidate, and recommended to him the continuation of the nation's efforts to stop the spread of communism. The two men also made arrangements for the orderly transition to the incoming administration. Eisenhower's staff members were not impressed with Kennedy's advisers, but they conducted plans for the changeover with efficiency and without overt rancor.

During the final weeks of his term, President Eisenhower

made two recommendations that he hoped would serve as guides to policymakers and citizens as well. The first, which was submitted to Congress, was Milton Eisenhower's seven-year-long evaluation of the executive office. The tasks facing the man in the White House, the report argued, were of such daily complexity and such enormous consequence that he should have the assistance of an office manager, a planning coordinator, an associate executive for defense and foreign policy, and a first secretary to handle purely ceremonial obligations. Moreover, coordination of executive budgets with congressional appropriations warranted the immediate consideration of presidential authority to veto items in money bills. Finally, the Congress should renovate the way in which a president was nominated and elected to office.

This recommendation on reorganization attracted slight notice, but Eisenhower's other legacy aroused widespread surprise and approval. Five days before he left office, he delivered a farewell address in the spirit of George Washington, the man he so greatly admired. Like the original, Eisenhower's contained a warning that was to be quoted by the generations who came after him. In it, he returned to the theme of his second inaugural address: the domestic impact of America's commitments around the world. Defense programs, he had long observed, were invariably subject to the selfish desires of pressure groups. While wrestling with Pentagon budgets before and after World War II, he had frequently been appalled by the way in which industrial lobbies tended to protect existing or potential investments when contracting for production of supplies and weapons. The debates over defense programs during his second term had provided Eisenhower with several opportunities to voice his understanding of the interrelationship between private aggrandizement and national security. But he chose instead to drop occasional cryptic remarks such as his news conference comment that "obviously something besides the strict military needs of this country are coming to influence decisions" on the subject.[13] In 1952, Republicans had warned that a barracks economy would evolve out of the Democrats' hazardous foreign policy; in 1960, Eisenhower warned that crash programs in weaponry could only result in a militarized America.

Halfway through his second term, the president decided to refer to the subject in a last major speech. Speechwriter Malcolm Moos drafted the sentences that would be quoted more than any others President Eisenhower used:

This conjunction of an immense military establishment and a large arms industry is new in the American experience. The total influence—economic, political, even spiritual—is felt in every city, every State house, every office of the Federal government. . . . In the councils of government, we must guard against the acquisition of unwarranted influence, whether sought or unsought, by the military-industrial complex. The potential for the disastrous rise of misplaced power exists and will persist.[14]

Those words were followed by a reference that went almost unnoticed at the time, a similar warning about the influence of the nation's scientific elite. When the Farewell Address was delivered in January 1961, many Americans were surprised to hear a professional military man bracket the military with big business as potential enemies of the national interest. They also wondered why he had not injected that warning earlier into the continuing debate over an "adequate" defense program.

During those last weeks, the president discharged several other final tasks. He arranged for the transfer of his public and personal papers to the new Eisenhower Library at Abilene, Kansas. At the urging of his staff, he awarded the Medal of Freedom to members of his cabinet and other close advisers. When he met the press corps for the last time, Eisenhower talked about the highlights and personal disappointments of his tenure and expressed the hope that his grandchildren would live in a peaceful world where both responsibilities and privileges would strengthen them—not only intellectually and materially, but spiritually as well. He signed a last treaty, one for joint American-Canadian use of the Columbia River. At the last meeting of the Eisenhower cabinet, the members talked about the recent election results, and Nixon urged them to continue to aid their party either as candidates for office or in other ways. As the meeting adjourned, they gave the president a moving round of applause.

Dwight Eisenhower and John Kennedy made a striking contrast of age and youth as they rode down Pennsylvania Avenue toward the inaugural stands at the Capitol. Their conversation enroute was far more cordial than the grudging remarks Eisenhower had exchanged with Truman eight years before. If the applause from the crowds along the way seemed as much for the man leaving office as for the man coming in, that was surely the first time such a thing had happened in half a century. Eisenhower listened intently to Kennedy's inaugural address, perhaps gratified that it reiterated his own emphasis on the interdependence of nations and a determination to be strong in the search for peace. Kennedy's call for individual responsibility, sacrifice, and self-discipline as the fundamental prerequisites for America's policies at home and abroad bore a striking similarity to his own public addresses. After the ceremonies ended, Ike and Mamie attended a farewell party, given in their honor by Lewis Strauss, and then drove off to their own first home, the farm at Gettysburg.

Instead of becoming the influential elder statesman he hoped to be in retirement, Eisenhower soon became a virtual anachronism. He was so completely identified in the public mind with the tranquility and confidence of the 1950s that he seemed like a figure from the distant past as domestic turmoil and international distress wracked the nation during the 1960s. His infrequent public comments were still newsworthy, of course, but they commanded far less attention now. To no one's surprise, he deplored changes that seemed to be based on self-interest, self-indulgence, or moral laxity. Yet he also recognized that old ways of thinking about many problems were, in some cases, no longer adequate. He had once, for example, vehemently opposed any suggestion that government should violate the privacy of citizens by becoming involved in a program for birth control; by 1963 he was speaking publicly about the great need for planned parenthood.

Apart from restrained generalities, Eisenhower made no critical comments about the new administration. Privately, he expressed strong criticism when Kennedy precipitously dismantled the White House staff system and appointed his own brother to be attorney general. Eisenhower also sourly noted that the Democrats found no "missile gap" once they were in office. In a private speech, he lamented their decision to commit the nation's resources to a race with the Soviet Union for the first moon landing. Above all, he was appalled by the administration's adherence to the tenets of the "new economics" and the administration's cavalier spending of tax dollars. The media's ballyhoo of Kennedy charisma and the rhetoric of instant achievement were, of course, the very antitheses of Eisenhower's own personality and principles. Characteristically, he made an oblique public judgment of those claims, saying that Moses-like leadership could lead the nation out of the promised land just as easily as it could lead it to a golden future.

President Kennedy sought Eisenhower's counsel on several

occasions: the Bay of Pigs disaster, the meeting with Khrushchev in Vienna, and the Cuban missile crisis. Although the record of Eisenhower's views on those events is not yet available, he may well have considered the president's policy properly firm and ultimately realistic in each instance. After Kennedy's death, Eisenhower called on Lyndon Johnson and urged his long-time adversary to address Congress and the nation in a call for unity and cooperation. The new president did so and, in turn, urged Eisenhower to take a diplomatic assignment in Europe or Asia. The former president's doctors, however, advised against it.

Eisenhower watched the international scene with increasing apprehension but did not change the convictions he had held as president. His response to the deterioration of affairs in Southeast Asia was notably consistent. Adhering to his earlier analysis of that conflict, he urged the nation to sustain the stance that his administration had taken to meet the sequence of threats to peace. He also called on Americans to give bipartisan support to the administration's policy in Vietnam. President Johnson was somewhat puzzled by the vigor of Eisenhower's advocacy until Eisenhower told him that he did not want to add criticism to the heavy burden of responsibilities Johnson had to bear. The two men had shared in determining America's initial response to war in that area and were still in general accord about the U.S. commitment there. As Milton Eisenhower recalled it, that reasoning was "purely Eisenhoweresque": the Gulf of Tonkin incident had made the war *de facto* for the United States, and the full resources of the nation had to be used to attain absolute victory; withdrawal from Vietnam would not only endanger the security of the United States, but would also erode its credibility among the nations of the world.

Eisenhower received top-level information about the conflict from the Joint Chiefs of Staff. Because he knew that this material was only a fragment of the complex evaluations the president had to weigh and consider, he made no public judgment of the administration's decisions. In private, however, he noted that the Vietnam War was as militarily unorthodox as the Korean struggle had been and was just as impossible to win on the ground without air pursuit to hit the sources of troops and supplies across the borders. Whatever possible alternatives may have existed, Eisenhower believed that Johnson's decision to employ direct and massive intervention rendered further discussion of alternatives purely academic. The president's decision now had to be sustained unconditionally in order to ensure the outcome.

Eisenhower did not alter his evaluation of the matter even after the bitter stalemate in Vietnam engendered widespread criticism within the United States and throughout the world. Questioned about his views on the terrible civilian casualties of the war, the former president gave an unguarded response. The United States, he asserted, should take "any action to win." He was asked if that included using nuclear weapons. "I wouldn't exclude anything," he answered. "When you appeal to force to carry out the policies of America abroad, there is no court above you."[15] When the media duly reported that he advocated nuclear war in Vietnam, Eisenhower was understandably angered. He had rejected that strategy in Korea, in Indochina, and twice in Formosa. He still believed in first seeking all possible alternatives short of any kind of war. But his statement obviously rested on the premise that "the policies of America abroad" were good and unquestionable, an assessment not shared by many of his fellow citizens. The harshness of these off-the-cuff judgments not only cast doubt upon his own record, but also added to the unfavorable opinion of the military mind, held by an increasingly large number of Americans. Unfortunately he chose to join with another superannuated general, his old wartime comrade, Omar Bradley, in making a sadly unimpressive defense of America's military involvement in Vietnam in a nationwide television interview. Recalling the days of the second Formosa crisis, Eisenhower once again denounced dissent as an obstacle to bipartisan foreign policy. Dissent provided the Communists with contentious issues, he argued, and could thus affect possible peace negotiations; criticism thereby passed beyond honorable bounds and verged on treason.

The confusion of voices during the 1960s reminded Eisenhower of the national mood at the beginning of the 1950s. Once again preservation of the two-party system seemed to be fundamental to a national unity of purpose at home and abroad. His own opinions on America's divided response to international problems reflected his continuing consternation about the impotence of the Republican party. While his confidence in Nixon had not been shaken by the defeat in 1960, Eisenhower was still dismayed by the party's inability to win votes. After Republicans lost additional congressional seats in the 1962 election, the Old Guard faction reemerged while right-wing extremism spread, led by the appeals of the John Birch Society. Eisenhower called for a return to the political middle of the road, insisting that the phrase did not mean a position so weak as to be meaningless. "My definition of the political road," he told an interviewer, "is all of its usable surface. That is where the road is highest and where the traction is best and where you can bring the most people along with you, as contrasted with the ruts and ditches on the extreme sides."[16]

Along with many other Republicans, however, he greatly underestimated the attraction of Senator Barry Goldwater's supporters. One of these was the former president's brother Edgar, who arranged for a meeting between the two men. Eisenhower shared the senator's belief in governmental restraint and decentralization. But Goldwater's claims to military expertise, his attacks on Social Security and TVA, and his vote against the civil rights bill of 1964 were, in Eisenhower's opinion, wholly unrealistic. The meeting produced no concrete results. Indeed, it ended with a discomforting replay of the Jenner incident during the 1952 campaign, when Goldwater publicly exploited photographs taken of the two of them together and gave out a version of their discussion that forced Eisenhower to issue a correction.

Eisenhower sadly diminished his own potential usefulness in 1964 by refusing to support any one presidential candidate. When he talked about the qualifications of the ideal Republican nominee, some newspapermen guessed that he had Governor Rockefeller in mind. But, after moderating a high-level party conference in Pennsylvania, Eisenhower persuaded Governor William Scranton of that state to enter the race. When Scranton did so, however, Eisenhower declined to endorse him publicly. And in the meantime, Eisenhower reportedly was encouraging Henry Cabot Lodge to seek the nomination. All of these efforts merely confirmed the Goldwaterites' contempt. Referring to the alleged timidity of the Eisenhower administration in both domestic and foreign policies, they adopted the slogan, "A Choice Not an Echo." The phrase was both an inference that Eisenhower had merely continued the Democrats' programs and a thinly veiled slur on the possible presidential candidates who had served in his administration.

Eisenhower's neutrality was distinctly out of place at the bitterly contested Republican national convention that year. Greatly upset by intraparty strife over the nomination, he tried to emphasize impersonal issues. Unfortunately, this caused him to join in attacks on the media expressed by extremists at the convention. In view of the fact that he had always been well treated by the press, it was plainly an unfair criticism. Although he privately concluded that the nomination of Goldwater was the result of maneuverings by a selfish pressure group, he noted no similarities to the manner of his own selection in 1952. After Goldwater's overwhelming defeat in November, party managers ruefully admitted that there was some wisdom in Eisenhower's definition of middle-of-the-road politics. Nevertheless, they ignored his repeated suggestions for reform of convention and election procedures.

The political embarrassments of 1964, together with advancing age, caused Eisenhower to withdraw from active participation in Republican party councils. His only public comments about politics were made during the subsequent debates on the Vietnam War. As the presidential race loomed in 1968, he issued a sadly impotent warning: "I don't regard myself as a missionary, and I don't want to convert anybody. But if any Republican or Democrat suggests that we pull out of Vietnam and turn our backs on the . . . Americans who died in the cause of freedom there, they will have me to contend with. That's one of the few things that would start me off on a series of stump speeches across the nation."[17] Finally abandoning his customary neutrality, Eisenhower issued an early endorsement of Richard Nixon as the man best qualified by training to be president. When Nixon received the party's nomination, he eagerly called upon Republicans to "win this one for Ike."

Apart from limited participation in public affairs, Eisenhower devoted much of his retirement to writing. He was able to elucidate the record of his actions as president more fully than any of his predecessors. A few months after his return to Gettysburg in 1961 he began writing an account based on files of personal papers and on his excellent memory. John Eisenhower and several other members of the old White House staff prepared topical outlines for him, but he wrote out his own emphases on the yellow pads he favored. His history was not broad in scope; it was confined to the decisions he had made. Because of that focus, because of his use of background information prepared by his assistants, and because of the guarded prose style he always employed, the results read like the "federal prose" he personally loathed

"My place in history," Eisenhower had said after the collapse of the Paris summit, "will be decided by historians. . . . And I don't think I will be around to differ with them."[18] In fact, however, he lived to run the gauntlet of historians' judgments and became greatly embittered by that ordeal. While he was writing his own account, there was an outpouring of criticism about his administration. These attacks had begun during the 1958 debate over defense programs and had coincided with the appearance of memoirs written by Eisenhower's former associates in war and peace. At that time, he had wryly predicted that he would probably be attacked by everybody who could write a book. One person eminently qualified to write a book was Emmet Hughes, his former speechwriter. The relationship between the two men during the presidential years had been one of mutual respect and confidentiality. In 1959, Hughes had told Eisenhower of his intention to write a differing judgment of the administration's policies. The president had encouraged him to do so, but took special care to correct Hughes's mistaken assumption that the spirit and direction of the administration's foreign policy had been determined by the State Department rather than by Eisenhower. In his book, pointedly titled *Ordeal of Power: A Political Memoir of the Eisenhower Years*, however, Hughes was sharply critical of Dulles's influence on the president's foreign policy. Angered by the author's treatment, Eisenhower later described Hughes as no more than "a part-time word carpenter" claiming expertise after brief service as a secondary member of the White House staff. "The idea of a man like that criticizing Dulles," he told an interviewer, "is like trying to get some ignorant African soldier to criticize Napoleon."[19]

A second judgment was rendered against Eisenhower at about the same time. Asked to rate the presidents of the United States according to their performance in office, a group of American historians described him as merely average. The estimate irritated Eisenhower because he believed that the problems his administration had faced were far more than average and that his careful handling of all of them had been most judicious. He was especially disgruntled by the techniques historians sometimes used to arrive at what he considered premature judgments. Instead of interviewing him personally (as historian Herbert Feis had done in 1960), another historian had now apparently taken a single speech, speculated loosely on its meaning, and consulted neither Eisenhower nor any of his close advisers before publishing his allegations. He felt that such scholars were far more interested in the decision-making process than in the quality of the decisions made. "They don't know a damn thing about such matters," he concluded.[20]

Eisenhower, however, did not write his memoirs in order to engage in contentious debate with these detractors. His purpose was simply to point out "a lesson learned, a principle proved, or an old truth emphasized."[21] Unfortunately, the two massive volumes, *Mandate for Change, 1953–1956*, published in November 1963, and *Waging Peace, 1956–1961*, published two years later, appeared against the backdrop of tragic events in America. Uncharitable reviewers found them impersonal, officious, and less-than-candid reconstructions. Some pundits and scholars used the occasion of their publication to claim that the Eisenhower administration had, by its passivity, contributed to the economic and social dislocations of the 1960s and had burdened the nation with continuing crises by its commitments throughout the world. These strained interpretations disgusted Eisenhower. "It makes me sick when I see sometimes how history is written," he later told an interviewer. "It's a hell of a condemnation of American common sense."[22]

In several magazine articles and interviews, he curtly dismissed the most persistent myth about his presidency: the claim that he was not in charge of his own policies. He also encouraged his former associates to contribute their recollections and papers to the Eisenhower Library so that responsible scholars could use them to evaluate his administration. But he abandoned all contentiousness in 1967 when he produced his last book. *At Ease: Stories I Tell to Friends* was an anecdotal evocation of his youth and military life, notably felicitous both in style and content. Because it offered an impression of the "Ike" most Americans wanted to remember, it was far better received by reviewers and readers than the memoirs had been.

Eisenhower also found private joys during those years of retirement. Congress restored his five-star rank and provided Mamie with a generous pension. No one seemed to care how often he went to the golf course now, he wryly noted; and when he made his first hole-in-one at the age of seventy-seven, he pronounced it the thrill of a lifetime. He attended the twentieth anniversary of D-Day and the fiftieth reunion of his West Point class and joined in two nostalgic get-togethers with his brothers. He spoke at the dedication of the George C. Marshall Library, the Harry S. Truman Library, and then at the opening of his own library and museum in Abilene. With Mamie he finally took the slow voyage to Europe he had always wanted to make; he later returned to England for the funeral of his great friend Winston Churchill. Eisenhower was greatly pleased when former White House aide Andrew Goodpaster assumed his old post as commander of the NATO forces and when his own son John was appointed ambassador to Belgium. Illness prevented him from personally participating in the happiest of all occasions: the marriage of his grandson David to Richard Nixon's daughter.

Unable to attend the Republican National Convention in 1968, Eisenhower sent a video-taped greeting to the delegates. His image on the television screen was shockingly frail, and the effort proved too much for him. Having already suffered two heart attacks in 1965, he was felled by a massive stroke the day after his greeting was shown at the convention. While the election campaign was underway that October, President Johnson proclaimed a "Salute-to-Eisenhower Week." The name surely provoked mixed feeling in a nation torn by civil disorders and dissent. Some voters who had been barely ten years old during the Eisenhower administration were quite unaware that he had ever appealed to young people and had encouraged them to participate in making the American system work. Some were vaguely hostile to him, both as the hero of their parents' generation and as a figure of the military establishment who supported the war in Vietnam. Few of them could recall that he had been the first to warn of "larger drafts of our youth into the Military Establishment" and the first to point to the ominous influence of the "military-industrial complex." But there were many older Americans who thought of Dwight Eisenhower as a link with their own past: the hero who had led them in the crusade in Europe and who later exhorted them to enhance material prosperity with spiritual confidence at home.

For his part, the former president respected both young and old Americans and refused to be pessimistic about the nation's future. He expressed these great hopes to President Nixon and members of the new cabinet when they came to visit him in the hospital. Although physically weary, Eisenhower continued to write and talk about all the things his country had given him. The pocket of his dressing robe carried a familiar inscription: "Feeling great again," but he was losing weight and soon had to undergo painful surgery for a recurrence of intestinal blockage. He flashed the famous grin and gave the thumbs-up sign as he was wheeled into the operating room, but afterwards, for the first time anyone could remember, he seemed to despair. Evangelist Billy Graham talked with him about spiritual things, and Eisenhower listened to a nurse read from the Bible, perhaps remembering the nightly readings in that small house in Abilene years before. To Mamie, he declared his lifelong love of family and country and thanked Milton for his loyal counsel over the years. When the Army Band serenaded him with old marching tunes on his seventy-eighth birthday, he waved his five-star flag from the window in appreciation. For a time, he thought of things that he still wanted to say to the American people, but finally he resigned himself to the end. Near midday on March 28, 1969, he softly gave his last command: "I want to go; God take me."[23]

In retrospect, the American people were mistaken in their initial assumption that a military leader would enlarge the power of the presidency. In that office, Eisenhower deliberately avoided the opportunities of heroic stance. In contrast to his Democratic predecessors, he preferred to restrain and even conceal his personality, while displaying his strength of character. Although he received overwhelming electoral support, he was unable to extend his triumphs to his adopted party's candidates. The self-effacement and preoccupation with scrupulous behavior that had earned him the highest positions in war and peace precluded conduct traditionally considered essential to administrative success. Indeed, he became a chief executive who did not even lead the federal government. His position was not intractable: he could carry the day in order to secure a measure about which he felt strongly, or to rally international cooperation, or to halt an aggressor. But in most cases he relied on allies and partisans with slighter perceptions and less talent. To have done otherwise, of course, would have belied his conviction that government was people, not just one man.

Eisenhower's flexibility was fixed on a rigid base. His defense of principles in which his countrymen believed took the form of merely holding fast to those principles. If his rhetorical definition of the nation's interest sounded nebulous, he himself recognized it precisely in each issue, each problem, each crisis. But personal certitudes proved to be uncertain in application. His belief in the separation of governmental powers could not by itself provide a base for effective domestic programs. And while his maintenance of the "shield" sustained the dominance of the Western nations in the world, he declined to deal with the wider implications of an American peace. The policies with which he had seized the day during his first term were not enlarged to meet the changes at home and abroad that occurred during his second term. At the outset, Dwight Eisenhower had shown that the presidency was not beyond his reach. By the end of his tenure, however, he had demonstrated that its great storehouse of powers was surely beyond his grasp.

Notes

CHAPTER 1

1. Dwight D. Eisenhower (hereafter, DDE) to a friend, Apr. 3, 1943, cited in Kevin McCann, *Man From Abilene* (Garden City, N.Y.: Doubleday, 1952), p. 110.
2. DDE to Milton Eisenhower, Oct. 18, 1947, cited in ibid., p. 143.
3. Excerpts from speeches, 1949, cited in ibid., pp. 178–90.
4. DDE to Edward Bermingham, Jan. 7, 1952, box 1, Bermingham–Eisenhower Correspondence File, Dwight D. Eisenhower Library, Abilene, Kansas.
5. DDE, oral history transcript OH 11 (unedited version):19, Eisenhower Library.
6. Sept. 27, 1948, cited in Peter Lyon, *Eisenhower: Portrait of the Hero* (Boston: Little, Brown, 1974), p. 390.
7. Dec. 21, 1951, cited in Henry Cabot Lodge, Jr., *The Storm Has Many Eyes: A Personal Narrative* (New York: W. W. Norton, 1973), p. 89.
8. Diary Memorandum, Nov. 1959, box 29, Papers as President File, Eisenhower Library.
9. Slogan and comment by Taft, cited in James T. Patterson, *Mr. Republican: A Biography of Robert A. Taft* (Boston: Houghton Mifflin, 1972), pp. 519, 536.
10. Merriman Smith, oral history transcript OH 160:13, 10.
11. News conference remarks, Dec. 10, 1958, *Public Papers of the Presidents of the United States* (Washington, D.C.: GPO, 1960–61), p. 856. (These annual volumes are hereafter cited as *Public Papers.*)
12. Richard M. Nixon, *Six Crises* (Garden City, N.Y.: Doubleday, 1962), p. 123.
13. Photograph, *Time*, Nov. 17, 1952, p. 21.
14. Robert Smylie to W. Smylie, Nov. 13, 1952, Personal File, Robert E. Smylie Papers, Idaho State Archives, Boise; R. Heminger to Walt Horan, Feb. 26, 1953, box 553, Political File, Walter F. Horan Papers, Washington State University Library, Pullman.

CHAPTER 2

1. News conference remarks, Mar. 21, 1956, *Public Papers*, p. 338.
2. News conference remarks, July 22, 1953, ibid., p. 502.
3. True D. Morse, oral history transcript OH 40, part 1, p. 25; DDE, news conference remarks, Feb. 17, 1953, *Public Papers*, p. 52; DDE, remarks at the governors' conference, Seattle, Wash., Aug. 4, 1953, ibid., p. 542.
4. News conference remarks, July 22, 1953, *Public Papers*, p. 503.
5. James Hagerty, oral history transcript OH 91, part 1, p. 56.
6. David Kendall, oral history transcript OH 142; Henry McPhee, oral history transcript OH 145; Donald Paarlberg, oral history transcript OH 52.
7. Mamie Eisenhower, "My Mem-

ories of Ike," *Reader's Digest,* Feb. 1970, p. 72.

8. John S. D. Eisenhower, *Strictly Personal* (Garden City, N.Y.: Doubleday, 1974), p. 172.

9. News conference remarks, May 13, 1955, *Public Papers,* p. 367.

10. McPhee, oral history transcript OH 145:35.

11. News conference remarks, Apr. 9, 1958, *Public Papers,* p. 303.

12. Kendall, oral history transcript OH 142:37.

13. Paarlberg, ibid. OH 52, part 1/1, p. 13.

14. DDE to Earl Warren, June 21, 1957, box 14, Papers as President File.

15. See, for example, DDE to Walter Williams, undersecretary of commerce designate, Jan. 13, 1953, Eisenhower folder, box 2, Williams Papers, University of Washington Library, Seattle.

16. Paarlberg, oral history transcript OH 52, part 1/1, p. 62.

17. Ibid., p. 65.

18. News conference remarks, Aug. 21, 1957, *Public Papers,* p. 617.

19. DDE to Everett E. Hazlett, July 21, 1953, box 2, Papers as President File.

20. News conference remarks, Mar. 30, 1955, *Public Papers,* p. 381.

21. Remarks at the Dartmouth College commencement, Hanover, N.H., June 14, 1953, ibid., p. 412.

CHAPTER 3

1. Remarks upon lighting the national Christmas tree, Dec. 24, 1953, *Public Papers,* p. 859.

2. Remarks to the Business Advisory Council of the Department of Commerce, Mar. 18, 1953, ibid., p. 102.

3. DDE, oral history transcript, OH 11:102.

4. DDE to Mark W. Clement, Dec. 21, 1957, box 17, Papers as President File.

5. DDE cited by Bryce Harlow in Emmet Hughes, *The Living Presidency* (New York: Coward, McCann and Geoghegan, 1973), p. 342.

6. Diary memorandum, Jan. 18, 1954, box 3, Papers as President File.

7. DDE, oral history transcript OH 11:72.

8. Ibid.

9. News conference remarks, May 11, 1955, *Public Papers,* p. 859.

10. DDE to Robert Woodruff, July 20, 1959, box 27, Papers as President File.

11. Hagerty diary, Mar. 1, 1954, James Hagerty Papers, Eisenhower Library.

12. Gary W. Reichard, *The Reaffirmation of Republicanism: Eisenhower and the Eighty-Third Congress* (Knoxville: University of Tennessee Press, 1975), p. 67.

13. Statement made after reviewing the case of Julius and Ethel Rosenberg, Feb. 11, 1953, *Public Papers,* p. 40.

14. DDE to William E. Robinson, July 27, 1953, box 2, Papers as President File.

15. Remarks at the Dartmouth College commencement, June 14, 1953, *Public Papers,* p. 415.

16. Address at the Sixth National Assembly of United Church Women, Atlantic City, N.J., Oct. 6, 1953, ibid., p. 639.

17. DDE, oral history transcript, OH 14 (unedited version):12.

18. DDE to Herbert Brownell, Jr., Mar. 29, 1954, box 2, Papers as President File.

19. News conference remarks, Nov. 4, 1953, Public Papers, p. 738.

20. Hagerty diary, Dec. 7, 1954, Hagerty Papers.

CHAPTER 4

1. News conference remarks, Dec. 2, 1953, *Public Papers*, p. 802.
2. Address, "The Chance for Peace," delivered before the American Society of Newspaper Editors, Apr. 16, 1953, ibid., p. 180.
3. Patterson, *Mr. Republican*, pp. 590–91.
4. David Halberstam, *The Best and the Brightest* (New York: Random House, 1972), p. 732.
5. DDE to Everett E. Hazlett, July 22, 1957, box 14, Papers as President File.
6. DDE to Nancy Bierce, Apr. 4, 1960, box 31, ibid.
7. Address, "The Chance for Peace," Apr. 16, 1953, *Public Papers*, p. 182.
8. Dec. 8, 1953, ibid., pp. 820, 822.
9. News conference remarks, Jan. 12, 1955, ibid., p. 59.
10. News conference remarks, Feb. 10, 1959, ibid., p. 168.
11. News conference remarks, Apr. 29, 1959, ibid., p. 346.
12. Diary memorandum, Jan. 24, 1958, box 17, Papers as President File.
13. DDE, *Waging Peace, 1956–1961* (Garden City, N.Y.: Doubleday, 1965), p. 223.
14. DDE, oral history transcript OH 14:10.
15. Robert J. Donovan, *Eisenhower: The Inside Story* (New York: Macmillan, 1956), p. 129.
16. Radio and television address announcing the signing of the Korean armistice, July 26, 1953, *Public Papers*, p. 521.
17. Hagerty diary, June 24, 1954, Hagerty Papers.
18. DDE, oral history transcript OH 11:65.
19. News conference remarks, May 8, 1957, *Public Papers*, p. 321.
20. News conference remarks, Feb. 12, 1955, ibid., p. 236.
21. News conference remarks, Mar. 16, 1955, ibid., p. 332.
22. News conference remarks, June 8, 1955, ibid., p. 587.
23. Address at the graduation ceremonies, United States Military Academy, West Point, N.Y., June 7, 1955, ibid., p. 575.
24. July 16, 1955, ibid., p. 707.
25. July 18, 1955, ibid., p. 710.
26. Charles F. Bohlen, *Witness to History, 1929–1969* (New York: W. W. Norton, 1973), p. 384; John Eisenhower, *Strictly Personal*, p. 178.

CHAPTER 5

1. News conference remarks, July 6, 1955, *Public Papers*, p. 674.
2. Notes on a conversation with Lucius Clay, Nov. 20, 1954, diary memorandum, box 3, Papers as President File.
3. Remarks at a breakfast meeting of Republican state chairmen, Denver, Colo., Sept. 10, 1955, *Public Papers*, p. 814.
4. Ibid., p. 816.
5. Sept. 12, 1955, diary memorandum, box 10, Papers as President File.
6. Hagerty, oral history transcript OH 91, part 4, p. 289.
7. DDE, *Waging Peace*, p. 546.
8. DDE, oral history transcript OH 14:44.
9. Hagerty diary, Dec. 13, 1955, Hagerty Papers.
10. Ibid.
11. DDE, *Mandate for Change, 1953–1956* (Garden City, N.Y.: Doubleday, 1963), p. 573.
12. Lucius Clay, oral history transcript OH 56, part 2, p. 108; Hagerty, ibid. OH 91, part 4, p. 309.
13. Sherman Adams, *Firsthand Report: The Story of the Eisenhower Administration* (New York: Harper and Brothers, 1961), p. 220.

14. News conference remarks, Feb. 29, 1956, *Public Papers*, pp. 265–66.
15. News conference remarks, Mar. 7, 1956, ibid., p. 287; DDE, oral history transcript OH 11:91.
16. DDE, oral history transcript OH 11:91.
17. Address at a rally in Cleveland, Ohio, Oct. 1, 1956, *Public Papers*, p. 833.
18. DDE, oral history transcript OH 14:31.
19. News conference remarks, Sept. 11, 1956, *Public Papers*, pp. 757, 761.
20. Emmet Hughes, *The Ordeal of Power: A Political Memoir of the Eisenhower Years* (New York: Atheneum, 1963), pp. 212–13.
21. Kennett Love, *Suez: The Twice-Fought War* (New York: Mc-Graw-Hill, 1969), p. 503.
22. Radio and television address, Oct. 31, 1956, *Public Papers*, p. 1066.
23. DDE to Alfred Greunther, Nov. 2, 1956, box 18, Papers as President File.
24. Ibid.
25. Arthur Larson, *The President Nobody Knew* (New York: Charles Scribner's Sons, 1968), p. 9.
26. News conference remarks, Nov. 14, 1956, *Public Papers*, p. 1108.

CHAPTER 6

1. State of the Union Message, Feb. 2, 1953, *Public Papers*, p. 30.
2. Radio address, Aug. 6, 1953, ibid., p. 556.
3. Ralph Cake, oral history transcript OH 111, part 2, p. 38.
4. Hughes, *Ordeal of Power*, p. 201.
5. May 19, 1953, *Public Papers*, p. 304.
6. News conference remarks, May 19, 1954, ibid., p. 491.
7. Ibid., pp. 491–92.
8. E. Frederick Morrow, oral history transcript OH 92, part 1, p. 103.
9. Cabinet secretariat, Chronological File, Mar. 9, 1956, Eisenhower Library.
10. News conference remarks, May 15, 1957, *Public Papers*, p. 357.
11. June 24, 1957, ibid., p. 494.
12. DDE to Everett E. Hazlett, June 24, 1957, box 14, Papers as President File.
13. DDE to Everett E. Hazlett, July 22, 1957, ibid.
14. News conference remarks, July 17, 1956, *Public Papers*, p. 546.
15. Diary memorandum, Oct. 1957, box 15, Papers as President File.
16. Ibid.
17. Sept. 14, 1957, *Public Papers*, p. 674.
18. DDE, oral history transcript OH 11:82.
19. News conference remarks, Mar. 23, 1955, *Public Papers*, p. 357.
20. Feb. 26, 1959, box 24, Papers as President File.

CHAPTER 7

1. Radio and television address, Nov. 7, 1957, *Public Papers*, pp. 793, 799.
2. Radio and television address, "Our Future Security," Nov. 13, 1957, ibid., p. 815.
3. Dec. 30, 1957, box 5, Hagerty Papers.
4. Anonymous flyer, Washington State Federation of Labor Papers, University of Washington Library, Seattle.
5. Address at the Economic Mobilization Conference of the American Management Association, May 20, 1958, *Public Papers*, p. 416.
6. Jan. 9, 1958, ibid., p. 10.
7. Jan. 21, 1958, box 18, Papers as President File.

8. News conference remarks, Apr. 9, 1958, *Public Papers*, p. 298; address to the American Society of Newspaper Editors and the international press, Apr. 17, 1958, ibid., p. 329.
9. Remarks at the fourth annual National Republican Women's Conference, Mar. 18, 1958, ibid., p. 221.
10. Ibid., p. 222.
11. News conference remarks, Apr. 2, 1958, ibid., p. 266.
12. News conference remarks, Feb. 26, 1958, ibid., p. 186.
13. Hagerty, oral history transcript OH 91, part 4, p. 275.
14. Diary memorandum, Sept. 17, 1958, box 21, Papers as President File.
15. DDE to Robert Cutler, cited in Cutler, *No Time for Rest* (Boston: Little, Brown, 1965), p. 409.
16. Jack Anderson, "The Little Watergate," *Seattle Post-Intelligencer*, May 20, 1973.
17. Address at a dinner in honor of the Republican members of Congress, May 6, 1958, *Public Papers*, p. 384.
18. Remarks to the Republican National Committee, May 6, 1958, ibid., p. 651.
19. Radio and television address, Oct. 20, 1958, ibid., pp. 758–60.
20. Hagerty, oral history transcript OH 91, part 6, p. 486.
21. Dec. 29, 1959, box 5, Hagerty Papers.
22. News conference remarks, June 17, 1959, *Public Papers*, p. 466.
23. DDE, *Waging Peace*, p. 388.
24. Remarks at a cabinet meeting, Nov. 27, 1959, box 29, Papers as President File.

CHAPTER 8

1. News conference remarks, Apr. 30, 1958, *Public Papers*, p. 358.
2. News conference remarks, May 28, 1958, ibid., p. 436.
3. News conference remarks, June 18, 1958, ibid., p. 487.
4. DDE, *Waging Peace*, p. 519.
5. Cutler, *No Time for Rest*, p. 519.
6. Harold Macmillan, *Riding the Storm* (New York: Harper & Row, 1971), p. 512.
7. Radio and television address, Sept. 11, 1958, *Public Papers*, pp. 698, 700.
8. DDE, oral history transcript OH 11:52.
9. DDE to Green, Oct. 5, 1958, *Public Papers*, p. 725.
10. DDE, *Waging Peace*, p. 339.
11. News conference remarks, Mar. 11, 1959, *Public Papers*, pp. 244–45.
12. John Eisenhower, *Strictly Personal*, p. 228.
13. DDE, *Waging Peace*, p. 342.
14. Hagerty, oral history transcript OH 91, part 3, p. 194.
15. DDE, *Waging Peace*, p. 353.
16. News conference remarks, Aug. 25, 1959, *Public Papers*, p. 593.
17. News conference remarks, Dec. 2, 1959, ibid., pp. 786–87.

CHAPTER 9

1. Hagerty to Thomas E. Dewey, Jan. 7, 1960, box 8, Hagerty Papers.
2. News conference remarks, Feb. 3, 17, 1960, *Public Papers*, pp. 145, 198–99.
3. John Eisenhower, *Strictly Personal*, p. 271.
4. News conference remarks, July 13, 1960, *Public Papers*, p. 525.
5. Jan. 7, 1960, ibid., p. 5.
6. Address at Gettysburg College convocation, Gettysburg, Pa., Apr. 4, 1959, ibid., p. 313.
7. Theodore E. White, *The Making of the President, 1960* (New York: Atheneum, 1961), p. 309.

8. News conference remarks, Aug. 24, 1960, *Public Papers*, pp. 657–58.
9. DDE, oral history transcript OH 11:89.
10. DDE to Barry Goldwater and Gerald Ford, Oct. 29, 1960, box 34, Papers as President File.
11. John Eisenhower, *Strictly Personal*, p. 285.
12. Smith, oral history transcript 160: 43.
13. News conference remarks, June 3, 1959, *Public Papers*, p. 432.
14. Radio and television address, Jan. 17, 1961, ibid., p. 1038.
15. *New York Times*, Oct. 14, 1967, p. 3.
16. Norman Cousins, *Present Tense: An American Editor's Odyssey* (New York: McGraw-Hill, 1967), p. 559.
17. Lyon, *Portrait of the Hero*, pp. 847–48.
18. News conference remarks, July 6, 1960, *Public Papers*, p. 553.
19. DDE, oral history transcript OH 11:113.
20. Ibid., p. 105.
21. DDE, *Waging Peace*, Preface.
22. DDE, oral history transcript OH 11:89.
23. John Eisenhower, *Strictly Personal*, p. 336.

Bibliographical Essay

SELECTED SOURCES

The papers of Dwight D. Eisenhower occupy more than a mile of shelf space at the Eisenhower Library in Abilene, Kansas. In addition to the vast official file, there is a large personal file containing diary memoranda and lengthy letters written to the president's friends both in and out of the federal government. While this group is important, it does not provide short-cuts to understanding the topics discussed therein. Scholars should first examine the official file, the records of members of the White House staff and the cabinet, and the records and papers of many of the men and women who served on presidential commissions and committees. These collections are supplemented by oral history interviews with dozens of persons associated with the Eisenhower administration. A guide to all of these sources is available from the director of the Dwight D. Eisenhower Library, Abilene, Kansas 67410.

The most accessible source of Eisenhower's official statements are the eight annual volumes of the on-going compilation, *Public Papers of the Presidents of the United States* (Washington, D.C.: GPO, 1960–61). In addition, selected documents, accompanied by useful introductions, appear in Robert L. Branyan and Lawrence H. Larson, eds., *The Eisenhower Administration, 1953–1961: A Documentary History*, 2 vols. (New York: Random House, 1971). Available at larger libraries are two comprehensive reference guides: Ralph J. Shoemaker, *The President's Words: An Index*, 7 vols. (Louisville: E. and R. Shoemaker, 1954–61); Robert Vexler, ed., *Dwight D. Eisenhower, 1890–1969, Chronology, Documents, Bibliographical Aids* (Dobbs Ferry, N.Y.: Oceana Publications, 1970). Margaret L. Stapleton's *The Truman and Eisenhower Years, 1945–1960: A Selective Bibliography* (Metuchen, N.J.: Scarecrow, 1973) is conveniently organized by topic and subtopic.

Eisenhower's memoir in two volumes, *Mandate for Change, 1953–1956*, and *Waging Peace, 1956–1961* (Garden City, N.Y.: Doubleday, 1963, 1965), reflects the rectitude of the official papers that he used as sources for his narrative. It does not reveal his strong personal views nor address many aspects of the subjects discussed. Far more revelatory of the man's character and personality is his last book, *At Ease: Stories I Tell to Friends* (Garden City, N.Y.: Doubleday, 1967). His prepresidential experiences and views may be found in Alfred Chandler, Jr., and Stephan Ambrose, eds., *The Papers of Dwight D. Eisenhower: The War Years* (Baltimore: Johns Hopkins University Press, 1970). Selections from those papers appear in Joseph Hobbs, ed., *"Dear General": Eisenhower's Wartime Letters to Marshall* (Baltimore: Johns Hopkins University Press, 1971). There are excerpts from Eisenhower's public remarks and private correspondence during the period between the end of World War II and his election as president in Kevin McCann, *Man from Abilene* (Garden City, N.Y.: Doubleday, 1952) and in Rudolph L. Trevenfels, ed., *Eisenhower Speaks* (New York: Farrar, Straus, 1948). At the Eisenhower Library are copies of articles he wrote and transcripts of interviews he gave during his postpresidential years. These statements recall the people and events of his tenure and present his retrospective views of the presidency.

Few of the men who worked under Eisenhower wrote or published their memoirs. One exception is a selection of George Humphrey's writings published as *The Basic Papers of George E. Humphrey, Secretary of the Treasury, 1953–1957* (Cleveland: Western Reserve Historical Society, 1965). Robert Gray, who held several positions on the White House staff, described that organization in *Eighty Acres under Glass* (Garden City, N.Y.: Doubleday, 1962). Another staff member, E. Frederick Murrow, offered a more personal view in *Black Man in the White House: A Diary of the Eisenhower Years by the Administrative Officer for Special Projects* (New York: Coward-McCann, 1963). Robert Cutler, secretary to the NSC, wrote a worshipful impression of working with the president in *No Time for Rest* (Boston: Little, Brown, 1965). Sherman Adams's *Firsthand Report: The Story of the Eisenhower Administration* (New York: Harper and Brothers, 1961) is an anecdotal outline that does not deal with many administrative matters and implies greater influence than other sources indicate. Milton Eisenhower's *The President Is Calling* (Garden City, N.Y.: Doubleday, 1974) presents a guarded and fragmentary account of his relationship with his brother; John S. D. Eisenhower's *Strictly Personal* (Garden City, N.Y.: Doubleday, 1974) is far more candid about his own, less important position during the last few years of the administration. Of the members of Eisenhower's cabinet, only Ezra Benson published a memoir, *Cross Fire: The Eight Years*

With Eisenhower (Garden City, N.Y.: Doubleday, 1962), a work that reflects the righteous convictions he shared with the president. Richard Nixon described his association with Eisenhower in *Six Crises* (Garden City, N.Y.: Doubleday, 1962). Henry Cabot Lodge, Jr., discussed his role in the 1952 campaign to persuade Eisenhower to become a candidate in *The Storm Has Many Eyes: A Personal Narrative* (New York: W. W. Norton, 1973) and his service with the administration in *As It Was: An Inside View of Politics and Power in the '50s and '60s* (New York: W. W. Norton, 1976).

Two books appeared too late for quotation in the present work. The first is George B. Kistiakowsky's *A Scientist at the White House: A Private Diary of Eisenhower's Special Assistant for Science and Technology* (Cambridge: Harvard University Press, 1976); it provides a far more candid and expressive account of working with Eisenhower than Lewis L. Strauss's *Men and Decisions* (Garden City, N.Y.: Doubleday, 1962). The second is *The Memoirs of Earl Warren* (Garden City, N.Y.: Doubleday, 1977). Instead of an exploration of his strained relationship with the president, Warren merely inserts a few denigrating anecdotes.

Robert J. Donovan's *Eisenhower: The Inside Story* (New York: Macmillan, 1956) is the remarkable transcript of the cabinet in session during the first years of the administration; and Merriman Smith's *Meet Mr. Eisenhower* and *A President's Odyssey* (New York: Harper and Brothers, 1956, 1961) are close-up views of Eisenhower by the dean of White House correspondents during the 1950s. Vignettes of Eisenhower in intimate social gatherings are offered in Cyrus L. Sulzberger's *A Long Row of Candles* and *The Last of the Giants* (New York: Macmillan, 1969, 1970). The 1960 edition of George Allen's *Presidents Who Have Known Me* (New York: Simon and Schuster) contains an added chapter on Eisenhower at work and play.

THE CYCLE OF EVALUATIONS

The first assessments of the Eisenhower presidency were made on the basis of his public record, before the end of his first term in office. They began with a series of articles by Charles Murphy in *Fortune* magazine: "The Eisenhower White House," July 1953, p. 75; "The Eisenhower Shift," January 1956, p. 82; "The Budget and Eisenhower," July 1957, pp. 96–99; and "The White House Since Sputnik," January 1958, pp. 98–101. In 1956, Merlo Pusey drew a courtly portrait in *Eisenhower the President* (New York: Macmillan). Richard Rovere's columns in *The New Yorker*, however, were more widely read; collected first in *Affairs of State: The Eisenhower Years* (New York: Farrar, Straus and Cudahy, 1956) and later in *The American Establishment* (New York: Harcourt, Brace and World, 1962), these pieces offered faint praise of Eisenhower as the beneficiary of events rather than their director. It should be noted that Rovere found no reason to change the doubts he had first formed in 1948; he saw little of Eisenhower during the 1952 campaign, and he never went to the White House during the presidential years. Punditry was also Marquis Child's only claim to understanding when he wrote *Eisenhower—Captive Hero: A Critical Study of the General and the President* (New York: Harcourt, Brace, 1958) during the period of public disenchantments in the second term. Perhaps the most widely read assessment was Richard Neustadt's *Presidential Power: The Politics of Leadership* (New York: John Wiley and Sons, 1960); primarily an account of the "battle of the budget," it showed the president as passive to the point of negligence and scrupulous to the point of impotence. Along with C. Wright Mills's strident *The Power Elite* (New York: Oxford University Press, 1956), Neustadt's book was used by some Democrats as campaign literature in 1960.

The first retrospective view, Emmet Hughes's *The Ordeal of Power: A Political Memoir of the Eisenhower Years* (New York: Atheneum, 1963), transcribed lengthy private comments by the president (although Hughes's limited duties in the White House made them suspect) and assumed that those comments were indicative of self-doubt and timidity, although they were obviously examples of the Eisenhower "act." Additional episodes from Hughes's speech-writing days appeared in a later essay, *The Living Presidency* (New York: Coward, McCann and Geoghegan, 1973). During the 1960s, liberal and conservative polemicists tried to sweep the former president into the dusty corners of history. He was a favorite butt for their cleverly vicious sneers in the pages of the *New Republic* as well as the *National Review*; and he was portrayed as a "conscious" tool of communism in *The Politician*— written, privately printed, and surreptitiously circulated by Robert Welch, president of the John Birch Society, in 1963.

The first group of more scholarly studies concluded that the Eisenhower administration had not met the nation's needs with competence or understanding. The best of these monographs are William R. Willoughby's *The St. Lawrence Waterway: A Study in*

Politics and Diplomacy (Madison: University of Wisconsin Press, 1961) and Aaron Wildavsky's *Dixon-Yates: A Study in Power Politics* (New Haven: Yale University Press, 1962). On the other hand, John W. Anderson's *Eisenhower, Brownell and the Congress* (University, Ala.: University of Alabama Press, 1964) is neither substantial nor accurate. David A. Frier's *Conflict of Interest in the Eisenhower Administration* (Ames: Iowa State University Press, 1969) relies almost entirely on liberal newspapers and magazines.

The passage of half a dozen years of presidential performances prompted journalist Murray Kempton to have second thoughts about his earlier judgments; and in "The Underestimation of Dwight D. Eisenhower" (*Esquire*, September 1967, p. 108), he started a period of reassessment by pointing up his subject's tactic of counterfeiting his true feelings. Arthur Larson, former assistant to the president, expanded on the workings of Eisenhower's self-restraint in *The President Nobody Knew* (New York: Charles Scribner's Sons, 1968). One of the most useful insights into Eisenhower's personality was historian William A. Williams's analogy of the hesitant but inexorable tide, mentioned in "Officers and Gentlemen" (*New York Review of Books*, May 6, 1971, p. 6). By that time even such irascible pundits as Gary Wills and I. F. Stone were finding complimentary things to say. Rovere, however, looked over their recantations in "Eisenhower Revisited: A Political Genius? A Brilliant Man?" (*New York Times Magazine*, February 7, 1971, p. 6) and reiterated his original views.

Studies of the American presidency published between 1965 and 1975 continued to rely on Adams, Hughes, and Neustadt and reasoned inductively about Eisenhower. The most notable exceptions are the more original essays by Arthur M. Schlesinger, Jr., and Henry Fairlie. The former's explanation of the rise of *The Imperial Presidency* (Boston: Houghton Mifflin, 1973) depicts Eisenhower's assertion of executive privilege as a source for his successors' abuse of that power. But Fairlie's *The Kennedy Promise: The Politics of Expectation* (Garden City, N.Y.: Doubleday, 1972) favorably contrasted Eisenhower's "drums" with Kennedy's "trumpets." The old myths were, nevertheless, still believed and still taught. In Paul Murphy's *The Constitution in Crisis Times, 1918–1969* (New York: Harper & Row, 1972), a volume in the prestigious New American Nation Series, Eisenhower is described as having no desire to strike out and initiate new approaches to government. Most amazingly, Murphy maintained that Eisenhower had only minimal concern for constitutional matters. "Eisenhower's Year," a prefatory chapter in

William O'Neill's paperback, *Coming Apart: An Informal History of America in the 1960's* (Chicago: Quadrangle, 1971), replaced the old caricature of the president as boob with a new one portraying him as Machiavelli.

The president's record was examined objectively for the first time some twenty years after he was first elected. Herbert Parmet's *Eisenhower and the American Crusade* (New York: Macmillan, 1972) argues that Eisenhower's accomplishments fell far short of his intentions at home and abroad, but does not adequately cover the sequence of crises in both areas that stalemated the administration during the second term. Two years after Parmet's work, Peter Lyon offered *Eisenhower: Portrait of the Hero* (Boston: Little, Brown, 1974); based upon additional sources and rich in relevant detail, this large volume is, nevertheless, marred by the author's impatience with Eisenhower's deliberative nature. Lyon underscored the contrast between what he called the "private Eisenhower" and the "public Eisenhower" but did not attempt to analyze the president's reasoning to account for the apparent difference between those two images. The secondary sources on which Charles C. Alexander heavily relied in writing *Holding the Line: The Eisenhower Era, 1952–1961* (Bloomington: Indiana University Press, 1975) are not solid enough or sound enough to sustain his thesis concerning the establishment, loss, and resurgence of an Eisenhower "equilibrium." The book is, however, a well-written introduction to the issues and interests of American life during those eight years.

By 1975, when primary sources became available at the Eisenhower Library and in other depositories, scholars began to put together the in-depth studies that will be the building blocks for evaluations of greater scope. One of these is Gary W. Reichard's *The Reaffirmation of Republicanism: Eisenhower and the Eighty-Third Congress* (Knoxville: University of Tennessee Press, 1975). Basing his narrative on quantitative analysis as well as on manuscript collections, Reichard substantiated the president's successful dealings with legislators of both parties and also offered data and details that will certainly stimulate other studies in legislative history and biography. Gary T. Schwartz traced one of the president's favorite programs in an extended article, "Urban Freeways and the Interstate System" (*Southern California Law Review* 49, no. 3 [March 1976]:406–513). The first assessment of Republican agricultural policy is Edward L. and Frederick H. Schapsmeir's *Ezra Taft Benson and the Politics of Agriculture: The Eisenhower*

Years (Danville, Conn.: Interstate Printers and Publishers, 1975).

While the historiography of the Eisenhower presidency seems to have come at least half circle, the specific theme of his conduct of foreign policy has not yet budged. Assessments must rely on the official documents published in *American Foreign Policy, 1950–1960*, 7 vols. (Washington, D.C.: GPO, 1957–64). Because of national security, access to essential materials in Washington, D.C., and elsewhere will remain restricted for many years. The complexities of diplomacy and the technicalities of weaponry have kept the field relatively free of the pundits who judged Eisenhower's domestic policies. But scholars have generally been critical in their evaluations.

John Gellin and K. H. Silvent early recognized "Ambiguities in Guatemala" (*Foreign Affairs* 34 [April 1956]:469–82), as did Philip B. Taylor, Jr., "The Guatemala Affair: A Critique of United States Foreign Policy" (*American Political Science Review* 50, no. 3 [September 1956]:787–806). Even before Suez, Norman Graebner's *The New Isolationism: A Study in Politics and Foreign Policy since 1950* (New York: Ronald Press, 1956) concluded that the Eisenhower administration was a continuation, not a corrective, of the Republican party's ultranationalist assault on Truman–Acheson foreign policy. M. A. Fitzsimmons was the first to analyze Middle East policy in "The Suez Crisis and the Containment Policy" (*Review of Politics* 19 [October 1957]:421–45). The debate over defense policy during Eisenhower's second term engendered many critiques; foremost among them are Maxwell Taylor's *An Uncertain Trumpet* (New York: Harper & Row, 1960); Emmet Hughes's *America the Vincible: A Brief Inquiry* (Garden City, N.Y.: Doubleday, 1959) and Albert Wohlsetter's "The Delicate Balance of Terror" (*Foreign Affairs* 37 [January 1959]:211–34). Walt Rostow summarized the thrust of Republican foreign policy near the end of the Eisenhower administration in *The United States in the World Arena: An Examination in Recent History* (New York: Harper & Row, 1960). When more primary sources became available, Kennett Love interviewed the former president for his comprehensive history, *Suez: The Twice-Fought War* (New York: McGraw-Hill, 1969); Elmer Plischke evaluated "Eisenhower's Correspondence Diplomacy with the Kremlin: A Case Study in Soviet Diplomatics" (*Journal of Politics* 30 [February 1968]:137–59); and Roy E. Licklider put "The Missile Gap Controversy" in perspective (*Political Science Quarterly* 58 [December 1970]:600–615). By that time, Eisenhower's role in the nation's involvement in Vietnam was questioned after the publication (in several formats) of "The Pentagon Papers" in 1971. The best brief presentation of the administration's deliberations on weaponry and disarmament policies is Charles S. Maier's introduction, "Science, Politics and Defense in the Eisenhower Era," in Kistiakowsky's *A Scientist at the White House*.

The relationship between the president and his secretary of state was examined in a dozen studies, ranging from Herman Finer's condemnatory *Dulles over Suez* (Chicago: Quadrangle, 1964) to Michael A. Guhin's admiring *John Foster Dulles: A Statesman and His Times* (New York: Columbia University Press, 1972)—the first to be based on the Dulles Papers. Neither of these authors examined that relationship as fully as Townsend Hoopes, *The Devil and John Foster Dulles: The Diplomacy of the Eisenhower Era* (Boston: Little, Brown, 1973). Because Hoopes did not use the materials at the Eisenhower Library, and because he respectfully employed the testimony of Hughes and of Harold Macmillan, in *Tides of Fortune* and *Riding the Storm* (New York: Harper & Row, 1969, 1971), he decided that Dulles was the conceptual fount, the prime mover, and the sole keeper of the keys in the foreign policy of the Eisenhower administration.

FOR FURTHER STUDY

There are obviously many more questions than answers concerning the Eisenhower presidency. Future scholars will undoubtedly take up the most important topics and events in the future and will, one hopes, include in their findings some consideration of the intent and execution of the president's policies. Whatever their theme, all of them must deal with the matter of continuity. As an example, in my *Dams, Parks, and Politics: Resource Development and Preservation in the Truman-Eisenhower Era* (Lexington: University Press of Kentucky, 1973) I found that the politics and materialism in the federal bureaucracy persisted both before and after the so-called mandate for change, despite the rhetoric of both parties. To what extent were other programs essentially an extension of policies devised by the preceding administration? A second question that confronts students of Eisenhower's presidency is the problem of his "watchfulness" as recommendations were translated into law. A case in point is the contrast between his concern for civil rights legislation and his apparent acquiescence in the termination of Indian reservations, a matter that also involved the social disruption and federal coercion that he abhorred. Can the difference in degree of interest be ascribed to the influence of his advisers?

Perhaps every researcher must eventually come back to the members of the Eisenhower team. It would be useful to know more about their education and background and their continuing associations with persons in and out of government. To what extent were the usual motivations of opportunity and status altered by a distinct sense of gratitude and respect for the president? The contributions of men like C. D. Jackson, Arthur Burns, F.ed Seaton, and Milton Eisenhower should especially be measured and described.

Other questions for future scholars bear on those subjects in which Eisenhower took a personal interest. Did his professed concern for states' rights elicit from governors any greater initiative in problem-solving or were state and local leaders preoccupied with political advantages for themselves? Similarly, did the administration's solicitude for business enable local enterprisers to take the initiative in housing, transportation, and resource development? Was the president's appeal to young people and to women as participants in the political process repaid with votes? Were his teachings about self-discipline and self-reliance dissipated by the materialistic prosperity ascribed to his administration? Each of these inquiries is relevant, of course, to the fact that many who led the protests of the 1960s came to maturity while Eisenhower was in the White House. Perhaps it is not wise, however, to evaluate an era solely to account for a subsequent time. The initiatives and responses of the 1950s may have a significance of their own.

Questions remain too about Eisenhower's role in foreign policy. How closely did he work with persons other than John Foster Dulles? To what extent did he rely on ideas and information that did not originate in the State Department? What, for example, was his understanding of the technical facts of weaponry and of the schemes of the intelligence agencies? Were his proposals for "open skies," disarmament, and control of nuclear testing merely gestures or calculated risks? Was the American "shield"—as Eisenhower applied it—another version of imperialism? A great deal of our understanding will depend on whether or not historians believe, as he did, that the containment of communism is "the struggle of the ages." Perhaps that is the key to every question involved in the foreign policy of the Eisenhower administration.

Index